EMOTIONAL ORPHANS

Memoir of a Young Therapist

Cate Shepherd

"Emotional Orphans tells the sad and moving stories of a number of lost children, young ones who had suffered abuse and abandonment and who had learned in consequence that trust in others was their most bitter enemy.

In this wonderful book, Cate Shepherd describes her clinical work and gives us moving accounts of her inspiring successes and her heartbreaking failures. She also opens up her own trauma history, and allows us to see how the wounds carried by the healer play an indispensable role in the process of healing itself.

This book should be read by every student and clinician who seeks to open the darkness of mistrust to the power of human understanding and connection."

- George Atwood, Ph.D.
  Author of *The Abyss of Madness*

FOREWORD

Teenagers can be tough.
Angry teenagers can drive you crazy.
Teenagers who have suffered early abuse can be impossible.

Dealing with the impossible is what *Emotional Orphans* is about. Because emotional problems related to early abuse remain encoded in non-conscious, or implicit memory, they are not accessible to conscious recall or to therapeutic interpretation. These teenagers cannot tell you where it hurts – they can only show you – often by doing to you what was done to them. And they do not learn from verbal dialogue or explanation; they only change through new experiences in relationships. Unfortunately, these young people often end up in residential treatment centers, group homes or juvenile hall where our system is oriented around trying to make them conform or punish them – a continuation of their experiences of abuse.

In this book Dr. Shepherd shows how to use inner hunches to understand, and counter-intuitive behaviors to connect with young adults who, while pushing you away, are desperately craving connection. Working with these teenagers is like adopting an abused puppy that you take home and offer loving care. When you try to pet or soothe it, it snaps at your hand. Interpreting the snapping as anger – not as protection – makes things worse. Leaving the puppy alone causes it to fuss and whimper. In her work, Dr. Shepherd understands that a teenager's anger comes from an instinct of self-protection. Like the fabled animal-whisperer, she is able to maintain a therapeutic distance, not too close and not too far, and wait patiently. Sometimes she waits for a very long time. The results are worth it as she shows how these troubled teenagers can eventually learn to feel safe and begin to trust. Her work is not without dangers, and she honestly describes how at times she gets hurt by the people she is trying to help.

In the twenty years I have known Cate Shepherd, as a student and as a colleague, she has become one of my most valued teachers. This book is a must read for all parents, therapists and court officials who want to help this very troubled population of young people.

- Sanford Shapiro, M.D.
  Author of *Talking With Patients*

Emotional Orphans is a fictionalized memoir inspired by resilient survivors who overcame impossible odds. All of their names and identifying characteristics have been changed to guard their privacy. In some cases, composite characters were created for additional protection.

I am deeply grateful to all of the precious people in these stories who let me share their lives for a time. It was a joy and an honor to travel with you.

Cate Shepherd
September, 2012

"Together, we are emotional
orphans no longer."

- my friend, Jeri

To emotional orphans everywhere.

And to Harry,
in all of his incarnations.

CONTENTS

Prologue: The Fool

"If you can't explain it simply,
you don't understand it well enough."
- Albert Einstein

THE FOOL

"Leap, and the net will appear."
- John Burroughs

"Bellies!" Miss B's booming voice echoed through Unit 400 of Los Angeles Central Juvenile Hall, and forty girls in blue prison uniforms dropped to the concrete floor, face down, arms at their sides. The girls stayed silent while brisk, muscular male guards handcuffed two troublemakers and dragged them to the isolation rooms at the other end of Juvenile Hall. I recognized Deandra, my favorite troublemaker. I would miss her in class.

Miss B whispered in my ear, "Deandra was about to rip Anchelette's face off."

Deandra picked fights all the time. She reminded me of that line from *The Karate Kid:*
> *Grief trapped in heart become big anger.*

I stood near the guards' station in my aerobics teacher leotards and *Flashdance* leg warmers, boom box in hand, and waited for Miss B's signal to start class. Every Monday evening I loped through the gauntlet of the boys' unit in my goofy getup, tuned out their chorus of lewd comments and smooching sounds, and made my way to the girls' unit for high impact aerobics and crisis counseling. I looked like a fool, but it was the only way in.

In a weird way, Juvenile Hall felt like home. Every week I had the same sobering thought: *That could be me...I just never got caught.*

"Line up!" Miss B yelled, and the girls jumped up and scrambled to form three lines with enough space between them to wiggle and kick. Miss B nodded for me to start class.

It was 1986 and I was 24, a psychology student and eager youth worker. School and work overstuffed my waking hours, yet I cherished Monday evenings when I volunteered at Juvenile Hall.

14

Every week we bounced and sweated together for an hour. After class, we formed a Soul Train line, and a gaggle of girls danced with me like they weren't in jail, and showed off their moves with explosive energy.

Kizzy, a feisty fifteen-year-old with a raucous laugh, tried to teach me *The Hammer*. When the boom box blasted, "Hammer time!" countless pairs of legs, ranging from pale white to dark brown hopped from foot to foot and pumped faster than I could track, much less imitate.

"C'mon, Cate! You can do it!" Kizzy shouted out her encouragement.

I struggled to keep up while sweat dripped from my red, freckled face. The girls burst into giggle fits. They loved to watch me make a fool of myself. For a few minutes each week, I distracted them from the shame of their uniformed incarceration.

After a few failed attempts at *The Hammer*, the music changed, mercifully, and we switched to the hip-hop version of *The Electric Slide*. I could do that one. I wiped the sweat out of my eyes.

Kizzy patted me on the back. "You'll get it eventually." She sounded so motherly, as I imagined she did with her three younger siblings who had been in her care since her mother's breakdown.

All of the girls I met in Juvenile Hall had suffered abuse or neglect at home. Many had been abandoned by their parents. Some had been ripped up and transplanted from foster home to foster home, after being abused by foster parents. Most had joined gangs to find family. Their delinquent behavior was an SOS they longed for someone to decode.

Frightened girls in bare cells will talk to kind visitors. I found my bliss on Unit 400. These girls needed someone who cared about them, and I needed someone to care for.

After Soul Train, Miss B rounded up the girls who needed to talk and sent them, one by one, to my counseling office, a few square feet of concrete floor in the far corner of the day room. Miss B was attuned to their emotional needs, but she couldn't serve as both Chaplain and Warden. And forty emotional orphans were a lot to tend, even for a heart as big as hers.

Locked up and frightened by their precarious fates, each girl poured out her angst while others hovered and paced by the pay phone, awaiting their turn to call a boyfriend or a probation officer.

Their pain tugged on me like gravity.

Follow-up work in the inner city was a whole other animal. On the outs, back in their tight jeans and midriff tops, the girls rarely bothered to keep their appointments with me. I tried to keep track of them after they left the Hall, but most drifted away. During my five years on Unit 400, I saw several return. Some more than once.

One summer afternoon, just after Kizzy was released on probation, I drove across town to take her out to lunch. I arrived to find an empty house. On my way home I watched her buy a bag from a drug dealer on 28th Street.

My psychologist friend who worked with troubled teens provided a metaphor to reframe lessons learned the hard way. One day, after a clever girl conned me, she told me the story of her favorite archetype, *The Fool*. She showed me a picture of him in his bold, multicolored coat, stepping off a cliff with a white rose in his hand, a serene smile on his face, as though his faith was enough to keep him from crashing on the rocks below. He didn't allow rationality to dim his passion. He leapt with his heart.

Sometimes fools grasp a kind of wisdom that more reasonable people can't see.

Therapists are drawn to this kind of work for personal reasons. I can trace mine back to the eleventh grade when I signed up for a psychology class, an exotic opportunity in Waynesville, Ohio, population 2700.

Mr. O was a progressive new teacher who had moved to our rural town from the big city, and he was a lot more interesting than the regular teachers. He told us juicy stories about all kinds of lunatics and perverts, like the guy with the poop fetish. *Blech!* Fascinated by his class, I worked hard to get an A.

One winter morning before school Mr. O called me into his office where he served as the high school guidance counselor.

"Sit down." He motioned toward the chair next to his desk and closed the door. He sat down in his chair, leaned way back, propped his wooden leg on the desk, and hiked up his plaid, polyester pants to reveal brilliant white cotton socks. His dark, fierce eyes peered out at me from beneath a black unibrow. A bemused grin sprouted as he lit a cigarette, looking pleased with himself.

"Why is a smart girl like you hanging around with those losers?" I had just returned from my morning smoke in the alley across the street, and I reeked.

Stunned by his directness, I sat in silence.

I had been ditching class and smoking pot with the bad kids since freshman year, but no one seemed to care. I felt accepted by the freaks. With them, I found family.

"You know, you can't wallow in shit without smelling like it." Mr. O leaned forward and looked into me with intensity that made me feel naked. He offered me a cigarette.

I stared at him and took the cigarette.

I didn't much like him calling my friends shit, but something more important was happening here. Smoking in the guidance counselor's office seemed oddly thrilling. His cheap filter cigarettes tasted nasty, but this smoking felt sacred.

"You know, you're smart enough to go to college, and you're pretty enough to have any guy you want there," he said. "Not like these yahoos around here."

I flushed. He must have been smoking something besides Newports.

Maintaining appropriate boundaries with female students did not turn out to be Mr. O's forte. Nevertheless, we enjoyed many soul-feeding talks in his office that year. He lent me his philosophy books, and I devoured the wisdom of Epictetus, Emerson, and Thoreau. I quit smoking, joined the volleyball team, and ran for homecoming queen. I made the honor roll for the first time.

He cared. So, I began to care.

Mr. O x-rayed through my tough, indifferent facade and recognized the wounded girl trapped inside. In a few months' time, he shifted the trajectory of my life enough to change my fate forever. I learned the power of a connection with a caring adult.

So, with heart on sleeve and boom box in hand, I set out on a mission to find other captives and free them. When I started, I didn't know that the kids I loved would sock me in the jaw, wipe boogers on my sleeve, dump Coke into my stereo, pee on my furniture, poop on my floor, brandish a broken beer bottle in my face, and heave a huge potted plant at my head.

Nor did I realize they would burrow into my heart, sometimes break it, and compel me to step off of cliff after cliff like a fool to follow them wherever they needed to go to heal themselves.

These kids molded me into a therapist. And when my own demons came to haunt me, I found myself in surprisingly good company.

SOUL CHILD

"One need not be a chamber to be haunted,
one need not be a house."
-Emily Dickenson

"Good morning, Jesse." I greeted my favorite girl with a warm smile, eager to hear about her weekend. Then I waited in the hallway, outside her dorm room, to escort her to my office for our weekly therapy session. For my kids, getting off the dorm for an hour was like getting out of jail.

Jesse's face loomed large as she moved toward me. Her left fist slammed into my right cheekbone.

Ouch!

I stood stunned, scared, confused. *What the...?*

Jesse looked panicked, like cornered prey. She stepped back and stared at me with haunted eyes.

I studied her face. *What could have triggered her?*

It is not unusual for emotionally disturbed adolescents to assault dorm staff, but they rarely hit their therapist. The therapist enjoys the special status of The Good Mommy who possesses power to grant weekend passes and carne asada burritos.

Perhaps it was Jesse's fear of growing closer to me during our three intense months together that made her push me away. The very attachment that could be life-saving and healing might make her feel unbearably vulnerable.

Jesse's surprise fist in my face felt like it belonged to another time and place, as though she was tilting at windmills and I just happened to get in the way.

I remember the hot summer afternoon when I met Jesse. Leslie, our program director, had grunted and waved me into the tiny room. Jesse crouched in the corner like a feral cat. I sat on the floor, five feet away from her, speechless and full of fear. "Meet your new patient," Leslie said, as she walked into her office in the adjoining room and closed the door; then eavesdropped through a big hole in the wall.

I assumed that Leslie's agenda was the same as her usual: *Counsel the kid into compliance.*

Jesse was fourteen years old, wild-eyed, and covered with cuts from her flight into the canyon ice plant an hour earlier. Four male staff had chased, captured and carried her back up the hill, struggling and flailing, to the group home. The guys said Jesse put up an impressive fight, and they had the scratches, bites, and bruises to prove it.

She looked so young. Too young to be in a place like this, with the most disturbed, violent adolescents in L.A. County. Her creamy complexion and rosy cheeks created an aura of innocence.

Jesse wore baggy boy's shorts and sneakers. Her cropped hair was dirty and disheveled, but her natural beauty shone through. Long lashes softened her intelligent, aquamarine eyes. Her lips were deep pink, like a young child's.

We sat in a space cluttered with office supplies and abandoned fax machines. It was a warm day, and she smelled like a child who had been playing outside. Two muscular men stood guard by the door in case Jesse tried to bolt.

Jesse's gaze was fixed far away. We sat together on the dirty carpet in silence. I felt an instinctive urge to comfort her, but heeded the stronger pull to keep my distance, sensing that closeness would threaten her.

I studied her face and strained to sense her inner experience. After a few minutes of silence, I spoke softly. "That must hurt." I pointed toward her lacerated legs.

She stared into space.

I felt like an idiot. Leslie listened from her office a few feet away. She often seemed exasperated when I failed to *take charge of a situation.* I imagined her shaking her head and writing me off as another wimpy therapist.

I had been employed at *Casa de Esperanza,* a long-term residential treatment center, for two weeks when I met Jesse. But my coworkers had already warned me that the Director's respect and support were with the paraprofessional staff who worked on the dorm, not the psychotherapists. It would take several months and at least one tragedy before I glimpsed the huge heart underneath Leslie's biker jacket.

I tried to sense what Jesse was feeling while she appeared disconnected from her feelings.

"It's scary coming to a new place," I spoke in a gentle voice.

She turned her head and locked eyes with me. My heart sped up. *Uh oh...am I about to set her off again?*

Jesse examined me like a dog sniffs a slab of poisoned meat. She pushed herself up into a straighter posture and propped the back of her head on the wall. A few minutes later, she stretched her legs out in front of her and crossed them at the ankle, like mine.

I had met a lot of disturbed kids during my seven years of therapy training, but I had never seen one this haunted.

After half an hour of Jesse's silence, accompanied by my self-conscious, empathic guesses, her tense muscles relaxed. She exhaled. As the minutes clicked past on a dusty clock radio, she transformed from a terrified captive into a tired girl. Later she would ask me, "Are you psychic?"

What have I gotten myself into? This girl should be in the hospital.

I felt dangerously inadequate to be Jesse's therapist.

The children's mental health system was structured such that children had to fail in several less expensive treatment programs before they were allowed to come to Casa for the long-term, intensive treatment they needed. Several years of failures and good-byes had formed layers of self-protective armor that guarded their broken hearts and battered self-esteem.

Some of our kids needed to live in a locked facility for their own safety, but little funding existed for that level of care. So, we did our best with the resources we could marshal.

Two dorms with long, bare corridors housed 25 girls and 25 boys. Stark rooms were furnished only with heavy wooden bed frames carved with initials, gang graffiti, and profanity. Cell block blue walls bore dents and holes from fists and feet. There wasn't much point in repairing the walls. A freshly painted wall was an invitation waiting to be engraved.

When triggered into a traumatic state, Jesse could only fight, flee, or freeze. She could not shift out of that state of mind on her own. Sitting calmly with her and not making any sudden moves for an hour gave her nervous system a chance to cool off. After she returned to a calmer state, Jesse could once again access the smarter parts of her brain.

While the staff escorted a more compliant Jesse to the dorm, I walked to my office, pulled out her fat file, and read her history. *Abandoned in infancy by a schizophrenic mother. Sexually abused in foster care. Abandoned by foster parents. Emotionally abused by adoptive parents. Abandoned by adoptive parents.*

Neglected, molested, discarded.

The only ones who stuck around were Jesse's latest foster parents, who reportedly hated her and blamed her for all of their problems. Yet, they fought to retain custody.

Jesse's wrists bore scars from self-inflicted cuts. She had been hospitalized several times for suicide attempts. When she cut, she cut deep.

During her first few weeks at Casa, Jesse assaulted the staff several times, and required physical restraint, sometimes for more than an hour. A burgeoning camp thought she belonged in jail instead of mental health treatment.

As Jesse's therapist, it was my job to find a way to connect with her, advocate for her, and hang on to her long enough to make an impact. If we could reach her at fourteen and fill in some of the gaps in her early childhood development, we might shift her life trajectory enough to improve her fate.

As a young child, Jesse never had a chance to form the kind of secure attachment that fosters the development of empathy and self-regulation. As a result, she could not regulate her emotions, and she felt little empathy for her caregivers.

If I could get a tube into this kid, I could meet some of those attachment needs and get some of her emotional development back on track.

After a few months of trying to reach Jesse, I realized that the dorm staff needed my support as much as she did. They worked on the front lines every day, and absorbed most of the blows.

I listened to the staff, empathized with their perspective, and let them use me for back up when they reached the end of their patience with Jesse's aggression. When they were short-staffed, I sat with Jesse in the quiet room to give them a break.

One morning, while I wrote chart notes in my office, the intercom buzzed. "Cate?"

"Yes."

"It's Essi. Can you come over here?"

"What's up?"

"Jesse's foster mother just called."

"Uh oh. I'll be right there."

The woman had an evil hold on the poor girl. No one knew what she had said on the phone, but after they hung up, Jesse stormed back to her room, ripped up all of her hip hop posters, and slugged one of the female staff.

I hurried to the girls' dorm.

The residential dorms at Casa looked just like Juvenile Hall except for the worn indoor/outdoor carpet that had completely forgotten its original color.

Three staff and I held one limb each to contain the flailing, adrenaline-charged adolescent who wore a pair of gigantic, black Doc Marten boots. After holding her powerful left leg for a few minutes, I shifted slightly to get comfortable on the floor. My Birkenstocked foot had fallen asleep.

In a millisecond, her boot heel smashed into my silver bracelet watch and sent it flying across the room. I liked my fancy watch. It was the most valuable piece of jewelry I owned, and I should not have worn it on the dorm.

Funny thing: I cared more about the girl than the watch. Jesse could have crushed all of my jewelry, and I would have come back for more.

The four of us held her, writhing, on the floor for more than half an hour. She just didn't give up, and her aggressive energy was not subsiding. If we had been at the hospital, we would have placed her in four point restraints and given her a shot of Haldol in her backside. But, we were a Level 12 group home, and our contract did not allow us to use restraints or give shots.

I often heard the staff say, "This kid should be in the hospital," and they were right. But, the hospital would admit her only if she was actively suicidal or homicidal, and they could only keep her for a few days due to funding constraints.

Molly, a freckled surfer with a sunny disposition, held Jesse's left shoulder on the floor and tried to talk sense to her. Molly was a real pro. She had been a team leader on the girls' dorm for several years. My funny, cynical buddy, Sean, held Jesse's right leg and rolled his eyes. He'd been through this routine many times. Sean tolerated Jesse as a personal favor to me. A.J., the dorm supervisor and picture of equanimity, knelt with perfect posture and held her right shoulder with patience.

Then he had a brainstorm. "How about some show tunes?"

A.J. loved musicals, and he always hummed as he went about his duties on the dorm.

With a bright smile, A.J. sang out, "Da da da da da...These little town blues..."

"Stop!" Jesse yelled.

We all joined in and sang merrily with Steve, "I want to be a part of it, New York, New York!"

"Stop it! I can't stand it! I'll calm down. Just SHUUT UP!!!"

"Okay, Jess, if you're ready to calm down, I'll release your arm," Molly said. "Okay? Are you ready?"

"Yes! Yes! Just stop singing!"

Molly gradually released the pressure on Jesse's left shoulder. Jesse broke free and swung her fist at Molly's head.

Molly ducked, grabbed her wrist, and returned to holding the shoulder again.

A.J. sang, "Don't know why there's no sun up in the sky, stormy weather..."

"No! Stop!" Jesse wailed, as though in pain. Then she started laughing, convulsing full body laughs into the floor. Trauma poured out of her body and into the dirty carpet in sobs of laughter, tears, and relief.

We all laughed. We couldn't stop laughing. Molly and I wiped tears from our cheeks. The storm was over.

It's a strange way to bond, but a strong one. Riding the bucking bronco, absorbing the blows, and consistently coming back for more forges an attachment with even the most hopeless heart.

Badly traumatized kids usually needed a nine-month gestation period to test us. Around that mystical nine-month marker, something shifted, and some transformation occurred.

With Jesse, it took eighteen months. As the months passed, it became more difficult for the staff to tolerate her intermittent explosions.

It also created an unexpected problem: when the county auditors came to examine our charts, I got into big trouble. Jesse's chart was practically empty. I had spent my paperwork time on the dorm stamping out fires. In my previous jobs, I had been the Paperwork Queen, praised for my perfectionism and penmanship.

Jesse uprooted my priorities and plunked them down on their heads.

My office mate, Elena, had the same problem, so we decided to attack it together. We spent all of our time and energy on the kids Monday through Friday, which was a huge relief to the dorm staff. Then we sneaked in the back door on Saturday mornings in t-shirts and cutoffs to do marathon paperwork catch-up sessions while the Indigo Girls blasted from Elena's boom box. I hid from my kids until I finished my work. If one of them spotted me, the chorus would start, "Cate! Cate! Cate!" and then they would pester the staff all day with urgent requests to talk to me.

Elena and I grew close raising our wild brood together. We had become friends in graduate school, and I had recruited her to work at Casa, assuming she would love the work as much as I did. After a few weeks on the job, Elena accused me of luring her into a nightmare.

But the kids eventually won her over. Several years later, after I had moved on to a cushy job at a quiet group home, I would return to visit my friends at Casa and find Elena's picture posted in the front office as Most Valuable Employee.

Elena reported to me daily about her dating adventures, and I told her scary stories about my interminable divorce. She yearned for true love as much as I yearned for peace and quiet. I gave her big sisterly advice about her love life, and she nagged me to jump back into the dating pool. If only there were lifeguards.

We decorated our dingy little office with cartoons, mostly Gary Larson, some homemade. My favorite was *Too many scientists, not enough hunchbacks.*

The kids' favorite was *Spam Farm,* a pasture full of spam-shaped creatures with toothpick legs. They found the whole concept of spam hilarious. At Christmastime, about nine months into Jesse's treatment, she and two of her friends put their money together, bought a can of spam, wrapped a bow around it, and presented it to me with cheesy grins.

Essi, the p.m. shift supervisor, swaggered around the dorm in her cowboy boots, jangling a massive wad of keys. A Latina beauty with long, voluptuous hair and dramatic makeup, Essi had been a tough kid in high school. Her life experience helped her connect with our girls.

Essi invited me to come out with the p.m. staff and drink tequila. We ended up at a dive bar, singing karaoke till the place closed.

I took my vocal stylings very seriously at that time. It was 1993, and I was keeping the 70's alive with classic rock and a Stevie Nicks hairdo.

After a few rounds, I got to hear what the staff thought of the therapists. Honored by their trust, I cringed and tried to be brave.

Naive. Weak. Stupid.

My time on the front lines with the staff had helped me shed the stereotype of the touchy feely clueless therapist. My job looked luxurious from their perspective, and I could do my job only because the staff secured my kids in the program structure 24 hours a day.

Sometimes I felt like Hawkeye Pierce in an episode of *M.A.S.H.,* performing delicate surgery while bombs dropped nearby.

The p.m. staff and I became war buddies. We took blows and survived together, and we blew off steam any way we could while we argued about whether to salvage the girl or ship her out.

Every Thursday morning in Case Conference, Jesse's psychiatrist, Dr. Sloan, insisted that Jesse was beyond hope. Sloan said Jesse's brain had been irreparably damaged by early childhood trauma, that she was permanently developmentally arrested, and that she would always be volatile, no matter how much therapy we gave her. In fact, therapy might make her worse, he said. He diagnosed her with *Borderline Personality Disorder* and prescribed an anti-psychotic, a mood stabilizer, an anti-depressant, and a sleeping pill. The staff could give her extra doses of anti-psychotic medication if she got too rambunctious.

Now, according to the *Diagnostic and Statistical Manual of Mental Disorders,* one cannot diagnose a personality disorder until age eighteen. Jesse was only fourteen. But in the residential treatment of welfare orphans, the rules bent. And, once a child was branded with an incurable personality disorder, there was no point in wasting valuable therapy on her.

It's not that I'm unsympathetic with the need to label. I myself once fell in love with a DSM, and pasted perfectly printed labels on each section for easy reference. Then I spent hours diagnosing my relatives.

As a graduate intern, I had flailed around in the deep end with disturbed patients, and learned that psychological theories and diagnostic formulations make good flotation devices. My mentors taught me to bear painful emotions and overwhelming circumstances. The first time one of my kids attempted suicide, my circuits overloaded, and I locked myself out of my office three times in the same afternoon.

Luckily, my mentors also taught me about the iatrogenic power of pathologizing labels to produce self-fulfilling prophesies in vulnerable patients like Jesse.

Perhaps the persistent nature of trauma creates the illusion that these children do not get better. But they do.

Attachment patterns are deeply embedded and can take years to change. Trauma is tenacious, and it never goes away completely. Healing these things requires hard work and patience over a long period of time.

It's certainly not for everyone.

While Jesse could still be triggered into flashback-like states, her development continued at a rapid pace. She *was* changing, and she would continue to grow and heal as long as we provided a safe, nourishing environment, consistent program structure, and the emotional responses she needed.

Terri, the staff psychologist, took Jesse to play in the sand tray once a week. One day, near Jesse's one-year anniversary with us, the two of them marched onto the dorm in triumph and told us about a funeral they had conducted – for a booger. They had named it Joey* and had given him a decent burial in the sand. [1]

Terri gave us a complex Jungian interpretation of the psychological significance of this ritual. Essi shot me a sideways glance, then fixed a big fake smile and nodded her head like she was interested. The other staff just laughed. It was heart-warming and relieving to see Jesse act like a normal kid.

Terri was an art therapist, and she loved myths and rituals. Her office provided a quiet refuge. Terri's devotion to the kids and her boundless energy inspired me. She reminded me of the Energizer Bunny the way she motored around campus from early morning till late at night, except instead of pink fur she wore long, flowing therapist skirts and leather boots.

She delivered soups, muffins, and other goodies to sustain me and Elena. Therapists never stayed long because of the stress, risk, and lousy pay, so Terri took it upon herself to provide fringe benefits.

Jesse charmed me with her intelligence and dark wit. Her poems and paintings provided a window into her inner life, and her childlike playfulness evoked a visceral joy in me.

Elena, my sweet office mate, watched in wonder. "You look like mother and daughter," she said one day after Jesse's visit.

I had an internal template for this kind of relationship. When I was in the third grade, a radiant woman named Olive drove to my house deep in the country and picked me up for Sunday school.

---

[1] The names of some boogers have been changed to protect the innocent.

She knew I was isolated and she came every week to take me out of my depressing home for a few hours.

In Olive's class I made macaroni wreaths and styrofoam angels. I listened to her stories, and sometimes I read stories aloud too. As the years went by, I grew secure in Olive's acceptance. In middle school, when I disrupted her class with clowning, she threw her head back and laughed freely at my jokes. Deep dimples framed her warm smile, and her eyes sparkled with unconditional love when she looked at me.

No matter how much progress Jesse made, she remained vulnerable to being triggered into terrified states, and when frightened, she became aggressive. At other times, when Jesse felt like she was falling apart, she carved on her wrists and stomach in an effort to glue herself together.

Jesse spent most of her time on the dorm. I was free to retreat to my office, while the staff worked in close proximity with her for eight-hour shifts. Sometimes, when they were short-staffed, they worked double shifts. And, no matter how sweet and charming Jesse seemed to me, her dark side emerged when she felt threatened.

I had started my own therapy during graduate school with a psychologist named Katherine. She was the best in town, and my psychologist buddies had all seen her during their training. Psychotherapy training programs required students to get their own therapy. Some teachers said it was the most important part of our clinical training. Katherine helped me understand my own wounds so that I could use them to enlarge my empathy with patients.

Therapists who try to heal others without working through their own pain are like surgeons who cut blindfolded.

On Tuesdays and Thursdays after work, I went to see Katherine. Sometimes I talked about Jesse more than I talked about myself. We discovered many parallels between Jesse's family and my own. I worked hard to understand Jesse's emotional experience. Sometimes the boundary between my story and hers became blurred.

I always sat in the same spot on Katherine's couch. On the wall across from me hung a large tapestry that looked like a young girl hiking through a jungle. I had to find my own way through that jungle before I could become a trustworthy guide for others.

On Tuesday mornings, I conducted family therapy sessions with Jesse and her foster parents. We met in a small trailer crowded with worn, mismatched furniture. Casa never had enough funding to fix up the place, so we made due with hand me downs.

One morning, a few months into her treatment, Jesse and I sat across from each other on two old, dusty sofas while her foster parents sat, fused at the hip, in straight chairs at the end of the sofas.

Her foster father launched into a tirade. "Jesse doesn't care about anyone or anything! All of our other children are normal. They appreciate all that we do for them. She acts like an animal! All she does is hurt us. She's just like her crazy mother!" His face looked like a distorted tomato that was about to burst from the pressure of his rage.

His rant seemed ill-timed since Jesse had been making good progress.

The foster mother sat like a grey mass frozen in martyr pose. I could see why A.J. called her Jabba.

While Jesse worked hard to make progress in the treatment program, her foster mother called me every day to remind me how much she suffered from Jesse's evilness.

These foster parents were locked into a shared delusion that Jesse was, in fact, the source of all their problems. Yet they refused to relinquish custody. *I hate you! Don't leave me!*

For several years, Jesse had been used as the scapegoat of a large, abusive family system, and she served as their trash can for poisonous projections. All of the shameful and despicable qualities disavowed by these disturbed foster parents were poured out on this chosen child like acid rain.

I could not leave her alone in her nightmare.

I held on to Jesse with a long look. She stared at me, eyes full of panic, as though she might bolt.

I looked up and saw a sadistic gleam in the foster father's eyes. He looked like he wanted to kill her. I looked back at Jesse. She grasped my gaze like a lifeline. My neck felt hot, my heart sped up. My ears became numb. My legs felt paralyzed. *Uh oh.*

My memory had recognized the hatred on the man's face, and my body had reacted - against my will.

I held on to the scratchy sofa. My nervous system flashed red, alerting me that I was in the presence of a dangerous man who wanted to hurt me.

I had seen that same gleam in my father's eyes when I was Jesse's age.

It's a cold Thanksgiving Day in Ohio. I stand knee-deep in trash, my hands numb underneath my father's stiff, dirty work gloves, and shovel out a bottomless wagon of garbage.

He glares at me with righteous eyes as hard as steely marbles, then climbs into his truck, drives away and leaves me there.

I can still feel the pain in my gut. The sadness. The suffocating loneliness of knowing that my cousins are playing, and my mother is chatting with her sisters a few miles up the road inside a warm house.

But most of all, I feel shame; the all-defining truth of that model scene, and others like it, that taught me where I belonged: in the trash wagon.

I loved my dad. I never understood why he hated me. Genetically, we were so alike. In good ways. And I don't know what he thought he was punishing me for. Perhaps for the sins of someone in his childhood. Perhaps for his own sins.

When I saw similar pain in Jesse, I felt validated. If Jesse's suffering was real, mine could also be real. If her circumstances could elicit empathy, maybe mine could too. We were two souls in the same darkness.

Parents who scapegoat their children can induce a special kind of desperation. While other children find comfort and support, the scapegoated child is deprived of a clear mirror for her emotional experience. The absence of validation can produce more trauma than the injury itself.

When a child is left alone with overwhelming, frightening emotions, or worse, blamed for them, she has no means to process her experience and make sense of it. Children who are left alone to make sense of painful experience will generally blame themselves. It's a lot less scary than looking at the reality of what the parent is doing to them.

The *folie a deux* (shared craziness) of Jesse's foster parents relieved them of any responsibility for their abusive behavior. To a scapegoater's mind, the child is simply bad and crazy. Or, as Gary Larson's sheep farmer says, "That sheep is a liar."

I drew a deep breath to calm my shaky voice and interrupted the frothing foster father. "Mr. Bachman, please."

He jerked his head to stare at me. The tomato got redder. His icy grey eyes narrowed like a raptor about to dive. He looked away and tore into Jesse some more. "You're going to spend your life in the loony bin like your mother!"

"Mr. Bachman." I raised my voice. I remembered what my psychoanalyst friend had told me about dealing with bullies: *Make a loud sound.* I stood up. "That's enough," I said, as firmly as I dared.

Without a word he rose and flounced out of the trailer, fuming. His martyr monument wife shuffled out behind him. They stormed into my supervisor's office and demanded a different therapist.

I took Jesse outside to walk laps around the athletic field.

We walked side by side in the grass while our breathing returned to a normal rate.

"Do your ears ever feel funny?" I asked.

"Yes! How did you know?"

"When your dad was yelling at you, my ears felt numb."

Jesse spun and stared at me, amazed. "Nobody ever knew that before," she said.

"Does he always talk to you like that?"

"Yeah, but never in front of anybody." She gazed at me with the trusting eyes of an innocent child.

After a few months of forging an attachment with Jesse, she revisited the terrible twos with an abundance of energy. She tested every limit and followed me around like a baby duckling. When I got too busy, she summoned me to the dorm with a flare in the form of outrageous behavior.

I don't really believe that patients go backward in time, but I became fascinated with the ways these kids, once they felt safe, appeared to revisit their early childhood gaps and re-do them. Sometimes they would even dress the part. One of Jesse's peers was a six-foot tall athlete who, once she bonded with her therapist, began wearing big bows in her hair, polka dot skirts, and mary janes that made her look like a giant four-year-old. We learned that if we wanted to meet their needs, we had to start where they were, however young.

Their development was not linear or orderly. It appeared random and chaotic, with long gestation periods followed by sudden spikes, and adolescent behavior mixed in with thrashing infants and tantruming toddlers. And, of course, adorable preschoolers and precocious ten-year-olds. It was a lot to keep track of in a relationship.

Jesse knew I had an M & M stash somewhere in my office and she never tired of pleading, conning, threatening and cajoling to get at them. I did not want to reward her with candy for harassing me, so I held the line. She needed to be relentless, so one afternoon I decided to make a game of it. I pulled a pad of paper out of my desk, printed at the top of the page, "101 Ways To Manipulate Your Therapist", and wrote a list of Jesse's tactics. She pulled her chair up three feet in front of me and leaned in with a mischievous smirk and the excited glee of a toddler with a new toy.

I took dictation.

#1 "I love you, Cate! Please give me some M & M's!"

#2 "Cate! I promise I'll do good if you give them to me!"

#3 " If you don't give them to me, I'll get Elena to give them to me."

#4 "Elena gives M & M's to her kids!"

#5 "If you loved me, you would give them to me!"

#6 Patient opens all desk drawers, searches for candy.
(Therapist uses Aikido technique to block patient's groping)

#7 "If you don't give it to me, I'll say you abused me!"
(Patient now doubled over, laughing)

#8 " If you don't give it to me, I'll kill you!"

Jesse's mission dissolved into hysterics. She was very pleased with herself when she saw the list.

The terrible twos eventually passed. Other developmental phases came and went. As we were approaching the two-year mark of intensive residential treatment, we seemed to have a young lady on our hands some of the time.

I decided to form a singing group, a pleasant change from the group home routine, and a powerful incentive for good behavior. Jesse and her friends loved to sing and dance. A.J. had a connection at a local recording studio where he could get us a free session.

Jesse and I sneaked off to my office and practiced singing with karaoke tapes. She dedicated a song to me: "The Wind Beneath My Wings." She sang it to me, earnestly and off key. After the music stopped, she looked down at me nervously. "I wish you could be my mom."

I tried to play it cool. You know, like a therapist: clear boundaries, not emotionally involved, not self-disclosing. As if she didn't know exactly how I felt. Probably before I did.

"That's a beautiful compliment, Jess. Thank you. You deserve a good mom."

The next day, Jesse brought me a 3' x 4' self-portrait she had drawn. I stopped what I was doing and helped her hang it on my office wall. In five-inch-tall letters, it read, "La La La."

"It means 'I love you'," she said.

Joy welled up in me. Giving Jesse the thoughtful care that I had longed for at her age satisfied my soul. Her love was my brass ring.

Singing group was a powerful motivator for these girls who had so little to feel good about, and they worked hard, practicing every day to perfect their performance. Finally, the day came when we all piled into the group home van and headed for the recording studio in colorful costumes, red lipstick, and with more excitement than senior prom. I felt like a minivan mom.

Sean came with us, just in case one of our AWOL risks got a sudden urge. Thrilled to off the dorm for a few hours, he chatted and joked with us. Four giddy girls bounced around in the back of the van like popcorn popping. Jesse's friend, Sonya, a young Latina gang member with a history of violence, had carefully shellacked her bangs into a four-inch-tall tidal wave. She shouted profanity at the neighborhood boys as we drove past.

"Sonya, roll up the window please." Sean was calm and firm. Thank God he was with us. Only a few weeks earlier Sonya and Jesse had erupted into a fistfight in the middle of my therapy group. One of them might go off at any moment, despite all the medications we gave them. Navigating their hot buttons was like walking through a minefield. A part of me thought I was nuts to take these four out together. Everything with them was a crapshoot.

When we arrived at the recording studio and piled out of the van, they looked like young ladies going to church on Easter Sunday in their pretty dresses. The studio manager treated them like VIP's, and they were full of fantasies about being discovered and going on MTV. He was patient and respectful as he lined them up and adjusted their mikes. The girls had selected a hip-hop remake of *Lean On Me,* which they sang a capella. The first time through they were so nervous I could barely hear their voices.

I made eye contact with Marquette, a playful African-American girl who loved to laugh. I grinned at her, sang loudly and badly, and did the white man's overbite as geekily as possible. The girls giggled.

"Stop that!" Jesse barked at me.

Then Marquette launched. She relaxed into her diva self, and her church solo voice rang out,

Sometimes in our lives we all have pain, we all have sorrow
But if we are wise we know that there's always tomorrow...

and they were off, singing and clapping, loud and free.

Jesse stared straight at me and belted out,

Lean on me! when you're not strong and I'll be your friend,
I'll help you carry on...

Chills rippled through my body. I stood in awe of something beyond me, overcome by the energy that connected us.

After the recording session, we took photos. The girls struck sassy poses they'd seen in music videos.

A few days later, I picked up a packet of gorgeous photos and gave them to the girls. The studio manager sent tapes of the recording session for each of them. The power and beauty of their combined voices stirred every listener at Casa. The girls played their tapes over and over and displayed their photos in their rooms.

A refreshing breeze of self-esteem blew through the dirty dorm.

But a funny thing happens when a trauma survivor makes a foray out of her cell and feels the wind on her wings. Intense fear. An overwhelming belief that the cell door will slam shut and she will be left alone outside to die. This threat of danger can activate a child's nervous system for fight, flight, or retreat to the familiarity of the cell.

On a Tuesday, after 23 months of intensive work with Jesse, I took a Mental Health Day and stayed home to get some much needed rest. I sat in my papasan chair with a cup of coffee and pondered. The phone rang.

"Hey, Cate. It's Essi. I've got some bad news."

My gut clenched. "What happened?"

"Your girl is going to the Hall. She assaulted Stacey."

"Oh my God. Is the baby okay?"

"Don't know yet. Stace is at the hospital."

Jesse had risen that morning, dressed for school, and done the most heinous thing she could: she kicked a pregnant worker in the stomach with her Doc Marten.

If only I had been there, I could have fought to keep her. Again.

But it was too late, and this was getting too dangerous.

Jesse's terror of abandonment was too much for her to bear. She had to seize control and eject herself before she was thrown out.

I curled up in my chair and wept like a mother whose baby had been ripped from her arms. I poured out my grief in a poem entitled "Soul Child".

36

When I read the poem, I knew the truth. I had seen myself in Jesse. In saving her, I was saving myself.

A few days later I visited Jesse in a bare, 6' x 10' cell at Juvenile Hall. I hadn't been there in a couple of years, and I felt like a different person in my work clothes with a brief case instead of leotards and a boom box. The guard at the front gate remembered me, and my old friend, Miss B, ushered me in ahead of the other visitors.

Jesse seemed calm within the confines of the holding cell, surrounded on all sides by concrete.

I sat on a wooden bench that was bolted to the wall and floor. Jesse slouched against the opposite wall and propped her leg up on the bench. She wore shorts and a t-shirt.

"Are you cold?" I asked. I was freezing, and I had a jacket on.

"No, I'm fine."

She was like one of those little kids who goes swimming in the ocean in December. She never got cold.

An odd sensation of excitement stirred my stomach. Or was it fear? I was inside Jesse's story now.

"Thanks for coming to see me." Her voice was strong, her eye contact direct. "I couldn't stay there any more."

"What happened?"

"The staff hates me. They don't want me any more."

Jesse's intuition was true. Most of the staff wanted to get rid of her. She frightened them. In spite of her progress, we could still misstep and trigger her trauma mines.

"Yeah, some of them are afraid of you. Where will you go?"

"My social worker is sending me to a placement. It's called New Vistas."

I knew the place. It would be a five-hour drive for her foster parents. *YESS!!!* I wanted to kiss her social worker.

I told Jesse the latest news from the girls' dorm and passed along greetings from her friends who wished her well.

"Is Stacey okay?' Her eyes grew wide. She fidgeted.

"Yes, she's fine."

Jesse swallowed hard. "What about the baby?"

"The baby is fine."

She exhaled and slumped back against the wall. "I don't know what happened," she said. "Please tell her I'm sorry."

"I know." I nodded. "I will." We'd been through many similar storms, and each time Jesse came away feeling she'd been possessed by a bad spirit. Sometimes she couldn't even remember what she'd done. Dissociation is weird that way.

After twenty minutes, a guard came to escort Jesse back to her cell. I watched her shuffle down the hall, shoulders slumped. She turned her head and looked back at me. She looked so forlorn. So alone.

Two months would pass before I could make myself write Jesse's discharge summary. Her chart was charged with intense emotion, like the ark of the covenant. I dreaded opening it.

Two weeks after Jesse left, Joanie, our wry, red-headed receptionist, buzzed me to announce a call. She was fond of Jesse and had singled her out for special attention like an adoring grandmother. Joanie could barely contain her excitement.

"Cate! It's Jesse on line two! She's calling from a pay phone. She AWOL'd from her new placement."

"Uh oh. Put her through."

"Jesse?"

"Cate! I ran away! I want to come back to Casa. I'll be good this time!"

"Jess, you know you can't come back. What's going on?"

She frantically fired off a story about the new treatment center. Hell Hole, she called it. She had lost her privileges for fighting with a peer, and she believed that everyone hated her. She asked my advice about what to do.

I told her to go back and finish the program. I explained why this was the smartest choice. She agreed without a struggle and walked back to the treatment center.

Jesse called me twice from pay phones in the following weeks. Then there was a quiet spell. She settled into her new program and graduated about a year later.

The bond that Jesse and I formed during our two years together provided a home base for her. She had internalized a new attachment experience that made her more resilient to life's disruptions.

It's tricky when the medicine is the monster. Jesse's deepest fear was getting close to another attachment figure who might abandon her. In moving close enough to treat her wounds, we had to survive the blows of her self-protective flailing. Much of Jesse's outrageous behavior contained the question, "*Now* are you going to leave me?" Our goal was to neither abandon her nor retaliate against her, no matter what. If we could pass her tests, we might disprove some of the fears that haunted her. Katherine called it *The Indestructible Therapist*. She said traumatized patients need to kill us off and see that we don't die. Our indestructibility is their only security.

Devotion is a prerequisite to this work. So is a willingness to plow through murderous anger and destructive behavior patterns to get to the child who is trapped inside. You can't take the aggression personally, any more than you would take the heat of the fire personally when pulling a child from a burning house.

Two years after Jesse graduated from Hell Hole, Terri brought news of her. She had broken out of the toxic orbit of her foster parents and she had a baby girl. The baby was healthy, and Jesse was going to therapy and parenting classes every week. She lived with a young couple from her church who helped her take care of the baby.

It's troubling to think of a child raising another child, but the need in Jesse was irrepressible. She had always dreamed of having a baby. She figured her baby would give her the love that she had never received from her parents.

Perhaps like the love she gave to me.

THE RESURRECTION

"The heart is a very resilient little muscle."
- Woody Allen

I'm sitting at my desk, writing a quarterly report about one of my kids, when a fist pounds fast and hard on the steel door six feet behind me. I jump. The steel vibrates, and an eerie echo bounces off the high ceiling and walls.

"Cate! Open up!"

Is that Essi? She sounds hysterical…

I hurry to unlock the door.

Essi's dark eyes are wide, like she's seen a ghost. She's out of breath. "Mariana tried to kill herself."

I run after Essi. We whisk past kids and teachers on our way to the girls' dorm. When we arrive, A.J. is bent over Mariana, administering CPR with his signature serenity.

God, I love that man.

Mariana was thirteen when she climbed up on her bed, wrapped a leather belt around her neck, around a light fixture, and stepped off into the unknown. None of us expected it. She had often flailed around on the dorm floor in traumatic states, but her feisty behavior was childlike compared to her peers. She reminded me of the baby ewok in *Return of the Jedi* the way she waddled around campus in her flip-flops and baggy clothes.

Mariana loved to be tucked in at night, so at bedtime, the end of my shift, I often stopped by her room, sang her a lullaby, and chatted with her before she went to sleep. Her sweetness seemed miraculous in view of the abuse she had endured at the hands of those she most trusted. The innocent child in her had remained intact.

Mariana had been tortured many ways: physically, sexually, psychologically. Her father had raped her and cut her with a hunting knife over a period of several years, leaving scars all over her body shaped like large pea pods.

The scar on her heart worried me the most. She believed that no one cared about her. In one desperate, lonely moment, she broadcast that belief.

Essi had been making her afternoon rounds when she opened the door to Mariana's room and found her hanging. Mariana's olive skin turned to grey, and her head, normally held high and proud, dropped to her chest like a marionette with no master.

The news ripped through Casa the way flames devour a parched village. Reactions popped and exploded in the heat. Staff sequestered the remaining twenty-four girls in the lounge and tried to soothe them.

I put on a calm face, hyper-focused on taking care of business, and tuned out the chaos. Elena had already left for the day, so I did what I could to tend her girls as well as mine.

Essi and Sean rode herd over the anxious kids and tried to reassure them. When the medics arrived, A.J. assisted them with the equanimity of a Zen master.

Mariana's peers were triggered like firecrackers in the blaze, blindsided by their own traumatic memories. Her despair mirrored their own, and her violent act terrified them. If we couldn't keep Mariana safe, maybe we wouldn't keep them safe either. And if Mariana stopped fighting and gave up, what did that mean for them?

When I ran back to my office to retrieve Mariana's chart for the medics, I found three therapists enjoying an extended break around my desk. They looked startled and guilty, and tried to engage me in conversation.

"What's happening on the dorm? Is she going to be alright?"

Anger shriveled my eyes. My talons popped out. We needed every team member on the dorm to take care of forty-nine traumatized kids. Essi had phoned every per diem staff to bring in extra help, and these three wanted me to bring them news while they sat on their butts.

"We don't know yet." I scowled and hurried back to the dorm. It was easy to understand why the dorm staff got so disgusted with these therapists. We were not much of a team.

Finally, around 10 p.m., the dorm quieted down. A few of the girls were able to sleep with the help of medication and one-on-one attention. Terri and I trudged to my office and collapsed, exhausted, but too wired to sit still.

"Did you see that coming?" I asked my seasoned psychologist friend.

"No. She's never done anything like that before."

"What do you think triggered it?"

"Could be anything. You know her history."

"Yeah. No shortage of reasons."

We squirmed with helplessness for a few minutes, then climbed into Terri's jeep and drove to the hospital where Mariana was in intensive care. We camped out in the hallway, waiting for news.

An hour later, her doctor came out to talk to us.

"She's in a coma," he said.

I did not know what to feel. My stunned, exhausted brain struggled to string four words together.

"What are her chances?"

"Well, she's young and healthy. We have that on our side."

I looked at Terri. She was in a trance.

"There's a lot we don't know yet. We're running some tests. There is nothing more you can do tonight."

We thanked him and shuffled down the hall to the elevator. Sorrow swelled from my chest into my throat and burned behind my eyes. My body longed to vomit out all of this horror.

We returned to Casa and told Essi what the doctor said. Then we drove to the beach, where we walked and walked in the damp, chilly air under a black sky. My heart ached with frustration. A torrent of anger gushed out of me.

"Why? Why her?! That poor girl has been tormented her whole life. She never had a chance! I wish her sleaze bag father was the one in a coma!"

"Oh, I think they deserve something worse than a coma."
Terri's boots crunched in the cold sand. She stared straight ahead. We both knew that Mariana's mother had served as accomplice

while the father raped and tortured her. It was the kind of story that made me long to spray some lead.

I could not imagine the torture Mariana had lived through, but I had tasted the terror of begging for protection from a mother who never responded. I had been living far away from my own violent family for fourteen years, yet I still woke up from recurring nightmares, calling out for help. When I visited friends for the weekend, my nocturnal shouts frightened them. So embarrassing. You'd think I could control it after all the therapy and training I'd had. But the unconscious has a will of its own.

The one thing that had kept me from going insane over the injustice of Mariana's tragic life was the hope of giving her a better future. I had assumed that we would have her for a couple of years and that we could change her fate.

I tortured myself for the times I had put Mariana off when she asked for my attention. Maybe I had made her feel more hopeless. It took so little to trigger fears of abandonment and states of despair in these children.

A few hours before her suicide attempt, Mariana had stomped past me in a huff and shot me a resentful glare. She was mad at me for making her wait.

"Jesse never has to wait," she mumbled as she stormed past.

I felt her jab in my chest, alongside steaming guilt about my favoritism. She was right to accuse me. Compelled by the more challenging kids, I spent more time with them. I believed they needed me more because others found them hard to tolerate. I figured the easier kids got attention from other adults. Terri nagged me about it. "The sweet kids need you too." I tried to treat them all equally, but my heart always ran after the hopeless and the hopelessly misunderstood.

I had been swamped and stressed that morning, and late for Case Conference when Mariana flounced off, flipping her long, dark hair. Attorneys and county mental health administrators waited to hear my cases. A crisis on the dorm held me up.

My twelve other kids wanted attention too. My boss wanted thirteen quarterly reports for next week's audit. Mariana would have to wait her turn.

Each of us who cared for Mariana created our own story about how her suicide attempt was our fault. We knew that if we had been more responsive, more attentive, more something, we could have prevented it.

We felt inadequate every day to meet the overwhelming needs of the fifty kids in our care. We were always short-staffed. The caseloads were too big. We spent more time saying, "not now" and "later" to the kids than we did responding to their requests.

This perpetual no-win scenario stirred up guilt and frustration. Some of us coped by overworking and overextending. Others survived by keeping an emotional distance from the kids. Sometimes we turned on each other, placing blame.

The staff could never understand why the therapists spent hours doing paperwork instead of helping with the kids, and the therapists felt misunderstood and disrespected by the staff. We were all burned out, and the kids felt frustrated and neglected.

While Mariana lay in her hospital bed, storm clouds of guilt gathered. We all stood accused.

Most of us had come from families where we had learned to be fine caregivers. We were the super-responsible ones, the rescuers. It was our mission to save the children, and we had failed.

In Case Conference, the morning of Mariana's suicide attempt, the staff/therapist split had climaxed over a boy named Mario who had been with us for eighteen months but made no progress. Mario abused the staff and expressed no remorse. His therapist did not like to get involved in the behavioral side of the program. "I'm Rogerian," she said, as though that relieved her of any responsibility to confront Mario's destructive behavior.

She took him out to buy comics, even when he was on restriction for assaulting staff, gave him treats, then sent him back to the dorm where he mocked the staff and gloated about his freedom.

Carl Rogers would sit up in his grave if he knew how his ideal of *Unconditional Positive Regard* was misapplied by conflict-avoidant therapists.

Outraged at being undermined, Essi and A.J. complained to Leslie, the Director, and obtained her permission to speak at Case

Conference. The pair stood together in the corner of the crowded room like scowling marble statues.

Case Conference was for the professionals. The staff were not invited. Enlisted men never mingled with officers. If they were lucky, the staff could grab a therapist's attention long enough to offer input before the meeting. If unlucky, the therapist would dismiss staff recommendations and forge ahead as she wished.

Essi and A.J. demanded to be heard that day.

"We can't do anything with these kids if the therapists are allowed to undermine us." Essi's nostrils flared, and her dark eyes flashed with anger. As Leslie's number one, she carried her power with confidence. "They think they can do whatever they want and their therapist will rescue them."

A.J. chimed in. "Mario assaults my staff after he comes back from his therapist."

The three therapists from Slackerville brooded in silence. Mario's therapist was out sick that day.

I sat at the head of the table, surrounded by medical records, and torn between the two camps. My boss, Marty, an administrator and pathological peacemaker, sat at the other end of the table, eyes bulging. This was supposed to be my meeting, but Marty grabbed the reins whenever my directness made him nervous. None of us respected or trusted him, but he wielded veto power. And he wrote our performance evals.

I didn't feel much sympathy for these therapists. Their behavior embarrassed me. While the staff worked closely with our kids eight hours a day or more, the therapists refused to dirty their hands on the dorm and treated the staff like peasants.

"A.J., what do you need from the therapists?" I asked.

"I need them to respect our decisions and enforce our rules. And I need them to check with me before they take kids off the unit or give them rewards."

The three therapists grumbled and muttered. They did not want any dorm staff telling them what to do.

Marty interrupted. "O.K., we're running late here," he chirped, his face stretched into a forced smile. "Let's discuss this in the therapists' meeting tomorrow. Thank you, A.J. and Essi."

Essi shot me a cynical glance and rolled her eyes as she stalked out.

It was complicated. The therapists did not trust the staff to be fair with the kids, and they certainly did not want to give them more power. We already had too many kids feeling bullied by staff. On the other hand, the therapists were never around when the kids were out of control, and the kids did not abuse the therapists like they did the dorm staff.

Leslie never came to Case Conference, but we all knew she didn't think much of therapists. Her daily stream of snarky comments could be overheard by anyone passing through the front office, and poking fun at therapist blunders brightened her day. She figured the kids' primary attachments were to the staff. Therapists rarely stuck around for more than a few months anyway, and she had her own feelings about being abandoned.

The staff said the therapists had it easy, and they fantasized that we made good money, even though we made about one dollar an hour more than they did with our masters degrees and Ph.D's. Therapists bent the rules and made exceptions for their favorite kids, which created a good guy/bad guy dynamic. We were one big dysfunctional family.

And then there were the staff soap operas. Mandy, who worked on the girls' unit, was embroiled in a stormy affair with LaRell, who worked with the boys. No one could keep track of when they were broken up or together. LaRell flirted with me openly and made disrespectful jokes about Mandy when they were feuding. When I walked onto the boy's dorm every afternoon, LaRell, a body builder in a tight muscle shirt, did a little dance and sang to me, "The Most Beautiful Girl in the World." Mandy seethed and sniped at me, and recruited her coworkers to make my life difficult. Self-conscious as a new therapist, I took her barbs to heart. It was just like middle school.

One evening I walked onto the dorm to pick up seven girls for Female Issues Group. Marty, my boss, famous for his emotional tone deafness, had decided that all of the girls who had been sexually abused would be assigned to a therapy group together to talk about being sexually abused.

I escorted the girls to the Case Conference room for privacy. Two staff stood guard outside the door.

"Quiet, please!" I shouted above the group chatter.

The girls scooted chairs around and giggled.

"Please take one of the handouts and pass them around," I instructed. We began with a simple group exercise called Wishing Well, a coloring sheet of a girl leaning against a well with two thought bubbles above her head. "You can color the picture however you want," I said, "or you can leave it blank. But please write in the thought bubbles something you wish for yourself and something you wish for our group. Any questions?"

The girls scrambled to grab crayons and markers. They loved to color.

"Yeah, I have a question," Jesse said. "How come Sonia wears her makeup like a ho?" Jesse bent over laughing. The other girls snickered.

"Jess, that is not appropriate. Let's keep it respectful. Who can remind us of the group rules?"

Three girls raised their hands. I called on Mariana.

"No name calling," she said. "No verbal abuse. Keep hands and feet to self. Use "I" Statements."

"Good, Mariana," I said. "Who can tell me what an I Statement is?"

They all raised their hands. I called on Sonia.

"It starts with I," she said. "I feel Jesse is a skanky bitch."

Jesse lurched out of her chair and across the table toward Sonia. Sonia jumped up and took a swing at Jesse. Before I could intervene, the two were standing on top of the conference table.

"Fuck you, bitch!" Sonia slapped Jesse's face.

"Shut your mouth, you stupid slut!" Jesse swung at her head. Sonia ducked. Jesse grabbed Sonia's long ponytail. Sonia punched her in the stomach.

Several girls egged them on with shouts. Mariana froze.

"Sonia! Jesse! Get down from the table!" I barked in a big voice. "Get down! Now!"

Just as I moved to put myself in swinging distance of the two big out-of-control teenagers, Mandy burst through the door with three of her friends and took control of my group.

She had warned me against running this group alone. "You need a staff in there," she bossed. Mandy treated me like an idiot child and assumed that I could not manage a group of kids on my own. To her mind, the therapists were an unnecessary annoyance.

I knew my group of girls would not talk with staff in the room. This was a therapy group, and they needed emotional safety to talk about hard things.

Without consulting me, Mandy and her friends escorted my group back to the dorm. She lobbed a disgusted look at me on the way out.

I dissolved into a puddle of humiliation.

I awoke at dawn on the morning after Mariana's suicide attempt and found a purring kitty watching over me. Daisy, my longhaired, redheaded Abyssinian, had been renamed by my friend, Warren, who never met a cat he did not rename.

"Good morning, Puffy."

I rubbed her head. She gave me that disdainful cat look as if to say, "Who are *you* calling puffy? "

I patted some eye gel on my scary bags and went to work.

When I arrived, Casa was still in crisis mode. The kids were frightened by Mariana's suicide attempt and eager to hear news about her. Most of them coped with their unbearable vulnerability by acting tough and aggressive, like a bunch of porcupines with their quills out.

I stopped by the front office to pick up messages. My buddy, Joanie, the receptionist, gave me a nervous heads up: "The Chief of Mental Health asked Dr. Young to investigate and write a report." Fear gripped my throat. I had been through this before. In these situations, some unlucky employee would end up taking the fall.

And I was Mariana's therapist.

When I walked into my office, Dr. Young was waiting for me. My gut clenched.

Harry Young, M.D., a wise, grey-haired psychiatrist, looked like a scruffy Sean Connery. He enjoyed hanging out in our dingy little office, and he read every cartoon I posted on the wall. Sometimes Harry brought in a cartoon of his own and taped it to the cabinet above my desk. On Thursday mornings, while I prepared for Case Conference, he sat in a folding chair next to my desk and asked me questions about my personal life and my work with the kids. Harry was a psychoanalyst, and I could hear the gears whirring in his head when he analyzed me.

He wasn't really a fan of Freud. Instead, Harry preferred contemporary psychoanalytic ideas like *intersubjective systems* and *sustained empathic inquiry*. He talked about *attachment patterns* and *disrupted development* rather than aggressive drives and mental disorders.

The previous day, Harry had been trying to figure out why I wanted to do social work instead of art. Even though he'd been devoted to these kids for decades, he tried to talk me out of it.

"Most people do this job because they can't do anything else," he mused. "You have other talents. Why do you want to be here?"

He laughed at my latest creation, a poster entitled *How to Spot a Narcissistic Man,* a parody of the kids' *How Do You Feel Today?* poster with cartoons of facial expressions and corresponding emotions. My poster featured caricatures of the men that Elena and I had endured. A thought bubble floated above each character, including Elena's most recent ex, who had told her, "My therapist says I have a great capacity to receive love."

Harry gave me advice. While I rushed around and tried to respond to every request, Harry moseyed across campus to get a cup of coffee and chat with the cafeteria staff.

"You have to take care of yourself first," he counseled.

I didn't buy it. Harry was cynical. He didn't realize how much the kids needed me or how overwhelming my workload was. And besides, that sounded selfish, and the last thing I wanted to be was selfish.

It felt like a year had passed since yesterday. Harry sat at Elena's desk, his tanned, sun-damaged tennis hand resting on top of Mariana's chart. The whole thing felt surreal, like being swept into a really bad parallel universe.

"You keep good notes, Shepherd." He looked up at me with kind, concerned brown eyes. I stood stiff, arms crossed against my chest, with enough tension in my neck to produce an atrocious headache.

"Yeah, right."

He was being nice. My documentation was crap.

"You know, some of the staff think it's their fault." He spoke with that sneaky psychoanalyst tone, like he was about to persuade me of something without me knowing it. "In situations like this, everyone thinks it's their fault."

"Yes, I imagine so." I remained clenched.

"Do you think you could have done something?" he asked in a soft voice.

"I *know* I could. I could have done a lot of things." Last night's horror re-emerged full force. I clamped my tears.

"Cate, these things happen, no matter what you do. You are not at fault."

I took a deep breath and sat down. Harry's gentle manner soothed me.

"Did you hear the report from the hospital?" I asked him.

"They said she's in a coma. Anything else?"

"They're afraid they got her too late. She might have brain damage."

"Well, you never know with children her age." He spoke with calm authority based in many years of experience. "Their brains are very plastic."

He showed me the report he had written. In a two-page document, he included a long paragraph that described the "over-heavy load" carried by the therapists. He discussed the chronic under-staffing, and noted that many of the children in our program were too sick for this level of care. The message was clear. He had our backs, and he intended to seize the opportunity to advocate for us. Harry assured me that no one at Casa would take the fall for this tragedy.

Amazing.

Harry went to the front office to fax his report while I walked toward the dorm. I ran into Essi, who had been working for twenty-three hours. She wore sunglasses to hide the dark circles under her eyes and stood strong, shirtsleeves rolled up, long hair tied in a knot.

She looked like I felt. The sight of her still standing strengthened me.

"How ya doin', old friend?" I sidled up to her so we could talk low, out of earshot of our nosy children.

"I'm okay. The kids are all going nuts and my staff are calling in sick."

"Great."

"Any news?"

"Nothing new. Just waiting. Harry's here."

"Yeah, he was already over here. He's a trip."

"Yes, he is. You need anything?"

"Nope, I'm good. As soon as A.J. gets here, I'm gonna go home and take a fuckin' shower."

"Yeah, do that, will ya?"

We both released a fatigued chuckle and watched the kids kick a ball around on the field.

I walked onto the dorm to check in with the staff. They greeted me with uncharacteristic warmth, eager to hear news of Mariana. I sat down in the dorm office with Mandy.

"Did they get the tests back yet?" Mandy leaned toward me with a soft expression I'd never seen before, her eyes red from crying.

"Not yet."

"Did you see her?"

"They wouldn't let us in last night. I'm going back today at lunch."

"We made something for her." Mandy tenderly lifted a huge yellow poster from behind the file cabinet and held it up. Forty-nine kids and their staff and teachers had written *Get Well* and *We Love You* messages decorated with flowers, smiley faces, and hearts. One of the boys drew a teddy bear. Mariana loved teddy bears.

Emotion swept through me as I read the poster. I looked up at Mandy with tear-filled eyes. "I'll take it to her."

Mandy cradled the poster and passed it to me with a sad, brave smile. Her flannel shirtsleeve brushed my arm. She smelled like lavender.

It was like we'd never met before.

Terri and I visited Mariana at the hospital every day and conjured ideas for waking her from her coma. We stood by her bed and talked to her about her friends and favorite staff.

I recorded a tape of her favorite lullabies, and one evening during our visit, Terri put headphones on her and played it. We held her warm, soft hands and watched her face while the machines beeped and hummed. The antiseptic air and crisp linens created a stark contrast to the grungy group home. I had never seen Mariana so peaceful. Her color was good and her skin had cleared up.

As the days passed, the hospital staff seemed pessimistic. Mariana had hung from her noose too long. Even if she woke up, she might be a vegetable.

But we ignored the prognosis and lobbied for a miracle.

Ingrid, the new therapist, brought her priest to the hospital to pray for Mariana. Ingrid was one of those happy, clappy Catholics who attended charismatic healing services at St. Vincent's. She said Father Tim had the gift of healing, and she had seen many miracles during her years as a nun.

Each time Ingrid visited Mariana, she anointed her forehead with blessed oil and laid her hands on Mariana's head while she prayed.

Terri was sort of a Catholic-New Age hybrid who sprinkled holy water, swung crystals, and visualized light healings. She figured she'd cover all the bases.

I just did my usual Protestant pleading.

Everyone prayed in their own way. Those without faith prayed anyway. Except for Harry. He was too rational for that stuff.

As the weeks passed, the staff/therapist conflicts got lost amid our shared grief and love for Mariana. We took time to get to know each other. Some of the therapists started hanging out with staff on the dorm. The guys bonded over Chargers games, and I heard stories about staff/therapist outings to the pub.

One afternoon, before her shift began, Mandy came to my office to talk. She asked my advice about graduate programs. She wanted to become a therapist.

On a Thursday morning before Case Conference, Leslie called me into her office. My stomach felt queasy. I had not entered the Director's inner sanctum since my initial interview a year earlier. Native American art adorned her walls, and a four-foot square painting of a green-eyed wolf hung behind her as she leaned forward and propped her elbows on the desk.

"Terri tells me you've been visiting Mariana every day."

Uh oh…I'm trouble for leaving during my shift.

I flushed. I felt exposed, as though Leslie had been watching me through that stupid hole in her wall. I remembered the day I sat on this nasty carpet with Jesse, feeling scrutinized and judged by Leslie.

"How are you doing?" Leslie's forest green eyes looked otherworldly, framed by long lashes and thick, black eyebrows. I had never seen her without her glasses before.

"I'm okay."

"Essi and A.J. like working with you," she said. "It's good to have a therapist on the dorm."

"They're amazing," I said. "I could never do their job."

"Cate, you did good work with Mariana. We all know that."

I swallowed. I didn't know what to say. A strange object on Leslie's bookshelf caught my eye, and I stepped closer to look at it.

Leslie smiled, stood up, and walked over to the shelf. She turned the object toward me so I could see inside. "It's a prayer altar," she said.

It looked like a little house with crystals, sage, rocks, and some kind of powder inside. A candle burned in the center. Behind it, a small picture of Mariana.

"If you need anything, let me know, okay?" Her eyes were kind and she spoke in a gentle voice I'd never heard before.

"I will. Thank you."

I can't believe she trusts me…

Several more weeks passed, and Mariana's condition remained the same. Our faith began to flag. We stopped visiting the hospital every day and turned our energy toward the remaining forty-nine kids.

On an afternoon when I had not planned to go to the hospital, Terri stopped by my office for a chat.

"I've been thinking about Mariana a lot today," she said, staring into space. She sat, slumped, in Harry's chair, her boot propped on my desk. "I had a dream about her last night."

"Really? Let's hear it."

"It was brief. More an image than a dream, really."

As a Jungian analyst, Terri was a dream fiend. She loved symbols and archetypes, and spent hours interpreting them.

"So what did you see?" I asked.

"She walked toward me with a peaceful smile, and an aura of white light all around her. She was wearing that blue t-shirt she likes so much, but I couldn't see anything else about her – just a lot of light."

"Sounds spiritual."

"I know." Terri looked at me. "I don't think I want to know what it means."

We looked at each other.

"Let's go see her," Terri said.

We climbed into the jeep, drove our usual route, and marched onto the hospital unit. It smelled like alcohol, and the air conditioning was turned up too high.

As we approached Mariana's room I heard a commotion; someone shouting, metal clanking against metal, a cacophony of anxious voices.

Oh no…that sounds like heroic measures…

My mouth went dry and sticky. I felt clammy all over.

I glanced back at Terri. She looked scared.

With my heart pounding fast, I hurried to Mariana's doorway. Five hospital staff flanked her bed. I couldn't see her, and no one appeared to be trying to resuscitate her.

"Oh, shit," Terri said.

A nurse turned to look at us. I recognized her as one of the regulars.

"What's happening?" I asked her.

Mariana's bed sheet rose like a ghost above her powerful kicks. Her hospital gown flew off one shoulder as she thrashed and flailed.

The eyes of the hospital staff grew wide.

"Let me out of here!" Mariana yelled.

Terri and I burst into gigantic grins.

Mariana struggled hard against the nurses and orderlies who fumbled to get a grip on her.

"Let go of me, dang it! Let me go!"

I took a step toward the bed. "Oh no you don't! You're on AWOL watch."

Mariana recognized my voice and jerked her head around to look at me. She stopped struggling and looked confused. The hospital staff stepped away from the bed.

"Cate! Get me out of here!" She looked more mad than scared. It was good to see her feisty face again.

I felt like that woman in the bible story who found the stone rolled away from the tomb. I couldn't wait to get back to the village to tell everyone.

Our nurse friend let us say hi to Mariana and give her a hug before we had to leave the room. Then we sped back to the group home where I bounded out of the jeep and sprinted to the dorm.

Essi sat at her desk, hunched over some paperwork. I flew into her office, out of breath, and blurted out, "she's awake!"

Essi looked up. "Huh?"

"We just came from the hospital." I tried to catch my breath. "Mariana just woke up. She's raising holy hell."

"Oh Dios mio!" Essi's face bloomed into a huge smile and she grabbed me in a bear hug.

"A.J.!" she shouted down the hall as she released me and bolted out the door.

We didn't get much work done that day.

We got our miracle and, for the first time, we all rejoiced together. Staff, therapists, psychiatrists, administrators, teachers, nurses, housekeeping staff, and kitchen staff chatted and hugged and chatted some more. The walls that had divided us were obliterated by our love for Mariana.

They say that relapse is always a part of recovery, and we backslid into bickering and turf wars from time to time, but we never forgot what Mariana taught us. We preserved her lessons in the program structure with policy changes.

Instead of waiting outside of Case Conferences for verdicts from the professionals, the staff sent a representative to every meeting. A primary staff was assigned to each child to work closely with the therapist and create a collaborative, inter-disciplinary treatment plan. The kids felt more secure when mom and dad were on the same team and, as a result, they spent less time maneuvering and more time working the program.

Therapists were required to spend some time on the dorm every day. At the beginning of each shift, staff and therapists met to discuss each child and fine-tune their co-parenting.

After a period of mild grumbling and resistance, both staff and therapists learned to like the changes. The new model reduced strife and made everyone's job easier. Staff and therapists learned to stick together under stress. We vented and laughed in our daily meetings, and came out looking like a unified front to the forty-nine kids who watched us like baby hawks in our nest.

Mariana did not return to Casa after she left the hospital. Our kids were too nervous about having her around after what she had done. We found a small group home where she could continue her treatment.

On a Tuesday morning, two weeks later, I walked into the front office to deliver some paperwork. Mariana stood in the middle of the room. A relaxed smile lit up her countenance. The hypervigilant tension and sad scowl were gone from her face. She looked more mature. Her hunched shoulders and baggy clothes were gone. She wore a pair of pressed, white jeans and a stylish blouse, and would have turned heads on any high school campus.

I could understand how she had lost a lot of weight at the hospital, but what was this new radiance and confidence?

Ingrid peeked out from the mailroom, beaming. She had already seen her.

Mariana looked at me with such joy. Her soft, brown eyes glistened when she smiled. No more haunted stare, jerking to and fro, scanning for danger. She was at peace.

Her CPS social worker of several years stood next to her. She knew we were eager to see her. "Cate, I want you to know that Mariana is doing very well in her new school."

"I got a A in Math and a B in Science." Mariana bubbled. "My shoshal worker is taking me to *Roberto's!*"

I always loved how she said her s's.

"That is so awesome, Mariana. Are you gonna get the carne asada fries?"

"Yeah." She nodded her head and leaned into her worker.

Mariana hugged me good-bye and I walked to my office, dazed with disbelief.

Weird…

Harry sat next to my desk drinking his morning coffee. "Did you see your girl?"

"I just saw her in the front office. I barely recognized her. How do you explain that?"

"Oh, it's not uncommon with children her age. Their brains are so plastic. Sometimes they can heal a lot more than we think."

I looked at him. That sounded like a lame explanation for such a dramatic transformation. I never dreamed we would get her that healed even if we had her for two years. *Where did all her trauma go? Where did that nasty, persistent hopelessness go? Where did that other girl, the haunted one in the baggy clothes, where did she go?*

I thought of my girlfriend who had lost her beautiful young husband in a motorcycle accident. She told me how the overwhelming trauma of that loss had wiped away all of the pesky old traumas that had plagued her for years.

Ingrid bounced into the room with a triumphant smile. "She is SO beautiful! She looks just like an angel!" She gushed with the toothy excitement of a young child.

Harry busied himself reading papers. He didn't think much of Ingrid or her nutty religion.

And Ingrid was not interested in talking about plastic brains. She knew this was a real miracle.

Funny the things you save...It's been almost twenty years, and I'm no pack rat, but I still have that little vial of Ingrid's blessed oil here in my desk drawer. She kept it in a Nordstrom sample bottle.

THE SATANIST AND THE SAINT

"It is a joy to be hidden, disaster to not be found."
- D. W. Winnicott

"Have you ever considered getting breast implants?" Mario welcomed me to my first session of Male Issues Group, his defiant stare searing into my chest.

"Yeah, I've thought about it." An unemotional Aikido move.

I passed his first test.

Mario had a special gift for seeing vulnerable spots in others, inserting a knife, and twisting it. At fifteen, he was a dreaded and despised button-pusher, the most hated and least wanted of all the misfits in our care.

Whose brilliant idea was it, I wondered, to send me into a group of adolescent boys who did not know me and did not trust each other, and to require that they talk about their experiences of being sexually abused? One could hardly blame Mario for his preemptive strike.

Mario's brand of abuse was familiar to me. I had been raised on it. The breast size comment was exactly the sort of thing my father liked to say to me at the dinner table until I learned to hide in my room. I saw my father's pain and rage in Mario and I found it irresistible. I couldn't heal Dad but, by God, I was determined to heal Mario.

Mario was an artist. His thick, black, curly hair had a presence of its own, sticking up and out in all directions, and his pigeon-toed shuffle matched the pout he formed with his chubby cheeks and plump lips. His belly pooched out, his shoulders slumped. He looked forlorn when he didn't know I was looking. But when he saw me, he lit up in a wicked grin that transformed the sullen waif into a lively mischief-maker. Every evening he assembled a bizarrely mismatched fashion ensemble to attract negative attention at school the next day. Plaids, cutoffs, leather, gaudy socks, rainbow suspenders, feather boas, you name it, he could make it not work.

In his free time, Mario read the Satanic Bible. He studied spells and curses, and tried to figure out how to put a hex on LaRell. He drew meticulous pictures of demons, pentagrams and writhing snakes that bared their fangs, and he plastered his walls with them.

Mario tormented the staff the way a cat twirls a mouse. Heaven help the new hire who innocently walked into his room. Mario would ask, "Do you like my artwork?" to set the trap for his prey. I winced at his cruelty. After he terrorized one earnest worker, he would lick his chops and look for another.

One afternoon, a few days after I met Mario in group, I walked past his doorway and saw three staff holding him down. A tall, muscular man shoved his knee into Mario's shoulder blade while LaRell stepped on his ankle and barked, "Shut up!"

LaRell did good work with some of the kids, but his tender ego retaliated when injured. And LaRell's self-esteem was Mario's favorite chew toy.

Disturbed by the scene, I considered who to tell. We all knew that LaRell and his buddies bullied the boys. The kids told us horror stories every day. It was the Director's responsibility to stop them, and I never understood why she didn't.

I had developed a bad habit of picking battles I could not win and taking on problems that were not mine to solve. So this time I decided to go through the proper channels and report the incident to Marty, my boss. It pained me to leave such an important matter in his jelly fish tentacles, but the last thing my kids needed right now was for me to become preoccupied with one of my crusades, trying to reform someone else's staff without the authority to do so.

I found some quiet time to sit in my office and read Mario's history: abandoned by birth mother at four, placed in a foster home where he was sexually abused, then another foster home where he was beaten. When he finally found a good foster mom in adolescence, he was too hurt and bitter to enjoy her. He busted up her antique furniture, keyed her car, and shoved her, which landed him at Casa.

Mario's previous therapist had burned out after eighteen months, bruised by his abuse and stymied by his tenacious indifference.

When she asked me to take over, I couldn't resist the challenge. I had felt a kinship with him since the first day we met. Terri teased me about my weird devotion to Mario and called me St. Rita, Patron Saint of Hopeless Causes.

My devotion was born of gratitude. When I was Mario's age, any teacher worth his salt should have been able to see that I was in trouble, but none of them seemed to care.

One day in Biology class, Mr. Robertson gestured with an arm wave, a little too close to my head, and I automatically ducked and covered. He made a joke about it in front of the whole class. "What's the matter?" he asked. "Are you used to being beaten up?"

Ha ha.

And in Art class, Mr. Barker noticed the dark themes in my drawings and asked me, "Do you have a personal problem?" Then he sent a note to the principal that said, "Cate may have a personal problem."

Gee, thanks.

But Mr. O never ridiculed me. He called me into his office and asked me what was going on at home. He persisted, so I told him. There was nothing he could do about it. Not in Waynesville, Ohio. There was no such thing as Children's Protective Services, and the town police officer was the jerk next door who abused his own kids.

Mr. O did something far more powerful than calling the authorities. He cared. And he understood. Yeah, his methods were a little unorthodox. He shared his cigarettes with me and swore like a trucker, but hey, strong language for strong feelings.

Mr. O saved my life. In a few months' time, his understanding lifted me out of hopeless isolation and catalyzed a transformation.

Fifteen years later, I remembered how it felt to be understood, and I recognized Mario's armor. I believed that a wounded boy was hiding underneath all that sadistic behavior, and I figured the best way to reach him was to survive his aggression and refuse to let him push me away. If Mr. O could save me, I could save Mario.

Mario's flamboyant hopelessness compelled me. He sabotaged all progress and harassed the adults who cared for him until they walked away, shaking their heads. When he accidentally earned some points, his primary staff, Tracy, got all excited and optimistic. Tracy was a graduate student and a true believer in the power of Positive Reinforcement. She trotted to Mario's room with a big smile to praise him. In response, he exploded in an abusive rant, called her a "skanky brainless cunt", and threw a chair at her.

Mario's hopelessness was his only remaining refuge.

I was two years out of graduate school, full of passion, and on a mission. I cruised through the barracks in my Birkenstocks, long skirt flowing, cross pendant bobbing. I had earned a reputation for reaching hopeless kids, and I felt confident that I could help Mario in a way that no one else had.

My spiritual practice grounded me and ordered my life. Freshly divorced, highly anxious, and living at the beach with my cat, I rose at 5:00 a.m. every morning for meditation. I walked barefoot on the beach, wrote spiritual poetry, and cleared out my cluttered soul before meeting the kids each day. I believed what Mother Theresa wrote, that if I was available and attuned, I could be a "pencil in God's hand". I didn't share her religion, but I loved her work, and my hungry little ego yearned for greatness.

My comrade, Ingrid, an ex-nun, had spent several years in a Carmelite convent, praying in silence after she raised her kids and divorced her husband. Ingrid was as fiercely devoted to our kids as she had been to Jesus. Her progressive ideas had gotten her the boot from the convent, so now she led a contemplative prayer group in her studio apartment where we lit candles and listened in silence. After group, we drank Heineken in the hot tub and giggled. At Christmas, when one of our orphan boys asked Santa for a $100 pair of purple Doc Marten boots, the prayer group made them appear under the tree.

Ingrid and I worked closely together with the kids and their families. She was the only woman who ever beat me at arm wrestling. She was tough. A stocky German with a thick accent, her beaming smile and fiery spirit evoked a protective aura in a barracks rife with conflict and violence. Ingrid told me stories about her life in the convent, like when the nuns went stir crazy from too much silence and threw rotten eggs against the convent walls to hear them explode. Her neighbors called the police, worried about gunshots at the convent.

When we prepared to meet with a particularly noxious set of parents, Ingrid and I joked about invoking St. Rita. For us, this was much more than a job. It was a calling. I was not a Catholic, but I resonated with her passion.

Harry seemed annoyed by Ingrid, but he loved hanging out in our skuzzy office, crusty carpet, cockroaches and all. He observed my antics with the kids, who came to visit during lunch break and after school. Their classrooms were only a few steps away, and they poured through the door to flood us with requests every day. Elena and I oohed and ahhed over their art projects, made our walls into an art gallery, and gave them Hershey's kisses.

Every kid had an angle. The nerdy boys schmoozed us for baseball cards and comics. The gang kids in their sagging pants tried to make contracts for Walkmans and boom boxes. Others begged for walks to the taco shop and trips to the mall. But not Mario. He didn't want anything. He was like one of those babies who never cries because he realized there was no point.

One afternoon, after a dark, provocative visit from Mario, Harry grinned at me. He stroked his grey beard, nodded, and said, "You're goofy enough to do this work." With those words, Dr. Young knighted me. I beamed.

You had to be goofy to do such dangerous, difficult work with a huge caseload of violent and suicidal patients for $12.00 an hour.

Harry said the most disturbed kids were treated by the least experienced therapists, and that young therapists, with their passion intact, often made the most effective healers. He tried to be a good mentor to me and Elena. Harry noticed that therapists became less effective later in their careers when they thought they were experts. "When you think you've arrived, that's when you're dead in the water," he warned.

I got lots of props from my coworkers for my ability to survive Mario. My friends buttered me up to ensure that none of them would inherit him. We were all stressed to our limits, and no one wanted to be abused by the Satanist on top of everything else.

Elena grew annoyed by my freakish patience with Mario. One morning she stomped back from the dorm after being eviscerated by Nikki, her newest patient, and launched into me. "It never gets to you!" Her forehead, normally smooth and crease-free, scrunched up above blazing blue eyes.

Elena was good when she was angry. I liked seeing it. I waited for it like Haley's Comet. She acted too sugar coated for my taste most of the time.

Nikki was Elena's Mario.

"These kids make me cry all the time." Tears flooded her big, pretty eyes. "Sometimes I hate them." She plopped down in her chair, deflated, and told me how Nikki had humiliated her in front of the staff.

The staff did not expect Elena to last, and they gave her a hard time, calling her "naïve" and "Pollyanna". Her youthful face and fluffy blonde hair didn't help.

Nikki was one of those telepathic kids who could ferret out your deepest insecurity. When Elena went to visit her with a warm, sincere smile, Nikki ripped into her like a honey badger. "You ain't nuthin' but trailer trash! You got a fat ass but no tits, girl, ain't nobody gonna want that!" The other girls laughed while the staff looked on, smirking.

"She is *evil*!" Elena yelled, "I hate her!"

"Yes! She *is* evil!" I egged her on.

"She is the *Antichrist*!"

"Yes! She *is* the Antichrist!"

Elena waved her arms and ranted while I sat on top of my desk and shouted out my full endorsement of every crazy thing she said. We laughed hard, and I thanked my lucky stars that that girl was not on my caseload. She would have brought my saintly equanimity to an abrupt halt.

After a cathartic spew and lots of belly laughs, Elena returned to the dorm to talk to Nikki.

I visited Mario every day. When I asked, "How's school?" He spat contempt for his teacher. "I hate that stupid pussy! He doesn't know shit!" Then he glared at me. "You have a big nose. You look like a witch."

When I asked how his foster mom was doing, he said, "You've been smoking crack again. You look like hammered shit." He stared into my eyes and waited for my reaction. I grinned and stared back.

As the weeks passed, I took Mario for walks around campus after school. He loved lizards and had a gift for catching them. They reclined in the palm of his hand while he gently stroked their bellies.

Mario had never spoken to anyone about his mother or his experiences in foster homes. He hated therapy and he hated therapists. They were all stupid. All they did was probe around in his tender spots and then leave him.

I would be different. I would be safe and dependable, and provide a new relational home that would resurrect his hope. I would make him trust me. After three months of persistent chipping away at his stony fortress, I found a crack in the wall.

Mario loved "fat mama jokes." He collected jokes like treasures and brought them to me.

"Yo mama so fat, when her beeper goes off, people think she's backing up!"

"Yo mama so fat, she's on both sides of the family!"

He threw his head back and laughed with raucous freedom. I told him the macabre jokes I'd learned in high school, and sick, deeply politically incorrect humor became our bond. Sometimes I felt a twinge of guilt and worried that my boss would get wind of my naughtiness. I couldn't really chart, "exchanged dead baby jokes with patient."

We walked around looking for lizards. We hung out in his room and looked at his Satanic drawings. He started to make other kinds of drawings. He replaced some of his demons with lizard pictures.

One day after school, Sean called me from the dorm. "Mario wants to talk to you."

"Really? That's a first. Send him over."

When Mario arrived at my door, he looked like a scared little boy. He sat down in Elena's chair and slumped over. He stared at the floor and spoke so softly I could barely hear him. "My foster dad hit me when I was in the first grade." He continued to look at the floor. "He hit my knees with a baseball bat."

A chill jolted my body.

That explained the limp that Mario refused to talk about. He became belligerent whenever someone mentioned it.

"I didn't do anything!" Mario erupted in a strained shout. He looked up and away into a distant corner of the room, as though addressing someone from another time. Tears trailed down his brown cheek. Emotions from the distant past flooded him.

His voice fell. "I didn't do anything."

Mario dropped his face into his palms and sobbed. An avalanche of pain tumbled out as his chest heaved. I rolled my chair closer to him and placed my palm between his shoulder blades. He sobbed louder, his back hot and moist through his t-shirt. The electricity of his pain crackled through my body. Tears blurred my vision.

I sat with Mario in reverent silence. I felt like a midwife catching a newborn.

After Mario's pent up pain broke loose, he began to heal. When he was ready, and when he was held securely enough by us, the developmental process worked its magic.

It's funny how breakthroughs seem to erupt out of nowhere. After months or years of invisible gestation beneath the surface, a dynamic system hits its tipping point, and everything appears to change in the blink of an eye. One minute it's all labor pains. The next, it's a baby.

His teacher, Mike, a sweet hippy with long hair, reported that Mario raised his hand in class, asked brilliant questions, and helped his classmates with their math problems. He even stayed after class to help Mike clean up, which Mike found a little unnerving.

Mario's stony, sullen expression softened, and he revealed his deep dimples every day. He loved to make me laugh, and I adored his dark, quirky humor. I enjoyed him so much that I had to be careful not to show favoritism around the other kids.

Mario made drawings for me: lizards, horses, unicorns. He stopped insulting me. The outrageous costumes disappeared, and he combed his hair. A calm came over him. Not the cold, creepy calm he used to exude, but the serenity of a child who feels safe.

One day after school Mario appeared at my door, escorted by Sean. He wore a pressed white shirt and black trousers, his hair neatly styled, and presented me with a pink cupcake that he'd decorated for Valentine's Day.

Sean raised his eyebrows and grinned, out of Mario's view.

I watched Mario's metamorphosis with deep joy. He poured himself into art projects and worked hard to earn extra money and decorate his room. The demons disappeared. He started building an elaborate car model with Terri. He acted like a regular kid, except that he made his bed every day and kept his room tidy.

Ingrid took Mario lizard hunting several times a week and delighted in all of their interactions. She marveled at his gentleness with the little lizards, and how they relaxed in the palm of his hand. She told me every adorable thing he said. Mario had a grandma for the first time.

Ingrid and I believed in the healing power of unconditional love. We figured that if we showed Mario acceptance and understanding in the face of all his testing, he would eventually let his guard down.

And so he did. Mario confided to Sean that he loved me, and he asked Sean to help him craft a letter. It was his first love letter. Sean delivered it to me one morning while Mario was in class, and sat with me while I opened the tightly folded square of notebook paper and read Mario's carefully printed words.

Dear Cate,
I want to tell you something
but you have to promise
not to show this to anyone...

"Soo…what does it say?" Sean asked with an eager grin.

"I can't tell anyone." I flushed.

"Aww…c'mon."

I looked up at Sean, smiled, and shook my head.

He chuckled and walked back to the dorm.

A little embarrassed, but moved by Mario's words, I tucked his letter into my briefcase.

That evening I visited the boy's dorm and knocked on Mario's doorframe.

He looked up from his book. His cheeks turned pink.

"Can I come in?"

"Yeah," he said. He fumbled around with his bookmark.

I stood a few feet away from him. He sat on his bed and clutched his book.

"Your letter is very beautiful," I said. "Thank you."

His eyes grew wide. He fidgeted.

"I'm honored by your words. You're a good writer."

"Thank you." A hint of a smile lifted the corner of his mouth.

"Don't worry. I won't tell anyone." I gave him a kind smile.

He smiled back. His dark eyes sparkled.

"I'll see you tomorrow." I turned toward the door. "We can go lizard hunting."

"Bye, Cate."

During the next few weeks, I handled Mario's feelings with all the reverence I could muster.

We balanced our relationship on the tightrope of his developmental needs for a surrogate mother, friend, and girlfriend, and his need to be protected by a professional with clear boundaries.

Every relationship was complex and unique in this way, and the balance shifted from day to day. As a therapist, I watched for cues from each child that indicated how s/he needed to use me in a particular moment. I tried to provide optimal emotional responses to emerging states of mind. On a typical day at Casa, I morphed from mommy to mentor to cheerleader to coach to twin and back to mommy again. Several times.

Those who had written off Mario acknowledged the change in him. He emerged from self-protective armor to connect with some of the staff, went on weekend passes with his foster mom, mended the rupture in their relationship, and rebuilt his family. To her credit, Mario's foster mom had always seen through his prickly defenses. She understood how frightened he was, and she patiently stood by him until he found the courage to drop the facade and reveal his vulnerable self. I looked forward to supporting the family through the rest of the program, graduation, and a successful reunion at home.

One of my girls posted a poem in the gallery that made me think of Mario. "*Don't be fooled by the face I wear for I wear a mask. I wear a thousand masks and none of them are me... Please...don't believe me!*"

Like a game of hide and seek with a toddler who covers his eyes and thinks you can't see him, I kept saying, "I see you!" And when Mario saw his true reflection in the eyes of people who cared about him, his hope revived. And, though it took a few bumps on the head, his hope survived.

On a Friday afternoon, my old boss at Chrysalis House called to offer me my dream job as Clinical Director of the Residential Treatment Program. As a clinical intern, I had trained there for a year and forged a deep connection with a gifted mentor. During that idyllic internship, I worked alongside delightful kindred spirits, found new friends, fell in love in one of them, and learned to be a therapist. Of course I would accept the job. It would be heaven, and I would also make a lot more money and enjoy a spacious office with windows. No more slogging my guts out in a stark, windowless room that reeked of Elena's abandoned French onion soup, or whatever that slimy brown gunk was that she foraged from the cafeteria.

Thrilled by the offer, but stricken with guilt, I shuddered at the thought of leaving my kids. If only I could time travel a month into the future and forego the gauntlet I was about to run.

Most of our kids had been abandoned by their parents and forced to move from home to home, transferred from therapist to therapist. I understood how disruptive my leaving would be.

I thought we should give the kids a few weeks to adjust to the news and say a proper good-bye. My mentors had taught me that the termination phase of treatment was important and should be managed carefully, allowing plenty of time to discuss emerging emotions.

But Leslie had more pressing concerns. She was responsible for the safety of fifty emotionally disturbed adolescents and the stability of a huge treatment center. She could not risk triggering my thirteen kids to act out their emotions on the dorm for several weeks. That would completely disrupt the milieu. No more than a week's notice, that was her policy.

With a humongous wad of anxiety in my stomach, I skulked into Leslie's office to tell her about my new job. I asked her for at least two weeks to say good-bye to my kids. She refused to accept my resignation and offered me a raise. She did not believe that I would really leave.

This was not going to be easy.

I was relieved to find Harry in my office when I returned with my tail between my legs.

"She won't let me leave," I whined. I sat down and slumped under a load of guilt.

Harry looked at my deflated form and laughed. "What are you going to do? Stay here and become one of the lifers? Grow some of those saddlebags on your butt like Leslie?"

I cackled. Too grateful to scold him, I relished the release of laughter.

Harry said healthy therapists never stayed more than two years. The lifers, he said, stayed long after they were burned out because they were afraid to leave. He thought they did more harm than good.

I hated to admit it, but I had hit the two-year mark. Elena and I talked about it every Friday, along with all the things we wanted to do on the weekend. But we were too exhausted. We both spent our weekends avoiding people and trying to get rested enough to come back on Monday. Funding cuts and burgeoning caseloads made our jobs increasingly impossible, and each wave of new kids was more disturbed than the last.

Leslie would not negotiate, and gave me the silent treatment, so I proceeded with her termination plan. *Termination*. It seemed like a scary word for ending a healing relationship, but in this instance, it felt appropriate. On Monday afternoon, my last week at Casa, Essi called in several extra staff for backup, and we gathered my thirteen kids in the group room to tell them I was leaving.

They knew it was coming. These kids had developed a sixth sense and could sniff out imminent abandonment the way puppy dogs sense an earthquake.

We knew our kids and we could predict which ones would run around like banshees, destroy furniture, kicks holes in walls, threaten suicide, assault the staff, AWOL, or caretake the therapist.

Mario was quiet. I could feel the storm brewing. I did not want him to hear this news in a group, but my boss forbade me to tell him in private. I was tempted to ignore the rules and give him a heads up, but I feared he would disrupt the dorm when we were short-staffed. Someone might get hurt.

After a painful group session that triggered thirteen sad, angry, frightened kids, I dragged my drained, depressed carcass to Terri's office and flopped down.

"Uhh..." I moaned.

"What?"

"I feel like I'm killing my babies."

"Your babies are survivors. They'll be fine."

"I'm worried. Becka gets re-traumatized every time someone leaves. She's been having night terrors again and screaming for her mom. And what about Mike? He's just starting to open up. This is his worst nightmare. And Mario. I can't even think about Mario. Maybe I can take him with me to Chrysalis."

"Cate, Mario will be fine. Everything you've invested in these kids is theirs to keep. They'll struggle for awhile, but they'll get back on track."

I studied Terri's face. She looked like she meant it.

"We'll take care of them. I'll help Gracie. Don't worry."

I had recruited my old friend, Gracie, from graduate school, to replace me. I trusted her to take good care of my kids. She was insanely devoted in her work and had a heart the size of the Pacific Ocean. I worried that the system would suck her dry.

"No matter when you leave, it will be like this," Terri said. "You'll always have a full caseload of kids, and they'll always be triggered and disrupted."

I knew she was right, but it still felt so wrong.

When I walked back to my office to wrap up paperwork, the emptiness hit me like a wrecking ball to the chest. My kids were not the only ones who would suffer loss. I wondered if they realized how much they meant to me. Overwhelmed by their own pain, the kids assumed that us therapists were rich and happy and went home to cozy, loving families. Little did they know they were the love of my life.

Later that day, Sean brought me a note from Mario.

If you were just going to use me and throw me away like a rag doll, you should've told me. It's not right to just use somebody like that and then just throw them away.
BAD BYE, Mario

Acid seared my gut.

I had planned to become Mother Theresa and now I was demoted to *Evil Seductress*.

Mario's rage jarred me. How could this be? I was *The Good Mommy*, the one who took the kids to the beach on Christmas Day and bought them meals I couldn't afford. I strained my limits to fill the holes in their souls with every teaspoonful of nourishment I could eke out.

As I sat alone at my desk, hunched over his note, I saw my mother's scowl.

"Don't be selfish!" was her refrain, the one I'd heard over and over for thirty years like a needle grinding in the groove of an old, scratched up LP. No matter how saintly I became, no matter how much of my life I sacrificed for her and others, the moment I tried to take care of myself, her gavel of judgment fell on my head.

This is part of the dilemma with narcissistic parents. The child believes something is wrong with her, and that if only she can do more, be more, try harder, she might win Mother's approval. It's a crazy-making role-reversal in which a child is used to serve the needs of the parent while sacrificing her own developmental needs. The child gives up her own life to feed the bottomless hunger of a needy parent. And when she dares to step out of role, rage and rejection ensue.

So, I learned to serve the needs of others and neglect my own. I could earn Mother's temporary approval by being cheerful, helpful, serving as nurse for my handicapped sister, and providing endless free psychotherapy for my mother. She wanted a child who smiled, looked pretty, tended her needs, and asked nothing of her. It was the kind of conditional acceptance than tends to make children highly anxious and prone to people pleasing. Or the opposite, as in Mario's case.

All my life I worried about being selfish. When I was thirty, a wise therapist said, "If you would just be selfish for six months, you wouldn't need any more therapy." That sounded like heresy. Harry told me the same thing. Years later, when I finally crumpled from exhaustion, I got it.

Mario refused to talk to me. He thrashed and raged like an infant in pain. His hopelessness returned, and he trashed his room and erased all of the progress he had made. He assaulted the staff and spent hours in takedowns and in the isolation room. He strapped his armor back on and attacked with nihilistic fury. Once again, he alienated the people who tried to help him.

I longed to explain myself. Surely we could find a way to stay connected through this storm.

I had committed an unforgivable sin. Though I knew it was time to leave Casa, a deeper, older belief coiled itself around the ventricles of my heart and choked out the joy of success.

I had betrayed Mario in the worst possible way. What did this say about me? What other atrocities was I capable of? Maybe my mother was right about me.

Mario's despair reminded me of a day when I was his age, curled up in the camper of my father's pickup truck, heartbroken by the unexpected loss of my best friend, Mr. O. He had given me hope. He was the reason I tried to do better. He was the only one who understood. And he was leaving, moving to another state. I would never see him again.

The loss of that relationship derailed me. My compass vanished. Grief flooded me till I choked. I huddled under a blanket with my journal and struggled to remember all the things he had told me. I wrote them down and clung to them like a sacred text. *Wise Sayings of Mr. O.* Even if I never saw him again, I wanted to make him proud. I still do.

Friday night, after a grueling week of grieving with thirteen frightened, aggressive adolescents, my coworkers took me out to an Italian restaurant within stumbling distance of my apartment where we drank too much chianti and got a little too rowdy. I still don't remember exactly why Darrell was sitting on my lap in the photos.

Terri and Elena gave me a wooden plaque carved with a hobo sign, a simple line drawing of a smiling cat with a heart in each corner. Terri explained that hobos drew the symbol for *Kind-Hearted Woman* in the dirt in front of a house where fellow travelers could stop for a meal. Essi and A.J. gave me a silver heart-shaped pendant with a card that read, "You have a big heart - save some for yourself."

I tried to absorb their loving compliments, but old voices rumbled in the back of my head. "Selfish! Selfish! Selfish!" Like a miniature mob chanting at a witch hunt.

I remembered what Harry said about *Invariant Organizing Principles*. He insisted that we all have a head full of unconscious beliefs left over from childhood that determine our perceptions of reality, no matter how much evidence we produce to the contrary. "They operate automatically," he explained, "outside of your awareness. And they never really go away. The best you can do is become more aware of them."

So I was fated to spend the rest of my life listening to the rival gangs in my head argue whether I was a selfish bitch or a saint? What good was all this therapy if the old beliefs are *Invariant*?

I left for my new job. Ingrid assured me that I was making the right choice and she promised to look after Mario. But it was too late. He had exhausted the patience of his caregivers. With no advocate fighting to keep him, Leslie sent him to another program.

When I visited Casa, Essi told me stories about Mario's antics at his new group home. He was destructive, but I had to admire his invincible spirit. He would go down fighting. I sent him a letter to try to explain myself. He didn't respond.

I loved directing my own treatment center. Unlike Casa, our little group home was quiet and fully staffed, the kids were stable, and we had time to play. We took our twelve kids hiking and swimming, and I recruited the kind of staff who made a healthy home. Laughter, creativity, and practical jokes flowed freely. Sometimes we had so much fun it didn't feel like work. I mentored interns with renewed passion, and regaled them with stories about my wild adventures at Casa.

When I thought of Mario, I felt ashamed.

I confessed to my friend over dinner one evening, and he asked me, "Do therapists fix to fix themselves?"

You bet.

I was no saint. Mario's pain resonated with the deepest part of my cloistered soul. In him, I saw my own isolation and wanted to stop it. We shared a life raft in the kind of storm where good company means everything.

When Mario opened to me, it felt like giving life. Leaving him, a lethal abandonment. I didn't trust the work I had done with him and I didn't trust myself. I had realized my worst fear and become another abusive parent. I believed that I had wounded him irreparably and destroyed all of the healing work we had accomplished together.

On a warm Sunday afternoon in June, seven years later, I visited a festival at the park. A cool sea breeze swished the leaves overhead as I stood in the sun under sprawling, gnarled trees, immersed in an exhibit of paintings created by children from a domestic violence shelter. A voice behind me interrupted my reverie.

"Cate?"

I turned to behold a tall, beautiful young man with a peaceful countenance and a familiar mischievous grin.

"Mario."

His soft eyes twinkled as he leaned over and wrapped his arms around me. So gentle. I couldn't believe how tall he was. And how grown up.

"How have you been?" he asked with a sweet smile.

"Good," I said. "How are you?"

"I'm good. I'm taking classes at City."

"That's great! What are you studying?"

"Art, of course." He grinned his lopsided smirk.

So much of our relationship had been about art. It was our first language together.

"Do you ever see Terri?" He asked.

"Oh, yeah, we still hang out. She's at Casa. She has your car model in her office."

He smiled. "That was a cool car."

"Is LaRell still there?" The old fire flashed in his eyes.

"Yeah. He's a supervisor now. He's mellowed out."

"That's good." He nodded and looked thoughtful. "I gave him a hard time."

What was this expression on Mario's face? Remorse?

"I gave you a hard time too," he said. His eyes grew sad, and he lowered his head.

Oh no. He blames himself.

"Mario, I felt so bad about leaving. It was not your fault. You had every right to be outraged."

He looked up and raised his eyebrows.

I nodded.

"Well, I'm sorry," he said.

"I'm sorry too."

I held his gaze. Our connection still felt intense. I squirmed.

"Did you get my letter?" I asked.

"Yeah, I got it. Sorry I didn't write back."

"That's okay. I just wish I could have helped you."

"You did help me. You were my best friend." He peered deep into my eyes.

I flushed with emotion and remembered Mr. O.

Mario looked straight through my shroud of shame and saw me. And when I found myself reflected in his eyes, the mob in the back of my head scattered.

We talked awhile in the sun, surrounded by the children's paintings.

I could not believe my senses. I felt like I was in a dream.

I listened with wonder.

He redeemed me.

BAREFOOT WARRIORS

"All that you have is your soul."
- Tracy Chapman

"FUUCK YOU, MOTHER FUCKERRS!!!"

Antonio's war cry rang out through the empty halls of *Casa de Esperanza*. He reminded me of Wind In His Hair, The Fierce One, who waved his spear at a naked Dances With Wolves and yelled, "I am not afraid of you!" But instead of a mustang, Antonio straddled a tall, wooden wardrobe, his dark, shirtless torso arched backward into a bow.

"La la laah! Blah! Lah! LaRell is a stupid ass monkey! LAHH!"

I tried to imagine how he got up there. The wardrobe was six feet tall and slick. He must have scaled it with his bare feet like a monkey.

Antonio had spent most of the day in takedowns and in the isolation room. That morning, before school, he trashed his room and kicked a large hole in the wall. As a consequence, LaRell removed all of his furniture except the wardrobe, which was too large to store, and left him in a bare room with no shoes, no shirt, and no belt.

But he still had his voice.

"Laah! La La LaRell! FUCK YOU, LARELL! You stupid FUCKER!"

I couldn't tell whether he couldn't carry a tune, or just chose not to.

Antonio was a beautiful boy with long, dark hair and flawless brown skin. He looked more like an Aztec warrior than an abandoned 14-year-old. And he was the only resident of *Casa* who was not afraid of LaRell, the beefy, steroid-charged supervisor of the boys' dorm.

My friend and martial arts mentor, Justin, stood at the end of the corridor like a soldier and barked at any boy who tried to sneak out of his room during quiet time. He had stopped barking at Antonio because it made him sing louder.

I knocked on the little troubadour's doorframe. "Antonio?"

"La! La! La! Blah! Blah!"

He looked at me for a millisecond, then resumed his song. He arched back and raised his voice, "LAAH!"

"Hi, Antonio. I'm Cate. I'm your new therapist."

His graceful movements reminded me of the boys at the black belt testing a few weeks earlier. Justin and I practiced Kung Fu and Aikido at Moon Tiger. Martial arts provided a strong counterbalance to the stress of our work, and the mental discipline came in handy.

Antonio looked up at the ceiling and bellowed. "JUSTIN! Tell LaRell I have something for him!"

Justin did not respond, but stood relaxed, with perfect posture. A tall, handsome surfer, he looked out of place here in our grubby quarters full of mismatched misfits.

With a conspiratorial grin, he leaned toward me and whispered, "strong *Chi*."

I smiled.

"Tell that stupid monkey I want my bed back!" Antonio yelled.

I sat down on the filthy carpet in my new sundress and leaned against the wall of Antonio's room, which featured two large boot-shaped holes in the dry wall. He ignored me, so I made myself comfortable and listened to the spaces between his notes.

My reverie conjured images…a monk setting himself on fire in protest…a memory of myself at Antonio's age…something sad…something funny… there was something humorous about this scene…a fearless jester thumbing his nose at the king.

Emotion swelled in my throat…a memory of Mr. O… a book he had lent me.

In the fell clutch of circumstance
I have not winced or cried aloud,
Under the bludgeonings of chance
My head is bloody but unbowed.

I hadn't thought about that poem in years, but I still knew it by heart.

I am the master of my fate:
I am the captain of my soul.

Funny how the kids who talked the least made me feel the most. I heard a chord of hope in his tuneless singing.

Leslie had lured me back to *Casa* from Chrysalis House after two years. She had predicted that I would get bored, and she was right. I missed the intensity of long-term work with traumatized kids. Chrysalis was great, but I needed a new challenge. I sauntered through Casa's barracks feeling special and entitled in my new role as Clinical Director.

Antonio couldn't be bothered with me. Oh, sure, he used me to get rolled tacos or rides to the store, but afterward he kicked me to the curb like an empty soda can.

I was just another clueless white woman who interfered with his freedom. All he wanted was to go home to his mom.

The raw wound that made Antonio insane with rage was the reality that his mother was long gone. He nurtured a fantasy that she would return for him, but she hadn't contacted him in years.

Antonio's father liked to remind him that his mother had abandoned him. He had beaten and berated Antonio for ten years before he lost custody, but he still had visitation rights. And I had the misfortune of supervising their visits.

Mr. Jimenez felt dangerous. When Antonio knew he was coming for a visit, he paced back and forth in his room like a caged animal, trashed his furniture, and kicked holes in the walls. He needed outrageous behavior to preserve his soul. His father was a soul killer.

On Wednesday evening, after dinner, Justin escorted Antonio to my office for a visit with his father. I felt relieved when I saw Justin's face in the doorway. I hated sitting alone with Antonio's father who ogled my body and oozed superficial charm. I couldn't wait to go home and shower.

"So what do you think of my son?" He waved his hand toward Antonio like he was selling him at auction.

Antonio hunched his shoulders and drew in his chin. His eyes grew wide and darted back and forth from his father to me to the door. He crossed his arms and stepped back.

"I think he's great." I put on my *I'm In Charge Here* face. "He's been through a lot."

I had never seen Antonio so vulnerable. He shrank into a frightened waif.

"Yes, his mother ran away. She has a lot of problems." His singsong voice did not match the hate in his eyes.

Antonio glared at his father.

"I raised him by myself. He's a little spoiled. He needs to learn respect."

"Where is Antonio's mother?"

"No se." He shook his head. Then he stroked his chin, "She's into the drugs, you know. She's a whore."

"Shut up!" Antonio yelled. He clenched his jaws and arms tighter.

"I'm just telling the truth, *Mijo*. She's trash." He forged an innocent face while Antonio seethed. "You better be careful or you will end up like her." He leaned toward me. "I hope you can help him, *Doctora*."

"I don't need any help," Antonio said. "I just need to find my mom." He looked at the door.

"You see, Doctor, he imagines things."

"Eres una mierda!" Antonio's rage erupted. He took a step toward his father, his fist clenched.

"No sirves para nada! Nunca vas a lograr nada!" Mr. Jimenez pigeon chested and spewed contempt in Antonio's face.

"It's time to stop," I said. "Mr. Jimenez, you can go now."

He shot Antonio a dirty look and slithered out the door.

I walked Antonio back to the dorm.

"I hate that bastard. He's a piece of shit." He stomped along by my side.

"Is that what you told him?"

"Yep."

"You need a kicking bag."

"A what?"

"A kicking bag. It's a big bag that hangs from the ceiling. You kick it to get your frustration out."

He looked at me like I was crazy and walked on in silence.

On second thought, Antonio *was* a kicking bag. His father had pounded him with shame and abuse till it poisoned and choked his soul.

I remembered what Harry said about aggression - how important it is for survival of the self. "As long as there is aggression, there is hope," he said. The kids he worried about were the compliant ones.

I thought about Antonio trashing his room and singing on top of the wardrobe. I remembered myself at his age, bent over my parents' king-sized bed in my new birthday dress and nylons, straining my vocal chords to produce defiant screams while my huge, angry father whaled away on my back and legs and arms. He used one of those wide 1970's belts with holes cut in the leather and metal rivets around each hole that left colorful welts and bruises to accessorize my high school wardrobe.

"Don't give me that go to hell look!" He glared at me with such hatred, his blue eyes crazed with rage, determined to beat me into submission.

But submitting to that man's abuse was never an option for me.

"Stop screaming!" He yelled with frustration.

He hit harder, I screamed louder. He would have to kill me to shut me up and he knew it, so he stopped.

I understood what Antonio was fighting for.

That evening, while practicing the Chinese broadsword, I visualized Mr. Jimenez.

> *slice down, cut head in half,*
> *slice left, cut head off.*

Ahh…that's better.

Antonio's placement worker gave me the scoop about the past. Antonio's mother had battled depression and substance abuse while living with her violent husband. She had neither the emotional nor the financial resources to care for a child, but she escaped a destructive relationship that endangered her health, her baby, and even her life. She took her infant daughter and fled, leaving Antonio alone with his father, who intercepted her letters and blocked her calls. Antonio never heard from her.

I tried to imagine how that felt to a precocious four-year-old.

In Case Conference the next morning I heard the controversy over Antonio for the first time.

"This boy shouldn't be here. He belongs in the juvenile justice system." Dr. Sloan had skimmed Antonio's chart and met him once.

"He seems depressed to me," Terri said. "I think we should try him on an SSRI." Terri used to be quiet in Case Conference, but her contempt for Sloan had grown during the two years I was away and she had learned to push back.

"He is a sociopath," Sloan said. "Treating him with anti-depressant medication is a waste of good pills."

Laughter erupted out of me before I could catch it. But he wasn't joking.

"He does not attach and demonstrates no empathy." He blathered on as though no one else was in the room. Antonio must have bruised the doctor's ego during their brief interview.

"He's never had an opportunity to attach." Terri raised her voice. "If I had his father, I wouldn't attach either." Her tone grew bitter.

I cut in from the head of the table. "Well, he's only fourteen, so we won't write him off yet. He just got here. Let's give him a chance." I didn't care what Sloan said. That diagnosis was *not* going into Antonio's medical record. "If you want to see a sociopath, come meet his father."

Sloan scampered off to his next meeting and the treatment team dispersed. Terri, Justin, and Mike the teacher stayed behind. The four of us saw something different in Antonio. He was a pretty good actor, but his eyes betrayed him. They were full of pain, sadness, and fear. He had not hardened yet. And, after beholding the horror show that was his father, I was ready to fight for him.

"Wow...did that guy go to some kind of special asshole school?" Mike asked, stunned by Sloan's proclamation.

We all laughed.

"Yes, I believe he is a founding member." Terri smirked.

"Justin, what do you think about martial arts for Antonio?" I asked. Justin had trained my boys before. It gave them something to feel good about.

"He'll have to earn it. He's lost all his privileges, and LaRell won't give him his shoes back until he stops kicking the walls."

"Well, he doesn't need shoes for Kung Fu." I grinned.

"Good idea," Terri nodded. "It will help him discharge some of that rage."

"He won't discharge it on us, will he?" Mike looked nervous.

"We'll focus on mental discipline and the right use of power." Justin reassured Mike.

"Let's teach him forms before we give him any kicks," I said. "See how he does with those."

"It's good for him to spend time with nurturing men," Terri said. "He's intensely avoidant of women. He reminds me of that baby in the attachment experiment who ignored the mother when she came back into the room."

"Yeah, he's heartbroken about his mom. You can feel the sorrow in him," I said. "It's worse because he's so smart and sensitive. He understands what happened to him."

"He's the only one here with no anesthesia," Terri said. "He fights back instead of going numb. I like it."

"Me too. Let's see if we get him to fight smart." I looked at Justin. He nodded.

As the weeks passed, Antonio treated me like a vending machine. He used me to get stuff and ignored me the rest of the time. He wouldn't talk to me and he wouldn't look at me. When I came to visit, he pretended I wasn't there.

I felt used.

Harry kept tabs on my kids, even though he had plenty of his own to worry about. He created nicknames for mine that were uncannily appropriate based on his brief interaction with them. *The Nervous One. Velcro Girl.*

Antonio was *The Normal One.* Harry said there was nothing wrong with him other than the pain inflicted by his parents, and that he was depressed because his life was so depressing.

No matter how Dr. Sloan tried to write off kids like Antonio, Dr. Harry Young always intervened with a more enlightened diagnosis, a compassionate clinical narrative, and the *cojones* to shut Sloan's mouth. Harry was my hero.

Around the two-month mark with Antonio, Harry stopped by my office to check in.

"How ya doin' with The Normal One, Shep?"

"He still won't talk to me. Sloan says he doesn't attach."

"You believe that?"

"Of course not. He never had anyone safe to attach to. But he sure is good at ignoring me to death."

"Well then, your job is to not die." He smiled at me like a proud teacher. "Keep watching. He'll show you how he needs to use you, and when he does, try to stay out of the way."

Stay out of the way. Good reminder. These kids always figured out how to heal themselves when we met their needs and kept our agendas out of their way.

On Tuesdays and Thursdays, after dinner, Justin taught Antonio Kung Fu forms out on the rec field. Antonio stopped trashing his room, but he still liked to draw caricatures of LaRell, which got him into trouble. I winced at the blatant racism in his half man, half monkey depictions with gigantic lips and a pointed head. But it was hard not to laugh at his drawings of the other staff. Antonio had a gift for capturing character in portrait. Terri and I were grateful he never drew us.

One afternoon Antonio asked to play Ping-Pong. I didn't have any interest in Ping-Pong, but at least he was willing to spend time with me.

Day after day we played Ping-Pong. My Ping-Pong skills improved.

I carried on a one-sided conversation to break up the long stretches of silence, and told Antonio stories and jokes while we played. Some days I saw him fighting back a grin. He had a killer sense of humor, and I figured there must be a way to connect with it.

One evening, while playing Ping-Pong, I told him a long, drawn-out, shaggy dog type story about The Legendary Fu Bird and the different kinds of horrible deaths that befell those who dared to wash off the droppings of the Fu Bird. I couldn't believe he fell for it.

"Do you know what the moral of the story is?" I asked him.

He stopped playing and gave me a serious look. "What?"

"If the Fu shits, wear it."

"Oh, God." He groaned and shook his head at me. Then he busted up.

Laughter relaxed his dour expression and brought his handsome face to life.

I felt like Luke Skywalker when he hit the tiny target and blew up the Death Star.

Justin helped me prepare for my upcoming belt test. It was my third belt, and I had to break a board with my hand. We met at Moon Tiger after work.

"So, how are you feeling about Saturday?" He smiled his movie star smile.

"I'm a little nervous about the board. I hear it really hurts if you don't break it the first time.

"But you will break it. The secret is to fully commit. No half way."

"I heard none of the other women could break it."

"That is true."

I was having second thoughts.

"Remember when you said you couldn't kick the bag above my head?"

"Yeah."

"Remember what happened?"

"You pissed me off. That's what happened."

Justin gave me a tender smile. "And then what happened?"

"I kicked it. Because you pissed me off."

"Same thing with the board. Mind over matter."

I changed the subject. "So, how's it going with Antonio?"

"He's improving quickly. He's excited about learning weapons."

"I'll bet! He probably wants to practice on his father."

On Saturday morning, I pulled on my pressed, black Gi, tied my belt, and lined up with nine men and five women for testing. Each time I watched one of the women hit the board and fail to break it, my anxiety grew. One of my classmates had injured her hand at a previous testing. But I had watched Justin bust through two of these boards with his fist at the Black Belt testing. I knew it could be done. I remembered the day I kicked the bag out of his grip two feet higher than I believed I could jump.

Mind over matter. Mind over matter.

It was my turn. I breathed deep and slow, stepped up to the board, and placed my feet in attack stance. Then I drew my knife hand behind my head and focused all of my mental and physical power in one strike.

"KYUUP!" My hand sliced through the wood in a clean break.

A room full of students and teachers applauded. Justin gave me a thumbs up.

Master Kim crossed the room, picked up the two pieces of wood, and scrawled across one of them with his pen, "Well done, Cate! Master Kim."

I glowed all day.

When I returned to Casa on Monday morning, I felt different. Taller. Powerful. I took Antonio outside to shoot some hoops.

"How do you like martial arts so far?" I dribbled the ball, shuffled back and forth, and struggled to evade his omnipresent arms. It was like playing one of those eight-armed Hindu gods.

"It's good. I want to learn weapons."

"Ah...yes. Which ones?" I distracted him long enough to shoot the ball. It ricocheted off the backboard. Antonio retrieved it.

"The club and the sword," he said.

"Is Justin going to teach you?"

"He says I have to show that I'm ready." Antonio leapt and swished the ball through the hoop.

"How do you do that?" I asked.

"He says I have to master my anger."

"Good idea. Make it work for you. Ride it like a wave."

"That's what Justin said." He grabbed the ball and held it.

"Great surfers think alike."

He rolled his eyes and smiled his stunning smile.

"Anger is your friend. It tells you when something isn't fair and gives you the energy to take care of yourself."

"Like with my dad?" He launched into a layup.

"That is a brilliant question."

It was also a timely question. His father was scheduled to visit that Wednesday evening.

On Tuesday, after school, we walked to the taco shop. Antonio lived for *Horchata* and rolled tacos.

"So how do I use martial arts on my dad?" He unwrapped his tacos with reverence.

"Aikido should work well with him."

"What do I do?"

"Do you remember that move Justin taught you where you pivot sideways when he rushes you?"

"Yeah. He fell down."

"Exactly."

"I don't fight back?"

"You don't have to. You've already won."

We sat at a picnic table in front of the taco shop and relaxed in the sun while Antonio munched on his rolled tacos. I congratulated him on his report card. Mike, his teacher, had invested extra time with him after class and it showed. Antonio was like a plant that hadn't been watered for a long time. As soon as he got a drink, he came back to life.

"So how am I gonna stay cool when I want to kill that asshole?" He crinkled his brow and jiggled a nervous knee.

I tried to think of a time when I had practiced what I was about to preach.

I remembered one. I was a little older than Antonio.

My father towered over me, itching to dump a load of his pent up rage. All he needed was an excuse.

Don't give me that go to hell look!
Don't try to con me with your baby blues!
Don't cry or I'll give you something to cry about!

But he didn't know what to do with a completely blank expression. I gave him my full attention, but showed no anger, fear, or vulnerability. I stymied his aggression with the face of a dutiful soldier reporting for duty.

I won that round. What was he going to say? *Don't give me that completely blank expression?* Even my family wasn't quite that crazy.

It was a weird war to wage with a Dad that I loved, but I guess it was better than nothing.

Dad always said I wasn't afraid of him. I sure thought I was. I don't know, maybe he was right. Maybe I saw a side of him that others couldn't see. Maybe I looked through the hate and saw the scared little boy.

I wrote a poem about him.

I never had a father
I had a monster instead
Sometimes I wished he loved me
Sometimes I wished him dead...

One day, in a rare moment of solidarity, my brother and I huddled up in my room and plotted Dad's murder. Most of the time my brother used me only as a sounding board and punching bag, but that day he was desperate for an ally.

I thought going to school with bruises and welts was the worst humiliation, but my brother had to sit out of P.E. class with a big bubble on his head after Dad slammed it into the driveway gravel a few times.

A tall, red vase stood on the mantle above the fireplace. I would distract Dad, and my brother would sneak up behind him and bludgeon his head with the vase.

We never did it, but we felt better knowing the vase was there.

Antonio finished his tacos and wiped his hands on his pants. He picked up his trash and mine, threw it in the appropriate can, cleaned the table, and sat down across from me.

"Can you teach me how to stay calm when I want to kill him?"

"I'd love to."

Harry was right. Antonio needed to use me on his own terms. He didn't need me to stare at him like a therapist and ask, "How do you feel?" Boys hate that. And he didn't need me to break down his defenses and make him cry. Antonio fashioned his own treatment plan.

Warriors have their own ways of healing.

Antonio leaned forward, alert, and waited for instruction.

"Well, the first thing we need to do is set some limits with you and your father so you feel safer. I should have established ground rules at the beginning of the first visit."

"He wouldn't follow them anyway."

"That may be true, but it's my job to keep you safe."

He looked at me with vulnerable eyes.

"Your job is to listen to your body. It will tell you what to do."

"What do you mean?"

"Like when your dad calls you names, what happens in your body?"

"I don't know."

"Close your eyes and try to remember."

He closed his eyes and sat in silence.

"A ball in my throat."

"Good," I said. "What is the ball?"

"Poison."

"Perfect. So, what would you do if your father poured poison down your throat?"

"Kick him in the nuts."

"Well… that's one approach. But then where is the poison?"

"In my throat."

"Right."

"How do I get it out?"

I mimed hocking a loogie at him.

He laughed.

"You're already half way there because you can identify the poison. The trick is to remember who it belongs to."

"What's the poison?"

"Good question." I tried to think how to explain concepts like *projection* and *shame* to a fourteen-year-old boy. "Here's one way to think about it: your father has things inside him that he hates. He can't look at them because it's too painful and it makes him feel like *he* is trash."

"That's what he calls me...and my mom."

"I know. If he takes the things he despises about himself and puts them on someone else, he feels better."

"That's kind of crazy."

"Maybe so, but a lot of people do it."

"Why?"

"I think people feel embarrassed and ashamed so they try to draw attention to someone else."

"Like when he called my mom a whore?"

"Exactly." I looked into his dark, sad eyes and nodded. "Antonio, your dad is probably not going to change very much. But you can refuse to believe what he says about you."

"It's hard."

" I know. You have to know the truth about yourself, and hold onto it in the middle of the mind games. Your father needs to make you feel like you are the problem, like there is something wrong with you."

"So what is the truth?"

"The truth is that there is nothing wrong with you."

"If there is nothing wrong with me, then why am I in this place?"

Hmm...this kid is too smart for me.

"Well, there is one thing wrong with you," I feigned a serious expression.

"Huh?" He scrunched up his forehead.

"You believe there is something wrong with you. That's what's wrong with you."

He shook his head like a wet dog after a bath.

That was enough deep thoughts for one day.

"Can I have another *Chata*?" He turned on the puppy eyes.

"Sure."

I had learned the power of validation, especially for kids who had been pummeled by their parents' projections. Little ones believe what mom and dad tell them, and it takes some heavy duty debriefing to convince them otherwise.

Antonio's father had been telling him that he was a worthless piece of trash since he was four years old, and there had been no validating presence in the home to contradict that message. Somehow, I had to counter the brainwashing of the Cult of Jimenez.

I couldn't erase Antonio's painful memories, but together our treatment team could create a Greek chorus loud enough to drown out some of the damage. If we could turn down the volume on the father's curses and soak Antonio in affirmation for a few months, his self-esteem would begin to heal.

I returned a well-fed Antonio to the dorm, then walked to his classroom for a consult. I loved having my kids in Mike's class. He was gifted and dedicated, and he had a thick enough skin to tolerate their ornery ways without getting grumpy.

"So, how's our boy doing?" I asked.

"Antonio is super bright. He can go to college if he wants to."

"Is he interested?"

"He's getting interested. He has a lot of talent for Art. You should see the portrait he drew of me."

"Uh oh…another portrait?"

Mike laughed. "It's okay. This one is benign. He made me younger. And thinner."

I smiled. "I saw his report card. His grades are coming up fast."

"Yeah, he won't have any trouble making A's now that he has some help. It's like it's all new to him. You'd think he was raised by wolves."

"Wolves would have been more humane."

The next day, Antonio asked to see me. The girls were using the basketball court, so we walked laps around the rec field.

"Why do I have to see him?" Antonio asked me in a frustrated tone.

"Good question. The court order says he gets two supervised visits per month."

"Are they looking for my mom?"

"Yes, your placement worker is searching for her. She is also trying to find a good foster family for you. Did you know that?"

"Yeah, but I'd rather go with my mom."

"I know."

"Cate, why do I hate him so much? I want to kill him."

"Of course you want to kill him."

Antonio whipped his head around and looked at me with a face full of surprise.

"Look at how he's treated you, Antonio. Your feelings are totally normal."

"He makes me feel crazy."

"I know. He doesn't see the real you. When he tells you you're bad and crazy, it's like he annihilates the real Antonio."

"That's exactly how it feels!" He looked amazed.

"That's why you want to kill him. It's a life and death struggle - kill or be killed."

"Wow. That really is how it feels."

"It's amazing how you've kept your spirit alive all these years."

He looked curious.

"Do you remember that story about Victor Frankl in the concentration camp?"

"Yeah."

"No matter what hell they put him through, he always found a small refuge for his soul. They locked him up in a little shed in the middle of winter, and he peeked out through a crack in a board and watched the sun rise and set every day. He wrote about the colors in the sunset."

Antonio nodded. "I remember. They killed his family."

"That's right. But he survived and told his story."

Antonio stared straight ahead, as though deep in thought.

We walked together in silence.

Antonio's resilient spirit reminded me of scenes from my childhood...climbing down the rope ladder my friends designed after Dad grounded me for six months... belting out Bob Dylan duets in the incomparable acoustics of the high school restroom with my friend I was forbidden to see…

Antonio would have loved those acoustics.

We walked back to my office and sat down.

"He'll be here at 7. Let's make a plan," I said.

"Okay."

"Like I said, we're going to set some ground rules this time."

"What rules?"

"No name calling, no verbal abuse, no Spanish."

"Why no Spanish?"

"Because of the things your father says to you in Spanish. If I can't understand him, I can't stop him."

"Oh."

Antonio had never been protected before. He seemed to like it.

"Now, your part. I want you to use your breath, like Justin taught you. Breathe slow and deep to calm yourself. Stay centered, focus, just like when you're sparring."

"I can do that."

"And I want you to visualize something for me. I want you to imagine that you are surrounded by an invisible shield, like a force field, and anything your father says about you or your mom will bounce off that shield and fall on the floor."

"Okay." His face brightened.

"That is all you have to do. Stay calm, stay centered, don't engage. You will win this round by not engaging."

At 7 p.m. Justin escorted Antonio to my office. Joanie, the receptionist, told Mr. Jimenez to wait in the front office. When we were ready, she sent him in.

I did not feel creeped out by Jimenez any more. I had beheaded him with my broadsword in Kung Fu class.

I hadn't thought about it consciously that morning but, instead of a cute dress, I wore a big jacket with massive shoulder pads. I exuded every badass vibe I could muster.

Antonio sat near me and checked my face every few seconds. His father sat across from us in Harry's favorite chair.

"Okay, let's get started," I said. "First, we need some guidelines for how we communicate."

"Guidelines?" Jimenez asked in a sarcastic tone.

"Yes, guidelines. I need both of you to keep it respectful. No name-calling, no verbal abuse, and no Spanish. Agreed?"

"Agreed," Antonio said.

Jimenez gave me a disgusted look and sighed. "You have a problem with your Spanish?"

"No, I don't have a problem." I frowned. "Last time we met, you insulted Antonio in Spanish. So now we speak English."

"Insulted *him?* Ha! He insults me." Jimenez grew agitated.

"Well, not today."

He crossed his hairy arms and simmered like a teapot about to whistle.

"Mr. Jimenez, I want to give you an update on Antonio's progress. He's doing very well in the program."

"Yeah?" He grunted through clenched teeth.

"Yes. His grades are all A's and B's now, and he has earned the highest level in the residential program."

"So he has you fooled." He looked at Antonio and smirked.

Antonio's eyes flashed with anger. Then he caught himself. He looked at me, drew a deep breath, and put on his Aikido face.

"No, I don't think so, Mr. Jimenez. This is a very difficult program, and Antonio has worked hard."

Antonio sat with perfect posture and said nothing. He stared straight ahead at a spot on the wall and avoided his father's gaze.

"You want me to be impressed?" Jimenez spat the words with uncensored bitterness.

"Well, I imagine that you must feel proud of your son."

"Oh, yeah," he mocked. "Really proud. Such a good boy."

Antonio looked at me with a composed face. I held him with my eyes. He glanced at his father then looked away. "I'm going to a foster home."

"A foster home?" Jimenez raised his voice. "They're going to coddle you after all you've done to me? *Que es estupido.*"

Antonio's eyes grew wide. His father's anger triggered old trauma. He looked like a frightened animal. I placed my palm on his shoulder.

"He's earned it," I said. "We're very proud of him."

Antonio exhaled and dropped his shoulders.

His father stiffened.

"After Antonio settles into his new home, you can arrange supervised visits with him there," I said.

Jimenez stood up, shoved Harry's chair up against the wall, and muttered in Spanish as he stalked out. The steel door slammed behind him.

I looked at Antonio with an innocent face. "Was it something I said?"

He let out a nervous laugh.

We kicked back in our chairs and sighed.

"So, how was that?" I asked him.

"Weird."

"Why weird?"

"I've never seen my dad like that. I think he's afraid of you."

"He should be!" I jumped into a goofy sparring stance, screwed up my face, and stuck my chin out.

Antonio laughed.

I took him to the taco shop for a *Horchata*.

Justin greeted us when we returned to the boy's dorm. "How did it go?"

Antonio looked at me. I nodded to him. He didn't know what to say. Success was foreign territory, and praise felt downright freaky.

"Justin, you would have been proud of this guy. He's an Aikido master."

"Good job, Antonio. I knew you could do it."

"Can I use weapons now?" He perked up and smiled at Justin with mischief in his eyes.

"Patience, Grasshopper." Justin patted him on the shoulder. "First, clean up your room and finish your homework, okay?

"Aw, man! Why do I have to clean my room? It just gets messy again!"

"Discipline, Antonio. Discipline."

The next morning, Case Conference felt like a celebration. Antonio's placement worker surprised us with a visit. She had found a good foster family for him, and they wanted to take him in two weeks.

"Two weeks? Ah! It seems like he just got here." I couldn't help it. I had grown fond of him and hated to see him leave.

"How was the visit last night?" Terri asked.

"He was amazing. So calm. His father didn't know what to do." I had to brag.

"Well, that was fast." Terri had grown attached to Antonio too. We usually had the kids for at least eighteen months, but he had transformed quickly and was ready to go in six.

"That's good." Dr. Sloan mumbled without looking up. He shuffled some papers. "Do we have any other cases to discuss?"

Terri grinned and winked at me. She loved to prove Sloan wrong.

I felt bereft that night as I drove to Moon Tiger. Antonio had finally let me in and now he was leaving.

Over time, my heart had become a revolving door for these kids. I learned how to attach, give 150%, love, lose, mourn, let go, and then love again. Several times each year. The process became more efficient with practice.

But it still hurt.

I thought about Antonio and his new foster family while I worked on my broadsword moves. He would be happy there. He could finish high school and start college, and his funding would follow him until he turned 21. By then, he should be well on his way. Who knows, maybe he would go on to study art like Mario. He had the talent. Now that he had solid connections with new friends, he could stop fighting and be himself. He could laugh again.

As I wiped down my sweaty weapons, inspiration bubbled up. My inner imp cackled.

I zipped the weapons into their carrier, shoved them into the trunk of my car, and drove to Casa. When I arrived, it was bedtime, and the boys were nestled in their rooms, reading or doing homework. I sneaked through the kitchen to the boys' dorm and hoped no one would see or smell me in my stinky *Gi*. Justin stood at his post. I hid around the corner.

"Psst! Justin!" He jerked his head around, saw my face, and walked over to my hiding place with a relaxed smile.

"What are you doin' girl?"

"Will you help me sneak Antonio outside?"

"What are you up to?"

I pulled the weapons bag from behind my back.

"Oh...I see. Sure. Meetcha out on the court in 5?"

"Cool. Thanks."

I crept out to the basketball court and unzipped my surprise package. The blacktop still held the heat of the day. It felt good on my bare feet.

A few minutes later, Justin escorted a confused Antonio onto the court.

"You have a visitor." He motioned toward me. Antonio did a double take. He had never seen me in full battle dress.

"Look what I've got." I pulled a cane sword, a club, and a broadsword from the bag. He lit up and ran to me, seized the broadsword with both hands, and sliced graceful curves in the air, as though reunited with an old friend.

"LaRell just left for dinner, so you have an hour. Have fun!" Justin grinned and strode toward the dorm.

"Show me how!" Antonio bounced up and down. The broadsword was always a favorite. So elegant and so deadly.

I showed him a sword form that had taken me several weeks to learn. It looked more like a dance than a fight. He looked bored - not what he had in mind.

I showed him the decapitation move. He liked that. He practiced it a few times.

"Can we spar?" I understood how he felt. Fighting was more fun than practicing forms.

I paused. *Why not? I trust him.*

"How about the club and the cane sword?" I asked.

"Okay."

He didn't care which sword we used.

I showed him a few moves with the club, then handed it over to him. Justin was right. He was a natural.

"Are you ready?" I asked.

He gripped his club and jumped into fighting stance. I wished I had my camera.

"Attack!" I yelled.

"Kyup!" He released the power shout Justin had taught him. I blocked his club with my cane sword, which made a loud, satisfying *Clack!* every time he struck it.

The *kyups* gave way to *Hah! Bam! Kah!* We sounded like a couple of little boys playing sword fight in the back yard. We made a terrible racket.

Antonio lit up with joy. We played and yelled until we both had to stop and catch our breath. We sat down on the warm asphalt, laughed together, and wiped the sweat from our faces.

Two seconds later, he jumped to his feet and challenged me. He grabbed the sword, grinned, and bellowed, *"KYUUP!!!"*

PARENTS' GROUP

"Sorrow makes us all children again..."
- Ralph Waldo Emerson

"Where do you fuckin' people get off tellin' me I can't see my kids?"

Michael Giraldi stood clenched in my doorway like a bull about to charge. He wore a muscle shirt and a snarl, and flames of rage flashed in his dark eyes.

If this jerk makes one wrong move, my buddies at the P.D. will gladly take him where he belongs.

"Come in, Michael." I exuded calm and motioned toward one of the comfy chairs that warmed my office at St. Jerome's Home for Children. As the new Clinical Director, I had inherited a spacious upstairs office that overlooked the lush landscaping of an historic Spanish mission. Monks padded through ancient archways downstairs into private prayer chambers.

A breeze blew through my open window and carried the scent of vanilla candles through the room. My backyard buddy, a red-shouldered hawk, sat among the sprawling branches outside the window, his breast feathers fluffed up like fur.

I remembered what Harry taught me: *Patients act aggressive because they feel vulnerable.* I spoke to Michael with a gentle voice. "How can I help you?"

"That new girl downstairs won't let me see my kids." He stood stiff, arms clenched across his chest, biceps bulging.

I glanced at the clock.

"It's dinner time, Michael. The staff are busy with children in the dining hall. Did you schedule a visit today?"

"Yeah, I told them I was coming. I was just running a little late. I got stuck in traffic."

"That's frustrating. Can you stay till the kids get back from dinner?"

He sighed, and shifted from boot to boot.

Then he switched tactics, unclenched his arms, and gazed at me with the same big eyes and long lashes as his four-year-old son, Michael Jr. "Can't I just visit them during dinner?"

My shoulders tightened. It sounded like a reasonable request, but the staff would kill me if I brought an angry alcoholic man into the dining hall where they supervised sixty children.

"Tell you what - I'll get you a plate and you can sit outside at the picnic table till they get back. It should only be about fifteen minutes."

"Okay." He sulked and walked out.

Maybe he could gnaw on a bone for a while and leave us alone.

As I walked down the stairs toward the dining hall, I found myself caught in the spell of Baby Amanda, Michael's one-year-old daughter, who sat surrounded by colorful toys on the patio. She looked up at me with sparkling blue eyes and a smile that made me swoon. Amanda had lived in protective custody with us for six months. I wished I could take her home with me. So did most of the female staff who took care of her. Every time Amanda heard someone on the stairs, she brightened and looked for Mommy, who had neglected her, then abandoned her during a bender. Michael had lost custody of both children after he beat his wife in front of them.

People like that should not be allowed to have children.

(All cynics are heartbroken idealists.)

When I reached the bottom of the stairs, I heard angry voices inside the children's dorm. I peered around the corner and saw two big men puffing up for a fight.

"What do you think you're doin' in here?" Tony, the dorm supervisor, stomped toward Michael, who had ignored my instructions and trespassed.

"What's your problem?" Michael puffed up and matched Tony's stare.

Baby Amanda looked up from her play, startled by angry voices.

A wide-eyed, young female childcare worker looked at me.

I scooped Amanda up and walked toward the open doorway to the dorm. "Michael," I said, in my authority figure voice, "the picnic table is over there." I motioned.

As he turned and slunk to the picnic table, his baby daughter tracked his movements with intelligent eyes.

Tony shook his head and made the universal *Up Yours* gesture behind Michael's back.

My old friend, Mark, had recruited me to create new clinical programs at St. Jerome's, a receiving home for abused children. He had taken over as Director a year earlier and redesigned every aspect of the program. Several staff from the old guard had resigned, and those who remained struggled to adapt to Mark's new, more enlightened culture.

Mark told me the staff blocked children's contact with their parents and treated the parents like criminals. Some of them were criminals. He asked me to develop programs to support and educate parents. "We have a responsibility to prepare them for reunification with their children," he said in our initial interview.

I would have preferred to deny this eventuality.

"They're just like the kids," he said, "only taller."

I tried to veil my reaction, but Mark saw the cynicism in my eyes.

"You'll see." He smiled. "They'll surprise you."

Yeah, right. On what planet?

My experience with abusive parents was different from Mark's. The ones I'd met took no responsibility and did not change. And their children, who held out hope for them, were re-traumatized again and again.

And, more to the point, *my* parents never changed. And they re-traumatized *me*. Year after year. Every time I gave them a chance.

My most recent mantra for dealing with abusive parents was *Keep Hope Dead*. I was sick to death of watching kids I loved get their hearts broken over and over. Just when they would start to heal and move on, some self-centered parent would pop by and rip open their wounds.

Nevertheless, I wrote a curriculum for a twelve-week parenting class to be followed by a support group. As an incentive, parents could enjoy playtime with their children after each group meeting.

Kit, a seasoned therapist with a dirty mind, a thunderous chuckle, and Whoopi Goldberg hair, helped me launch the new program. She had been doing double duty in the absence of a Clinical Director, and made her rounds through the building, darting from room to room like a guppy among the coral. I surmised that she survived that way, never lighting long enough to become entangled in drama. The rest of the time she hid out in her tiny office with cool jazz and lots of snacks. Kit possessed the gift of spinning darkness into dark humor. It was impossible to be depressed when she aimed her dimpled grin and twinkling eyes at you. I've never met a more magical jester.

I was Kit's new boss, but most of the time I felt like her student. She had worked at St. Jerome's for ten years, watched administrators and programs come and go, and survived the wackiest system dysfunction I had ever heard of. Her big eyes bulged when she explained how the orphanage was built on Native American burial grounds -- hence the bad spirits and perpetual chaos.

I had never taught a parenting class, and my memories of running parent groups at Casa made me nervous. I had no kids of my own, and parents loved to pick on that fact.

Kit didn't have kids either, but she and her partner had adopted two fluffy, white Maltese puppies who provided fodder for funny anecdotes.

I had two cats, both renamed by my friend Warren, who never met a cat he didn't rename. Puffy, for obvious reasons, and Marty for her Marty Feldman eyes. I didn't need any more pets in my little beach cottage, but my biological baby alarm kept shouting *Baby! Baby! Baby!* until I found myself driving to The Uptown Pet Store every weekend to play with the little fur ball Shih Tzu puppies. I became obsessed.

On a Sunday morning, two weeks before Christmas, I lounged with my coffee and scanned the classified ads expecting to find puppies advertised at prices out of my reach. An ad caught my eye.

Shih Tzu puppies, $200.00

Wait a minute… what's the catch? They're normally three or four times that…

I called the number, and a nice lady answered.

"I'm calling about the puppies."

"Yes, there are five left - two boys and three girls." She lowered her voice. "My mother already has fifteen Shih Tzus here in the house. If I don't find homes for these five, she will keep them." She sounded desperate.

I must have been in some kind of altered state. Shih Tzu fever? What was I thinking? I had never trained a puppy. My landlady wouldn't like it. But, what the heck, she was in Japan for six months. Besides, I was just going to look at them. I wouldn't really get one.

The nice lady wasn't kidding. While I sat on the crusty living room rug and interviewed puppies, a herd of fifteen Shih Tzus, in varying states of hygiene, wandered in and out of the room. Some had long, scraggly hair. Others were clipped short. A couple had little ponytails atop their regal heads. They all had the same little smoosh face, button nose, and plume-tailed sashay as their Tibetan ancestors. The dark, dusty living room smelled like wet dog food.

"My daughter thinks I have too many dogs," Mrs. Cooper said in a loud whisper. Her husband sat in a recliner, engrossed in his Sunday paper. "We are Christian Scientists." She rolled forward over mounds of belly to hand me a church pamphlet. Her grey beehive hairdo, heavy with bejeweled combs, leaned to the side when she moved. Two of the longhaired Shih Tzus settled on the floor next to me.

I glanced at the pamphlet, and noticed that similar literature covered every tabletop in the room. Antique mahogany tables tried to peek out from under the piles.

"Thank you." I laid it aside. "Are they still nursing?"

"No, they've been eating dog food for several days." She hauled her mass out of the sunken chair with a few focused grunts and shuffled into the kitchen. I pondered the five puppies. A moment later, she returned with an aluminum pie pan of wet dog food. I watched the puppies lick food from her fingertips.

Her daughter, a slender, neatly dressed young woman, knelt on the floor in front of me. "Look at this little guy." She pointed to the biggest pup of the litter, who kept popping out of the basket, trying to charge me.

"He's adorable." I laughed at his frantic scramble toward my lap.

But he was not the one. A tiny black and white girl with a perfect panda face lay curled up in the corner of the basket. I don't know what it was, but it felt like we had met before.

I couldn't leave her there.

On Monday morning, I packed a tote bag with puppy supplies and puppy and reported to work. Our regular projects and problems became eclipsed by the question: *What do we name the puppy?*

Happy, Lucky, Sparky, Susie, Lucy, Alexandra (?), Bandit, Scooter...

Everyone came to visit and each one promoted the perfect name.

That afternoon Mrs. Heydel, an eccentric German woman, arrived for her weekly visit with her two children. I invited her to join our Parenting Class, but she had no means of transportation. The social worker could only bring her to visit once a week in the daytime. She rushed into the playroom, excited to see her children.

"Ohh! My leetil Shnuckies! My leetil Shnuckies!" She pinched their cheeks and kissed their faces.

Kit stuck her grinning mug out of her office to watch the scene. She shook her head and chuckled. "Little shnuckies."

Kit, who could make a comedy routine out of any mundane event, went nuts doing impressions of Mrs. Heydel. In no time, the staff were calling each other "My Leetil Shnuckie," and an epidemic of cheek pinching ensued. When it spread to the puppy, it stuck.

We named our baby *Shnuckie*.

On the night of our first Parent Education Class I tidied up the rec room and set out some cookies and juice. Michael was the first to arrive.

He sat down and crossed his arms. "Where is everybody?"

"It's not quite 7:00 yet."

"What's this?" He picked up one of the handouts: rows of faces with different expressions, labeled with corresponding emotions. He pointed to an inebriated face labeled *borracho*. "That's me...heh heh." He seemed proud of it, though it had cost him his family.

Kit had told me about Michael's drinking and drugging. And temper. She said he should not join the class until he had 90 days of sobriety because he might disrupt our group. As a former Marine, Kit liked structure and discipline, and we both had been trained that you don't do therapy with someone who abuses substances. There is no point. But, Michael had completed six weeks of residential rehab, and he wanted to participate, so I gave him a chance.

A young woman peeked through the open door. She was barely five feet tall with a tiny voice. "Hello?"

"Hello. Come in." Sonia's dark eyes radiated pain, and she slumped under a burden that reminded me of poor old Scrooge stumbling under the heavy chain of his sins. I reached out to shake her limp, clammy palm. Sonia sat down without a sound and watched me with the vigilance of a frightened child.

Mary, a tall, pale woman who had suffered from schizophrenia for many years, arrived next. She wore the blunted expression of the long medicated. Her grey hair hung in uncombed strands that clung to her forehead.

Right behind her came Alex, a dark-skinned, boyish young woman with haunted eyes. When I spoke to her, she responded in barely audible monosyllables. Alex had lost custody of her children after she failed to protect them from her husband.

Cindy made a loud, manic entrance twenty minutes late. She wore an Ozzie Osborne tank top and bleached hair with black roots. "Hey everybody! Sorry I'm late!" She spun around and focused on the refreshments. Her cheery façade could not hide a cracking, fragmented self, barely glued together and running fast. Cindy had lost custody of her three children after her relationship with crystal meth led her to prostitution and burglary. She had neglected her children, and allowed her boyfriend to molest them.

It's easy to stereotype addicts. In graduate school, I learned about *Character Disorders* and *The Addictive Personality*. My social work professors characterized addicts as narcissistic, exploitive, irresponsible, and incurable. They had a *Disease* over which they were *Powerless*, and they were not to be trusted.

Harry disagreed. He said people used drugs and alcohol to anesthetize unbearable pain and isolation. In his psychoanalytic practice, he treated many patients who used substances. When they healed and felt more connected, they used less. It made sense when Harry explained it, yet his point of view was considered radical, even heretical, in the 1990's.

I had watched the brilliant, talented husband of my youth self-destruct with alcohol. He tried to drown the demons of his childhood, but there wasn't enough beer. And when we removed the beer, the demons remained.

Kit told me awful stories about the things these five had done to lose their children. It had to be bad for CPS to place children in protective custody. During the previous ten years I had filed dozens of child abuse reports and the response was always the same: a 5 1/2" x 8 1/2" slip of paper in the mail that said *NO ACTION TAKEN*.

"Welcome to Parenting Class. I'm Cate and this is Kit. We're glad you all could make it. Please help yourself to some cookies. The chocolate chip ones are pretty good."

Michael hopped up to get cookies. The others sat still and watched me.

"I'd like to go over some of the topics we'll cover in the next twelve weeks. If you have a question, please raise your hand."

They stared.

I described a program of basic parenting skills, stress management, communication, and self-care. I hoped they could learn how to deal with their emotions under stress so they wouldn't need to use their children as punching bags. I didn't realize at the time that most of their behavior patterns were automatic, and operated outside of their awareness. Like a computer program running in an endless loop. With no screen.

Michael slouched in his chair and munched cookies with his mouth open. "Are you gonna talk to CPS about us?" He needed to know how much power I wielded and how I planned to use it.

"Good question, Michael. Everything said in this group stays in this group."

He raised his eyebrows, surprised. "Hmm," he grunted and sat up straight.

I handed out a class schedule and set some ground rules.

"First, let's talk about stress. How many of you have ever felt completely overwhelmed by parenthood?"

Six hands went up.

"Puppies don't count, Kit." I gave her a playful look. Michael laughed. Kit lowered her hand with an impish grin.

"Okay. Now, how many of you have done things you regret when you were overwhelmed?"

Seven hands went up. Kit and I both held our arms high and nodded to the group.

With a little coaxing, we got them to talk about their stress, which they managed with Budweiser and other medicines.

"Would you like to learn some new ways to decompress?" I asked.

They all nodded.

"Great. Let's get started."

We practiced deep breathing for a few minutes. Then I led them in a meditation called *Ten Minute Vacation*. Kit turned out the lights while I lit candles and played the *Garden of Serenity* tape. We visualized a safe, peaceful place where we could get away from all the stresses of life.

At the end of ten minutes no one wanted to stop.

"Wow...that was cool," Cindy said.

We discussed the stresses of raising children. That's when the confessions started.

They told stories about fistfights, meltdowns, blackouts, and frightened children. Guilt and shame gushed out of them, as though too long pent up behind a crumbling dam.

Stunned by their jaw-dropping honesty, Kit and I listened with reverence. They were telling the truth for the first time.

Sonia swiped at a torrent of tears as she talked about losing her baby. She had battled methamphetamine addiction since adolescence. When her first child was born with a positive tox screen, Children's Protective Services took the baby girl and placed her in a foster family. Sonia was willing to do anything to help her baby. All of her friends used drugs. She struggled to cope and stay sober alone.

Alex reached over and patted Sonia's hand. Michael fetched a box of tissues for her.

Where was all the bullshit? The shucking and jiving I'd heard about for so long? Aren't these people supposed to be *The Most Resistant Patients?*

These young parents felt utterly overwhelmed and unable to cope. They had done the best they could and, by their own accounts, failed miserably. Their eyes were full of pain and fear. Each of them had suffered abuse as a child. Repeating their parents' mistakes was their worst nightmare. They felt possessed by the demons of their own abusive parents, could not escape the haunting, and looked to us for help.

After they all left, Kit and I sat dazed.

"Whoa..." Kit jiggled her shoulder-length dreadlocks.

"Yeah. That's not what I expected."

The next morning in staff meeting, Kit and I introduced the new parenting program. More than forty clinical and residential staff gathered in the high-ceilinged meeting hall curious to hear about Mark's latest idea. He was always changing something, but never without a fight from the old guard.

Tony, supervisor of the dorm staff and kingpin of the old guard, leaned against the back wall, his furry arms folded and propped on top of his belly. He only moved to groom his long, thick mustache. A dozen faithful followers clustered near him.

Kit suspected that Tony and his buds were involved with the Mexican mafia in Tijuana. She spied on them in the parking lot and saw them move large parcels in and out of Tony's van. It was hard to tell when Kit was joking. "Don't piss him off!" She warned me. He and his friends could make life difficult.

The huge group rustled and murmured. "I want to thank all of you who helped recruit parents for our new program," I said. "We met for the first time last night."

The rustling and murmuring grew louder in Tony's corner. He stepped forward. "What about the safety issues of letting those people on the dorm? You know, some of them have restraining orders. That Michael Giraldi is a hot head. We got a lotta little kids..."

Kit cut him off. "You know, Tony, we handpicked these parents."

"How do you know they're not just conning you?" Tony scowled. Stupid therapists, so clueless.

"Well, for one thing, they're gonna have to work hard to be in the class." Kit sat up on the edge of her chair and stuck her head out like a banty rooster. Her dreads swung to and fro. "What do you think they're conning me for, the cookies and punch?"

The group laughed. Tony flushed.

"Okay, guys." I would have enjoyed watching Kit take a few more comedic slices out of Tony's ego, but Mark paid me to be the grownup. "The reality is that these children are going home with these parents in a few months. Don't we want to prepare them for that?"

Sandra, our dedicated nurse of twelve years, spoke up. "You know, Tony, some of these parents are trying really hard to get better. They're working their recovery programs, and sometimes they come to my office and ask for advice. I think they need our help."

Sandra was a kind grandmother who nurtured everyone she met, whether they deserved it or not. Especially if they did not. The staff respected her.

Tony re-inflated. "I'm just sayin' they can stir up a lot of trouble. You know how these kids get when they're scared. They're goin' off all night and we can't get 'em to sleep."

"It's true, the children can be triggered when they see a parent who abused them," I said. "But they also get upset when they can't see their parents. Most of these kids would rather see their parents than anything else. They are a lot more forgiving than we are."

I remembered a story my therapist once told me. She wanted me to stop kicking myself over my repetitive, futile opera of trying to reach my father. A little girl came into the E.R. with third degree burns all over her body. Her father had poured gasoline on her and set her aflame. The little girl was frightened, in horrible pain, and she screamed, "I want my Daddy!"

I understood Tony's perspective. During the previous ten years, I had served as a surrogate parent. My role had been to protect, validate, and support my kids, and to help them heal the damage done by their parents. I had focused on *my* relationship with each child, and I was their savior.

Tony spoke the truth about frightened children. I remembered the morning Jesse socked me in the jaw after talking to her mother. There is no trigger more powerful for an abused child than contact with the abusive parent. Well, that's not true. There is one. Most of these children would rather be hit than abandoned. When you're hit, someone cares enough to hit you. Being left all alone feels like a death sentence to a child. Like Frank Poole drifting off into space after HAL severs his oxygen hose. Or like those astronauts who got stuck in space and had to choose between orbiting indefinitely or burning up while returning to earth. They chose home.

My days as a surrogate parent were over. My role now was to herd this unruly group of staff in a new direction. "Tony, we'll do everything we can to avoid triggering the kids. If you need backup, call me." Little did he know that I welcomed invitations to help out with the kids. I missed them.

The group settled, and we went on with the rest of the agenda. After the meeting, several staff stopped by my office to express their support of the new parenting program.

They really came to play with the puppy.

Our little parenting class met every week. We learned about positive reinforcement and anger management. We talked about how to build a support system, a completely foreign concept to all of them. And, when the time was right, we talked about how they got here.

At the end of week five, I introduced the topic for week six: *Childhood Emotional Patterns*. "I want you to spend some time this week thinking about your parents' parenting styles. What you liked, what you didn't like, and what you have imported into your new family. We're going to identify and label the baggage. The patterns we are not aware of, we repeat. Automatically, unconsciously."

No one spoke. They hurried out.

Cindy did not show up for week six. Michael heard through the N.A. grapevine that she had relapsed. That night in group, he looked distraught.

"What is it, Michael?"

"I should have helped her."

"What do you mean?"

"I could tell she was having a hard time. I should have talked to her. Maybe I could have stopped her."

"Michael, you're not responsible for Cindy's choices."

"I was being selfish."

"What?"

"My sponsor says I have a problem being selfish. I only think of myself."

"Michael, you're here to focus on your own recovery. Part of recovery is learning healthy boundaries. You are responsible for your own sobriety, not for Cindy's."

He stared at me, puzzled.

"Does Cindy have a sponsor?" I asked.

"Yeah."

"Does she have a treatment program?"

"Yeah."

"It's not your fault."

"Then why do I feel guilty?" The muscles in his face and neck pulled taut. He teared up.

"Good question. Cindy relapses, and you feel guilty. You believe your selfishness is the cause. I wonder where you learned those ideas."

Michael squirmed. He had never shown his soft underbelly before, and he looked like he might bolt. I backed off to let him regain composure. I figured he could use an experience of someone respecting his boundaries. For once.

"Okay, let's get started. Did anyone think about the assignment from last time?"

Silence. Wide eyes. Alex and Sonia held their breath.

"I did." Michael raised his hand.

Hmm…he's a resilient one. "That's great, Michael."

He pulled a crumpled piece of notebook paper from his pants pocket and unfolded it. "I wrote some stuff."

"Would you like to read it?"

"Okay." He cleared his throat and sat up straight. "I was born a poor black child." He looked up with a sheepish grin.

I laughed before I could stop myself. Michael caught me off guard with his reference to the silly Steve Martin movie. The tension in the room fueled my laughter.

No one else got it. Kit raised her eyebrows.

"It's a line from a movie. I'll explain later." I smirked at Michael. "Please proceed."

"Sorry." He looked at his confused peers, then back at me like a little boy, worried that I was angry. I wasn't.

He clutched the wrinkled paper and read aloud. "I was the oldest of five kids. My dad drank a lot and he was a real mean drunk. He ran off when I was twelve. I got a job working at a gas station to help my mom pay the bills. She cleaned people's houses when she could, but she was sick a lot. My mom was real sad but she worked hard to take care of us kids."

Michael had dropped out of school at 16 to support the family. His father did nothing to help, but popped by once every few months to berate Michael and compete with him. Sometimes the visits erupted into fistfights.

Michael's story reminded me of my Dad's childhood.

Michael looked older when he told his story. He sat stiff, like a soldier.

At 17, his girlfriend became pregnant and, at 18, he was married with a child. Unable to support his little family with a minimum wage job, he sold drugs. He continued to help his mother as much as he could. Until he was arrested.

Michael spoke with reverence about his mother, who died alone at home from undiagnosed heart disease. "I wish I could've given her a better life," he said. He started to cry, then quickly shut down and shoved the paper back into his pants pocket.

We talked about the intergenerational transmission of patterns. Children learn what they live. They form attachment patterns intertwined with their caregivers, and sponge up the emotions and behavior in the home. Children believe the way their family does it is *normal*, until they experience something different. For these parents, our group was their first experience of something different.

After group that night, around 9 p.m., Tony knocked on my door with an attitude. I had been working for twelve hours and I was packing up to go home.

"Hey, Cate, you said if we needed backup on the dorm we should call you," he said. I recognized the passive-aggressive look on his face.

"Sure," I said. "What's up?"

He looked disappointed when I didn't react. "Well, little Michael is all stirred up after seeing his father. Maybe you can help us calm him down."

"Okay. Why don't you bring him up, and he can hang out with me for awhile."

He looked blank. "Uh…okay." He shuffled off toward the stairs.

Just like the kids…he picks the perfect time to test the limit. I was exhausted, but I intended to prove my point.

A few minutes later one of the female staff buzzed me on the intercom. "Cate?"

"Yes."

"Tony said to tell you Michael is okay now."

"Great. Thanks for letting me know."

Ha. I hurried out before he could think of another test.

Later that week, I visited Harry at his swanky Santa Monica office, a long way from our old roach infested room at *Casa*. From his sixth floor window, I watched the blue Pacific sparkle in the sun.

Harry nestled into his soft, leather chair. "So, Madam Director, how's life at St. Jerome's?" I absorbed the warmth of his proud father smile.

"Good. We're really busy. We have a lot of projects going."

"How's Mark?" Harry had trained Mark in his psychiatry fellowship several years earlier.

"He's doing well. He's really transformed that place. You won't believe what he has me doing now."

"What's that?"

"Remember how I used to be afraid of the abusive parents?"

"You had some doozies."

"Well, Mark has me running a parents' group."

Harry laughed. "So, how's it going?"

"That's what I'm here to find out."

I told him about Michael and Sonia, and their apparent remorse. I confessed my fear of being conned. Again.

He listened, nodded, stroked his beard.

"Do you think these people can actually change this late in the game?" I asked.

"Yes."

"How?"

"The same way the kids change."

"Hm."

"Do you remember reading Selma Fraiberg in your Ego Psychology class?"

"Is she the one who wrote about the blind babies?"

"That's her. *Ghosts in the Nursery.* She worked with mothers who had tried to kill their babies."

I shuddered.

"The mothers went numb and abused their babies, driven to repeat their own traumas because they had never owned them emotionally. Fraiberg helped the mothers connect to the emotions of their own abuse. After they mourned the traumas of their own childhoods, they spontaneously became good mothers."

"Reminds me of Mario."

"Who?"

"Remember the Satanist?"

"Oh, yeah," he chuckled. "After he did all that crying he wasn't much of a Satanist, was he?"

Thinking of Mario made me smile. "So we're on the right track?"

"Sounds like it. If they can attach to you, they can make use of you."

I nodded.

"Let me know how it goes." He gave me one of those wonderful hugs that feels the way family should.

Ideas bubbled up as I left Harry's office. I stashed my shoes in the car and took a long walk on the beach.

My thoughts turned to my father and the ghosts in his nursery. I'd heard about some of them, but I needed to know more. When I got home, I called Aunt Barb, my father's older sister. Unlike the rest of the clan, she had always been a friend and fan of mine. Like me, she had worked her way through college and grad school, and also like me, she had been branded the family weirdo for *Tryin Tuh Git Abuv Yer Raisin By Gettin Edicated*.

"Can I ask you some questions about Dad's childhood?"

"Oh, gosh, Catie, I haven't thought about that in a long time." I could hear the dread in her voice.

"I am trying to understand some things. Is it true that Grandpa used to beat Dad up and throw him through windows?"

"Oh, yeah. He beat us every day whether we deserved it or not. I hated that old bastard."

"What was Grandma like?" My Grandma Cate had always been good to me. I was her favorite.

"She was *crazy*. But then, who wouldn't be? Living with a no 'count husband and five rotten kids. We probly drove her crazy."

"What do you mean by crazy?"

"She used to go nuts and chase us around the yard with a butcher knife. Maybe she had PMS." She let out a sarcastic chuckle.

"Barb, I don't understand how Dad can be so loving with my sister and with other people but so vicious to me. He acts like he hates me."

"I'm sure he loves you as much as he can, Hon. He's just damaged."

"Yeah."

"He probably feels safer with your sister. She's no threat to him."

My little sister suffered from severe cerebral palsy and never spoke.

"Why am I such a threat? I've never done anything to him. If I was going to retaliate, I would have done it years ago."

"I don't know, Honey, but I know it's not you. He's doing the best he can. You have to go on with your life."

If only it were that simple.

With Harry on my shoulder, I came to the next Parents Group in search of ghosts.

Sonia talked about her mother, who called her *Puta*, and kept her home from school to cook and clean. Sonia wept and trembled when she recalled the humiliation of being molested by her stepfather.

"I couldn't get away from him! He always got me in the kitchen when I was washing the dishes. He sneaked up behind me..." She gasped for breath. "He hurt me."

She hunched over, sobbing. "I feel like trash. I can't even wash the dishes without a panic attack."

Alex wrapped her arm around Sonia's shoulders. "It's okay, *Mija*, it's okay." A tear trailed down her brown cheek.

Michael leaned forward and patted Sonia's hand. "It's not your fault."

In between bursts of grief, Sonia described her unbearable loneliness. At thirteen, she learned to numb the pain with drugs and alcohol. She had nowhere to go and no reason to feel hope.

Sonia used drugs to turn down the volume on the ghosts who haunted her, and to numb the pain of being unloved and abandoned. The drugs became her surrogate mother.

When Sonia was finished, Alex spoke. She had grown up in the barrio with three brothers. Her father worked with a traveling crew in fields far away. Alex's mother did not speak English, so Alex conducted much of the family business.

"My brothers were mean," she said. "They d'int protect me like a brother is s'posed to."

The eldest was in prison for gang-related crimes. Brother number two had been shot and killed in a drive by. Alex's baby brother ran with a tagging crew. "He's an artist," she said.

Alex had been badly beaten and jumped into the gang at age fourteen. At seventeen, she found herself pregnant and, at nineteen, she married an older man who turned out to be a violent alcoholic.

By the time she realized what she had done, it was too late. She couldn't go home to her mother, and she had nowhere else to go.

After group, Kit and I reverberated with the sorrow of their stories.

"I feel like we're on sacred ground," I said.

Kit nodded. "We are."

Meanwhile, back at the beach cottage, my little black and white fur ball was molding me into a mommy. Every morning, before dawn, she woke me up and demanded to go outside.

Now, that may not seem like a big deal to some people, but I don't do mornings. I had been running to catch the bus, sometimes missing it, since the third grade. I couldn't even get out of bed the night our house caught fire. Dad had to carry me out still asleep. I was like that proverb in the Old Testament:

> *The sluggard turns on his bed like a hinge.*
> *He says, "There is a lion in the street."*

But the little lion dog got me out of bed. Before dawn. Every morning.

Not only did she completely disrupt my sleep, but the little Shih Tzu ate every piece of paper in the house. One day I came home to find that *Shnuckie The Shredder* had gobbled up my W-2 forms. Try telling that to the IRS.

Shnuckie made lots of friends at St. Jerome's. All of the children loved to play with her, and the staff brought her treats and toys. Some of the older gang girls who acted all hard and bad the rest of the time cuddled the puppy in the privacy of my office. Shnuck was the only one who could penetrate their armor. She was the secret weapon.

Sandra, the most maternal nurse in the world, fell in love with Shnuckie. I finally figured out that when I couldn't find Sandra, she was sneaking into my office. One day I walked in and found her curled up on the floor, talking baby talk to the puppy. She flushed and crept out.

117

Gradually, over time, Tony and his staff warmed up to our parents whose children lived downstairs. Sometimes they chatted after Parents Group.

One afternoon I found Tony at the picnic table with Mary and two of his staff. He introduced her to the women who took care of her daughter.

Our staff served as surrogate parents for these children, night and day, for many months, and they grew attached. Of course they felt protective.

We finished our twelve-week Parenting Class, and transitioned to a Support Group. We talked about the daily struggles of staying sober, and applied the new skills we had learned. Cindy never returned, but our faithful four kept coming.

The group discussion weaved in and out, back and forth between day-to-day life, ghosts from the past, and group dynamics in the moment. The group organism had a life of its own, and the four took turns leaning on each other.

Mark decided to host a Summer Picnic and invite all of the parents who had visiting rights with their children. I met with him to discuss a strategy. We anticipated a riot in staff meeting.

On Tuesday morning, I sat next to Mark in my grownup suit while he announced his crazy idea.

Tony raised his hand.

Mark's jaw tightened as he called on Tony. "Yes?"

"My brother has a restaurant downtown," Tony said. "He could get us a good deal on some Mexican food."

Mark exhaled and regrouped. "That's great, Tony," he said, with a hint of disbelief.

Tony continued. "And he's got a couple of vans for moving tables and stuff if you need them."

Kit leaned forward and whispered in my ear, "That's those vans I was tellin' you about. It's Mexican Mafia, I'll bet you." She snickered.

She was so full of it.

All of the staff pitched in to help set up for the massive event. They supervised the kids, served the parents, and stayed late to clean up. It was after 11:00 p.m. when we finally dried the last pan.

"That was a good one." I smiled at Tony, still intoxicated by the success of the day.

"Yeah." He nodded, so exhausted he could barely hold his head up. He'd been working since 6:00 a.m. "Hey, you wanna take some tamales home?" he asked.

"Sure. Thanks."

The next week before group Michael knocked on my doorframe. "Cate, do you have a minute?"

"Sure, come in."

"I was wondering if you have any books that I could read about this stuff?"

"Which stuff?"

"You know, about getting over childhood. Stuff like that."

"I sure do."

"Could I borrow one till next week?"

I looked through the shelves and selected a book for Michael called *Healing The Child Within*. Dr. Whitfield used concepts from the 12 Step recovery model. I thought Michael would like that.

"Tell me what you think of it." I handed him the book.

"O.K. Thanks." He started to walk out, then turned back. "You really care about us, don't you?" He stared into my eyes with disbelief and studied my reaction.

I nodded.

As our group progressed, sheet after sheet of self-protective ice melted in our presence. These parents were eager to heal and, given the opportunity, they changed. As they learned how to care for themselves and manage the stress in their lives, their capacity to care for their children improved. After they released their pain and rage in the group, it no longer bubbled up with the same intensity at home. Feeling accepted and supported by our little family, they became more affirming and nurturing with their children. And as they became more aware of their own demons, they were not as vulnerable to being possessed by them.

Michael and Alex completed all of the court's requirements and earned the right to take their children home. Alex divorced her husband and enforced a restraining order to protect her children.

Mary could not manage the stress of full time parenthood, but she developed a cooperative relationship with her daughter's foster parents and visited every week. Sandra helped her find a day treatment program with other adults who struggled with mental illness. She found friends there.

Sonia relapsed and failed the court-ordered urinalysis twice. Her baby remained in foster care while she continued to struggle with sobriety. She decided to live in a women's recovery home where she could get the support she needed.

Every week after group, Kit and I sat together in the messy rec room, shaking our heads in wonder. Something beyond us was at work in these battered, brave lives.

The parents became our heroes.

Humans are not designed to cope with overwhelming circumstances alone. When young parents get into trouble, they don't need to be punished. They punish themselves enough.

These four weren't monsters after all. They did monstrous things because monstrous things had been done to them. Trauma is an intergenerational phenomenon and no one is to blame. And connecting to the child in the parent can stop the transmission pattern.

Every Christmas, St. Jerome's was overrun with donations of toys and clothes for the children. That year, Tony and his staff shared some of the presents with the parents.

One day while the staff were wrapping gifts I overheard Tony talking to Michael on the patio, teaching him how to use time outs with Michael Jr. The two men swapped stories about the rambunctious little boy. They were trying to decide which Transformer to give him for Christmas.

A few days before Christmas, Sandra stopped by my office with presents for me and Shnuckie. She had found a framed needlepoint that read,

We are not here to see through one another,
but to see one another through.

That pretty much summed up Sandra's philosophy. She got it long before I did. I was still throwing around diagnostic labels and hiding behind my cynicism while she was parenting the parents.

It's easy to lose sight of the humanity of flailing parents when working in the massive, impacted bureaucracy of children's services. And it's hard to keep opening your heart after it's been broken repeatedly.

Social workers see horrors that no one should ever have to see. Getting burned goes with the territory. So does burnout. Or, to use the new P.C. term, *Compassion Fatigue*. Almost sounds glamorous.

If we want to help families heal, we have to open up and find a deeper empathy for the parents, which in no way excuses or exonerates them.

The following week, Michael and his son came to visit after group. The proud four-year-old clutched his dad's right hand and grinned. Michael Sr. cradled a box under his left arm.

"We thought you could use these in your sandbox." He held the box of toys out to me.

Michael Jr. looked up at me. "We cleaned out our closet after Christmas."

"Mikey told me about your bathtub." Dad looked curious.

"Wanna see it?" I led them into the adjoining room where I had painted a sunset on the wall and filled the bathtub with sand. The sink and toilet had been replaced by rows of shelves full of toys for play therapy.

"Wow, that's neat." He smiled at his son and nodded.

"Look, Dad. Transformers!" Mikey grabbed a toy from the shelf.

"Let's ask permission first, Hon." Michael spoke in a sweet voice.

"Can I show my Dad the Transformers?" Mikey asked me.

"Of course you can." I smiled. "Thank you for asking."

Dad knelt beside the tub while his son showed him how to change the robot into a tank. He was so gentle and patient with the little boy.

"Okay, kiddo. It's time for us to go," Dad said. "Let's thank Cate for letting us see her toys."

"Thank you, Cate," Mikey said. He turned to pet the puppy, who jumped up on him, her tiny plume tail swishing with excitement.

"Thank you for sharing your toys, Mikey," I said. "That's very generous of you."

"You're welcome." He looked up at his dad with a worshipful gaze.

Michael Sr. held his gaze for a moment, then looked at me. "You know, I was thinking. There are two kinds of therapists..."

I smirked and waited for one of his dumb jokes. "Yes?"

"No, I'm serious. It's like you're sinking in quicksand. One therapist tells you everything he knows about quicksand, and everything you're doing wrong. The other one throws you a rope."

MESSAGES IN THE SAND

"All play means something."
- D.W. Winnicott

I'm standing in the hallway outside my office with Sandra the nurse when a waist-high blur of color zooms past us. He roars like a wild beast. "Grrr!" and his red cape sails behind him as he dashes into the playroom.

"It's one of those cloth napkins left over from the holiday banquet," Sandra confesses with a sheepish smile. "I pinned it to his t-shirt collar."

Luke was the most popular five-year-old at St. Jerome's. Wiry, freckle-faced, and funny, Luke tore through the halls every day with sound effects loud enough for a much bigger boy. His superhuman energy exhausted the staff, and they grew more attached to him because he was such a handful.

Luke loved Batman, and talked about him nonstop. In his little cape he became Batman. Sometimes his flights of fantasy made his caregivers nervous. They were familiar with PTSD, but none of them had met a child with hallucinations or delusions before.

One afternoon on the dorm, Luke became an evil king who terrorized the younger children. "You will do as I say or you will die! Bow before me!"

Fueled by rage, he swung his toy sword around fast, out of control, and hit his little brother, Nathan, in the face. Nathan screamed and cried.

"Luke! Put the sword down! Now!" Tony yelled to snap Luke out of his trance.

"Bow before me, you little piece of shit!" Luke lunged at Tony with the sword. Tony grabbed it and wrapped his arms around Luke. He held the squirming little hellion in his lap till he calmed down. After a few minutes, Luke went limp and stared off into a black hole.

Dr. Peterson, the consulting psychiatrist, diagnosed Luke with childhood schizophrenia. This label made Luke exotic among his peers and intimidating to young therapists. After a few weeks of wild behavior, Dr. Peterson wanted to prescribe anti-psychotic medication.

Luke had been removed from his family at age four because of suspected abuse, but Children's Protective Services found no physical evidence. His medical records revealed little. And when Luke's fantasy life started to look more psychotic, Dr. Peterson's focus shifted from trauma to *mental illness.*

After hanging out with Harry for a few years, I was skeptical of Peterson's diagnosing. Harry had become disgusted by the de-evolution of child psychiatry, and called it the *Disease of the Month Club.* One month it was ADD, the next it was Bipolar Disorder. He was appalled to see psychiatrists prescribe medications which had not been adequately tested to young children who were not thoroughly evaluated. "There is no way to predict how these medications might affect a child's brain," he said.

The medical students in psychiatry no longer studied psychotherapy or psychodynamics, and they paid little attention to a child's environment and relationships. "It's all about the meds now," Harry grumbled. "That's all they're trained to do."

I had trained alongside psychiatry fellows for several years. Senior psychiatrists quizzed medical students about symptoms, syndromes, and medications while psychotherapy trainees learned to do BioPsychoSocial assessments that included environmental and cultural variables, developmental history, losses, traumas, underlying dynamics, etc. But when the therapy interns raised questions about a child's home environment or traumatic experiences, the docs were dismissive. Biological psychiatry ruled in our neck of the woods. Not like Northern California, where cutting edge programs took children off of all psychotropic meds and provided intensive attachment therapy. The new med students seemed to think they could fill in developmental gaps with chemicals.

At St. Jerome's, children's behavior was typically driven more by trauma and family dynamics than by mental illness, though the symptoms initially looked similar. But if all you have is a DSM, everything looks like a mental disorder.

We were lucky to have a Director like Mark who understood each child in context, and did not rush to pathologize a traumatized child. And when he did prescribe medication, he prescribed therapy along with it to treat the underlying source of symptoms.

Mark said the whole diagnostic system was evil. "The DSM is based on deficiency from some arbitrary ideal instead of development," he said. "These children are expressing the violence to their souls. You have to look deeply into the so-called pathology to find the child's coping and striving for life."

We were fortunate to find therapists and interns who wanted to learn Child Psychotherapy. They had been trained to do talk therapy, but that is not the language of young children.

I had remodeled the abandoned restroom attached to my office and made it into a sandplay therapy room. The sink and toilet were removed, leaving space for rows of toy shelves. I painted the inside of the bathtub aquamarine and filled it with play sand. On three walls around the tub I painted a bright orange and red sunset. The ledges of the tub were gold with sand imbedded in the paint.

After the paint dried, I hung an Annie Leibovitz photo over the tub: a portrait of Whoopi Goldberg in a bathtub full of milk. Now that's a girl who knows how to play.

The staff of St. Jerome's helped me fill the shelves with nature objects and toys. This was a language children understood. Every week my new friends appeared at the door bearing bundles like sacred offerings. Most of the objects were hand-me-down toys from their own children. Sandra the nurse went hiking on weekends and brought in special rocks and pieces of wood which sat on the top shelf, out of the teething puppy's reach.

One of Luke's rewards for good behavior was playing in the sand tub. He loved our collection of action figures, and lost himself in the world of play. And though the staff adored him, they appreciated the break.

When Luke first visited the sand tub, he scooped dozens of toys off the shelves, loaded up his arms, and dumped them into the sand. He wasn't quite sure what to do after they were all in the tub.

I sat with him and sorted through the pile.

"Look! It's Batman!" I smiled at him.

"Yeah!" He snatched the action figure from my hand.

I rooted around some more. "Look! Ninja Turtles!"

He picked up one of the Ninja Turtles and examined him from all sides, while clutching Batman in his other fist.

We plowed through the pile until Tony called him for dinner.

After Luke left, the sand looked like an archeological dig.

The following week in Case Conference, Dr. Peterson pushed for meds. He had fallen in love with the *Childhood Schizophrenia Study* at the university, and its accompanying clinical trials. And, of course, the yummy lunches catered by pharmaceutical companies, and the coveted drug rep dinners at L.A.'s finest restaurants.

"I think it is important to get this boy started on medication as early as possible," Dr. Peterson said. "Children who are medicated younger have better outcomes. We can stop these patterns in the brain before they become intractable."

He made pronouncements as though they were facts, even though the drugs had not been adequately tested. Our children served as lab rats.

A few years earlier, I had worked at the psych hospital where I learned that overwhelming experience can produce psychotic symptoms in children. I remembered Joana, a straight A student and track star, who became floridly psychotic, nearly catatonic after her long struggle to keep incest secrets. Her healthy, high-functioning nervous system reached a melting point and broke down. Medication didn't help until she spilled the secrets that had derailed her.

And, of course, I remembered Jesse's wild traumatic states in response to her foster parents' abuse. Sometimes Luke's outbursts reminded me of Jesse.

Dr. Peterson had seen Luke twice for fifteen minutes before prescribing an anti-psychotic.

Sandra the nurse tried to stall him. "He's awfully young to take such a strong drug," she said. "And he's so tiny. There must be some other way we can help him."

I chimed in. "I think we should do a more thorough assessment. Luke's behavior could be disorganized for a lot of reasons."

Dr. Peterson looked at Sandra, then at me. Everyone knew that Mark backed us up when we disagreed with one of the consulting psychiatrists.

Dr. Peterson was nice enough, but he was sort of a one trick pony when it came to treating trauma. "Well, we can wait till next week if you want to observe him a little longer." Dr. Peterson looked down and scribbled on his prescription pad. "Who's next?" He went down the list of children, assuming that each one needed at least one prescription.

The next time Luke came to play, he picked out a few superheroes, some soldiers and tanks, and made war. I couldn't make much sense of his noisy battle, but it seemed cathartic. He lost himself in play. Bombs exploded, warriors shouted, machine guns went rat a tat tat. Batman roared.

Sand swished through the air and smacked against the colorful walls. Some of it flew out of the tub. Luke stirred it around on the floor with his busy little body.

The following week when Luke came to play, he grabbed a red and blue rocket ship, about ten inches long, in his tiny right hand. In his left hand, he held a small Batman action figure.

With the fury of a madman, Luke thrust the rocket into Batman's little bottom again and again. He channeled a deep, gruff voice that I had never heard before

"Fuck you, bitch! Shut up, bitch! I'll give you something to cry about!" He looked possessed.

Chills shuddered through my body.

Luke smacked Batman around with the rocket.

I knelt beside him on the sandy floor and laid my palm between his shoulder blades. I spoke softly, "Hey, Luke, what's happening?"

Luke was in a trance. He stopped shouting, but continued to poke Batman and whispered, "Stupid bitch. Piece of shit."

Sorrow swelled in my throat.

My old friend, Terri from Casa, came to St. Jerome's to teach the new psychotherapy interns how to do Sandplay Therapy. She brought a gift of two shoeboxes full of magical sandplay miniatures from her collection: witches, unicorns, Hindu gods, dragons, Mary and Jesus, angels and devils. She even gave me her favorite piece: *The Sandplay Wizard.* He stood five inches tall and wore a purple robe with white fur trim. In his outstretched hands he held a magic wand and a crystal ball. His bewitching grin looked so real, I expected him to say something.

For her Sandplay Workshop, Terri used her Jeep to transport a regulation sized tray full of sand and several tubs of miniatures from her massive collection. We set them up in the rec room, along with her slide carousel and projection screen.

She taught us about *right brain interventions* and how they can bypass the defenses to directly access unconscious material. She told the stories of children who had worked through traumatic experiences by playing them out in the sand.

"Children are pre-programmed to heal themselves," Terri said. "All we have to do is create and hold a safe play space for them. And keep our agendas out of the way."

"Sandplay is like wakeful dreaming," she said, "with its archetypal symbols and unconscious meanings. The tray is designed to be the size of the child's visual field, and the child's internal world is represented in the sand."

Terri showed us slides of sand trays created by traumatized children. One little girl had buried all of her secrets in the sand and then unburied them, one by one, week by week, for nine months. After she dug them up, all of her retrieved symbols marched in a parade around the sand tray, led by The Wizard. After that parade, her nightmares stopped.

I figured the Wizard was Terri, but only the little girl knows for sure.

Terri asked me to present a case as an example for the interns. I chose Luke.

"How old was he when he came here?" Terri asked.

"Four," I said. "CPS suspected sexual abuse by the father, but they didn't find any physical evidence. The mother had died, and Luke and his two-year-old brother were neglected for several months before a report came in."

Terri nodded.

"They said he went completely nuts when they tried to do a rectal exam, but they didn't find anything. He was constipated and smearing poop for awhile when he first got here."

Poopers were not my specialty, but I had worked on the same hallway with an Encopresis expert in grad school. An odor worse than dirty diapers hung in the air outside her office every day. I could not imagine why anyone would choose that as a specialty.

The Poop Lady was passionate about her work with children, and she told me her theories about trauma and nonverbal communication. When one of my young patients began making poop murals on the walls at home and leaving poo surprises around the house, her theories made sense. In a weird way, it wasn't so different from art or play therapy. The little boy was sending messages, hoping someone might decode them and help him. Poop signals instead of smoke signals.

Terri frowned and pondered Luke's story. She scrunched up her forehead and propped her fingers over her mouth. "He may not have words for what happened to him if he was traumatized before he had the language to make sense of it. But he has emotional memories. And body memories."

"Like Jesse," I remembered hours spent on *Casa's* dirty carpet, trying to contain her terrorized flailing.

"Exactly. Pre-verbal trauma. That stuff can be nasty."

"Especially when they wear big boots."

Terri smiled. We could never talk about kids without thinking of Jesse. She was our firstborn.

"But back to Luke," I said. "I'm not sure how best to help him with his play. He gets pretty psychotic at times. I don't want to re-traumatize him."

"Focus on your connection with him while he plays," Terri said. "Be very present and follow his lead. You'll know what to do."

"Just trust the Force, eh?"

"Yeah, that's it. The Force." Terri smiled. The interns laughed.

After listening to Terri's inspiring stories, all of the interns wanted to use the sand tub. I made a sign-up sheet so they could take turns.

Terri never accepted payment for her workshops, so I rewarded her that evening with homemade pizza and Kendall Jackson cabernet. We sat on the deck behind the beach cottage and watched the surfers while Shnuckie bounced around in the grass.

As Shnuckie's self-appointed Godmother, Terri always brought her puppy treats and toys. Terri was the kind of pet owner who bought rotisserie chickens from Whole Foods for her dogs, and cooked organic brown rice and vegetables for them every day. They ate better than I did.

We chatted and philosophized while the sun went down. Surfers still straddled their boards in wet suits when it became too cold for us to sit outside.

As she was packing up to leave, Terri dug around in the back of her Jeep for some more sand play goodies she wanted to give me. Puffy, my redheaded outlaw kitty, jumped up into the Jeep and climbed into Terri's sand tray. It was about twice the size of Puffy's litter box and full of clean sand.

"Puffy! No!"

But it was too late. I gasped in horror.

Terri just laughed and scooped out the sand.

The next morning, I cleared a spot for Terri's magical sand play wizard on the top shelf. I could use all the help I could get.

The sand tub schedule filled up fast. I loved listening to the interns play with their kids while I worked in the next room.

They made magic in there.

Luke came to see me twice a week. He played out the same scene over and over. He assaulted Batman with the rocket, smacked him around, and berated him. After a few reruns of that disturbing scene, intuition led me to join his play.

One afternoon while Luke played, I scanned the shelves for an ally. Spiderman, Catwoman, Hulk, Hercules...Luke Skywalker! Perfect.

Nervous about how Luke might react to my intrusion, I approached with care.

"Uh oh, Rocket...you're in trouble now..." I held Luke Skywalker up and waited for Luke's reaction.

He whipped his head around and looked startled. His eyes grew wide. His breathing sped up.

Uh oh.

He stared at the toy in my hand with the tunnel vision of fight-flight.

"Luke Skywalker is coming to save Batman. Vvvh! Vvvh!" I made lightsaber sounds.

Luke snapped out of his trance and looked at me. He grinned and sat up straight.

"Take that, Rocket! Vvvh! Vvvh!" I smacked the rocket with Luke Skywalker's lightsaber.

Luke chuckled, and tightened his grip on the rocket.

"Come with me, Batman! The shuttle is waiting!" I gently pulled Batman out of Luke's sweaty little hand. He didn't resist.

"Here we go! I grabbed a space ship off the shelf and zoomed them away to safety. "Vroom!"

Sand crunched under Luke's tiny boot as he pivoted to watch the ship. His intelligent blue eyes tracked Batman. He didn't say a word, but dropped the rocket into the tub.

The rocket lay upside down, engulfed by sand, surrounded by Luke's allies.

The next time Luke came to play, he rescued Batman with Catwoman. In the weeks that followed, he rescued him with Spiderman, Hulk, and Hercules. Sometimes they all piled on.

After Luke's allies rescued Batman a few times, Batman fought Rocket on his own. And after Batman kicked Rocket's ass for a few weeks, Luke's rage faded. His play became calmer and more contained. He was able to keep all of the sand inside the tub.

When Dr. Peterson saw Luke for his quarterly follow-up he noted the absence of delusions and hallucinations, and stopped talking about schizophrenia. But he wanted to prescribe the new drug for ADHD.

One afternoon while Luke played, he smacked Rocket hard against the side of the tub and broke him in two. He gasped and looked up at my face with wide eyes, clutching Rocket's tail in his hand.

"Ah ha! Take that, Rocket!" I shouted and clapped my hands.

Luke chuckled his deep, funny chuckle, and looked down at the broken toy.

"Now what do we do?" I asked.

"Leth bury him!" He sprayed through his missing tooth. His eyes glistened above a lopsided grin.

I grabbed a plastic shovel and scooped out the sand. Luke dug with his hands. We dug a deep hole, big enough for lots of rockets.

I placed the broken rocket pieces in Luke's palms. He looked at them for a moment, then dropped them into the bottom of the pit, shoved sand on top of them, and patted it flat.

The smooth sand looked so peaceful.

Mark taught us that trauma was determined by the response of the environment. Kids could survive horrible injuries, losses, and despair if they didn't feel alone. Empathy and validation helped them metabolize their experiences. But children who were left alone with overwhelming pain and fear became far more disrupted. Without connection or support, traumatic memories remained raw, unprocessed, and easily triggered.

We never learned what happened to Luke before we met him, but he was no longer alone in his nightmare.

A few weeks later, Luke brought his little brother to play. Nathan's long, blonde curls formed a cherubic afro, and he wore fat, padded pull ups instead of pants. He was the cutest toddler in the world and I wanted to squeeze him.

I greeted the little boys at the door. "Hey, guys, wanna check out my new toys?"

"Yeah!" Luke yelled.

"Yeah!" Nathan mimicked.

Luke grabbed Nathan's hand and led him into the sand play room. "Look." He held up the Batman action figure. "Batman ith the motht powerful. Grr!"

Nathan plopped his padded bum down on the sandy floor and watched his big brother. Luke introduced each of the superheroes and explained their powers. For a moment, he seemed so grown up.

Nathan stood, scooped an armful of toys off a shelf, and dumped them into the tub.

"No!" Luke yelled. "Nathan!" Luke propped his fists on his hips and shook his head. He looked up at me with an exasperated expression. "I'll thow him how to do it."

Luke sorted through the pile in the tub and put some of the toys back on the shelf.

"Here, Nathan, you can be in charge of the soldiers." Luke picked soldiers out of the pile and showed them to his brother. Nathan picked up a soldier and studied it.

Luke shoved the pile to the foot of the tub and lined up soldiers and tanks for a proper war.

It was a hot summer afternoon, and I stood near the doorway of the playroom to catch the breeze that blew in through the open windows.

Luke cackled as he smacked soldiers and tanks together. Sand flew and swished against the sides of the tub.

Nathan picked up fistfuls of sand and watched it cascade through his chubby fingers. He giggled at Luke's noisy play.

These kids had an amazing ability to create moments of joy even while going through hell.

As I watched the little boys play, my mind drifted back in time. I remembered a poem I wrote for my brother.

...we never got to frolic on childhood's happy lawn;
innocent abandon harshly stolen early on.
We never got to form the sacred bonds of kindred souls;
too busy much too early trying just to plug the holes...

Tears welled. I willed them away.

The breeze blew sand off the shelves and onto my sandaled feet.

After a few minutes of rowdy play, Luke grew bored. "Hey, Nathan, leth go play thordfight!" He looked at me. I nodded, and he scampered out the door with baby brother trailing behind.

I looked around the playroom and remembered afternoons with Luke. The light seemed brighter than before. It was that late afternoon low light that makes everything glow.

I picked the toys out of the tub and returned them to their shelves. The warm sun beamed in and animated tiny metallic specks in the sand as I raked it smooth.

As I rose to leave, a flash of light startled me. Terri's grinning wizard sat on the top shelf among Luke's action figures. His crystal ball refracted a sunbeam.

I grinned back at him and planted him in the glowing sand where he belonged.

THE SNOTROCKETS

"When one finds a child...who is relatively intact
after surviving a horrendous childhood,
one should look for the making of art. Art heals."
- Elan Golomb, Ph.D.

I'm stretched out on Lali's hardwood floor, elbows propped on a pillow. It's September in the desert, the hottest month of the year, and nine therapists have gathered for this last day of training in expressive arts therapies. We've lived through four intense, intimate weekends together. All eyes are riveted to the monitor, watching the psychodrama we filmed yesterday, the story of a young dancer who was beaten and crippled by an angry man.

A hill of soggy tissues grows on the floor under my chin as I sop up a geyser of grief. I haven't cried this much in years.

The play is about me and my father.

Our class met at Lali's secluded retreat center, where red-tailed hawks screeched as they circled, and golden eagles flew low over the house in moments of breathtaking synchronicity.

Lali decorated her breezy ranch house with paintings, sculpture, Native American art, drums, feathers, and souvenirs from her travels. Her spacious family room housed a collection of costumes and props for psychodrama, musical instruments, glue guns, and art supplies.

Lali had studied with a Native American shaman after she finished her psychology training. Her multi-colored jewel eyes were more lion than human.

I had experienced a variety of different therapies and healers over the years, but nothing as powerful as this. Art circumvents the intellect to penetrate the heart.

My roommate, Karen, and I drove an hour each way on winding country roads to Lali's house. The wind whipped our hair while

Ani DiFranco tunes blasted from Karen's car stereo. In the evenings, after long days of intense emotional work, we debriefed in the hot tub while I practiced playing Eine kleine Nachtmusik on my beer bottle.

We lived in a funky house near the beach with Karen's boyfriend, Will, and his golden retriever. And Karen's fat orange cat. And her Jack Russell terrier. And, of course, Puffy and Shnuckie.

Karen was a lot like her Jack Russell - smart, hyper, and always getting into mischief. She ran marathons, won surf competitions, and made all kinds of art. Karen was striking with her deep tan and thick, dark curls. She had grown up at the beach, and her surfboard had become another appendage like John Lee Hooker and his guitar.

We spent weekends surfing and hanging out at home. Will was a wizard with the barbeque, a standup comic, and a jazz musician. He owned a collection of classic jazz CD's that made a super groovy soundtrack for our leisure time. Except for Wednesday nights when we all huddled up together to watch the latest episode of *South Park*.

Will told stories about his adventures as a jazzman and ghost buster. He and his buddy saged rich people's houses and drove out spirits for a fee that supplemented what they made playing gigs. Then he became a psychologist, and wore a suit to his administrative job every day, which seemed to depress him.

Karen and I worked at a group home called Canyon Ridge, way out in the desert. My job at St. Jerome's had become too administrative after a few years and squeezed out my time with the kids, so when a former intern recruited me to work as a therapist at Canyon Ridge, I pounced on the opportunity.

Karen and I couldn't wait to use our new art therapy training with the kids. We shopped for supplies, collected magazines for collages, and gathered clothing and accessories for a psychodrama wardrobe. A few of the group home staff donated dress-up stuff while the more cynical staff razzed us about trying to do art with our wild pack of girls.

My friend, Jim, supervisor of the girls' dorm, encouraged his staff to be supportive. "Karen and Cate have some great ideas," he said. "Let's help them any way we can." He talked like one of those responsible dads from a 1950's T.V. show.

Jim was such a good grownup. I counted on his steady, conservative style to balance my spontaneity. We teased each other about our differences, but we made a good team. Jim helped me move furniture. I rewarded him with a foot-long, plush Mr. Hanky, The Christmas Poo, to hang from the ceiling in his office.

Mr. Hanky was our totem.

Jim always wore a Dodgers cap to work, and he looked about twenty years old with his chubby face and pink cheeks. The only thing more fun than making Jim laugh was making him blush.

He humored us while he waited for our crazy idea to blow up.

In Case Conference the previous week, Jim had pressed to discharge our wild child, Nicole. A dozen or so staff and therapists and a couple of psychiatrists sat around the conference table. Most of them agreed with him.

"She hasn't made any progress in twelve months." Jim sat stiff and spoke in an agitated tone. "I have to pull staff out of the classroom every day to sit with her in the quiet room. While she's getting all this attention, we're neglecting the other girls."

Maggie, long time house parent of the girls' dorm, backed him up. "I don't see any signs of remorse in her." Mag spoke with the raspy voice of a heavy smoker. "She don't belong here. She oughta be in probation, not in mental health."

Karen leaned forward with angry eyes. "She is only twelve years old. She's had nothing but abuse and abandonment since she was in the womb. You want to send her to jail for more trauma?'

Jim flushed. A deep number 11 scrunched up between his eyebrows. "Remember how she had those boys arrested for rape? Then laughed when she admitted there was no rape?" He looked at me for support. "What if she makes false allegations against one of us? You know she's a pathological liar."

"The girl has no conscience and no impulse control." Maggie's voice cracked. "We're doin' nuthin' to help her and she's endangering the other girls." She glared at Karen and shoved her cat eye glasses up her nose with her middle finger as she looked down at Nicole's chart. The chain on her glasses swung back and forth while she scrawled notes. "I think she's a sociopath," she muttered without looking up.

A hard-core AA veteran, Mag had no patience for codependent behavior. Especially mine.

I listened. Jim and Maggie were my friends, and I felt their frustration. Keeping Nicole was risky. Several staff had been injured in take downs, and she said vicious things to them that were hard to forgive.

It is almost impossible to keep a child in residential treatment when the staff want them gone. These children had a sixth sense for sniffing out abandonment and pre-empting it.

I wished I could agree with my friends, but I could not abandon Nicole. If we let her slip away into the juvenile justice system, her fate would change forever.

"Tell you what," I said, "if you guys can hang in there a little longer, I'll see her every day and you can use me for backup. Call me when she blows out of the classroom and I'll take her to my office. Give the staff a break."

Jim tightened his lips and gave me his long-suffering look. Maggie waved her hand in the air without looking up from her notes. "Okay, who's next?" She re-filed Nicole's chart. I'd get an earful from her later.

They think I'm nuts, but we bought the kid some time. Good trade.

I looked across the table at Karen. She winked.

On a Thursday evening after dinner, Karen and I corralled eight adolescent girls in the big conference room and told them about the art therapy group. The high-ceilinged room was bright with florescent light. A long conference table took up most of the space, and extra chairs and audio-visual equipment were stacked along the walls.

Shelly, a stout sixteen-year-old who always wore boy's clothes and spent many afternoons in the time out room for aggressive behavior, stared at me with brewing annoyance. She had no interest in art or in groups of girls. She preferred to hang out with the boys. Sometimes I thought of Shelly as a porcupine: self-protective quills, soft underbelly.

Susie, a severely depressed heroin addict who rarely got out of bed, propped her chin on the table and waited for the show to start. Underneath her nose sat her most recent drawing of Kenny, the South Park character, in his little orange coat with a bloody spear through his head. Susie loved Kenny, and found many creative ways to kill him off in her drawings. Sometimes when I arrived at work in the morning I found a portrait of Kenny taped to my office door that indicated Susie's current state of mind. The decapitations were my favorites.

Alice, an awkward redhead with horrible acne, sat hunched over, her hands tucked underneath her legs. Her eyes darted from face to face. The girls often scapegoated Alice, and she looked like she was bracing herself for more abuse.

Patrice, a charismatic African-American girl sat next to Karen and whispered in her ear. Patrice and Karen were tight. Karen had been her individual therapist for six months, and though she tried hard not to play favorites, everyone knew she loved Patrice. It was hard not to. Patrice exuded warmth and humor. Her radiant smile lit up the grey hallways, and her raucous laugh busted up the dark clouds on the girls' dorm.

Jillian, the only child of wealthy parents, posed with perfect posture and looked down her nose at the rest of us. She made straight A's, weighed less than 100 pounds, and felt she did not belong here with these troublemakers. I suppose she was right, but there were no long-term residential programs for eating disorders at that time. Like so many of our kids, she got the treatment that was available rather than the treatment she really needed.

Jane, who had grown up in England, sat quietly and drew a picture in her sketchbook. Jane seemed older than the other girls, though she was only fifteen. Her chart said she'd been admitted for depression, but she acted like a normal, healthy teenager. Maybe her artistic temperament had gotten her diagnosed. It was weird how the healthiest family member often became the identified patient.

Rhiannon, proud to be Wiccan, slouched in her chair, twirled her long, dark hair around her index finger, and chewed on it. Ry liked to cast spells on the other girls when they annoyed her.

Nicole, who was on permanent AWOL watch after running away and hooking up with strange boys, bounced in her chair like an excited preschooler. At twelve, she already had a long rap sheet for drugs, theft, assault, and more. Nicole was intelligent and creative, but possessed the impulse control of an untrained puppy.

My stomach fluttered when I imagined this combination of characters armed with paints and markers.

Patrice bellowed. "Let's vote on a name for the group!"

"The Furbies!" Nicole shouted, holding up her furby baby.

"The Foxy Mamas," Susie slurred.

"West Side Ho's!" Patrice's big chuckle rocked the room.

The girls laughed and shouted increasingly crude names.

Jane raised her sketchbook and displayed her drawing of a rocket. With her proper British accent, she enunciated the name printed on the side of the ship – *Snotrockets*.

"Yeah." Susie nodded.

"Yay!" Nicole jumped up and down.

They all clapped and cheered. "Snotrockets! Yay!" Shelly did her deafening wolf whistle.

I felt like I was leading a pep rally.

Karen and I rode herd over the rowdy group for another thirty minutes, explained the rules, and showed them some of the art projects we had made in our expressive arts therapy training.

After a few minutes, Patrice grew bored. "Hey, Alice, is that a hickie on your neck?"

Alice flushed and looked scared.

"I heard you and Ricky were doin' the nasty out there last night." Patrice giggled.

"Patrice!" Karen scolded her.

"Sh-shut up!" Alice stammered. She was slower than the other girls and could not defend herself against Patrice's quick wit.

"Let's keep it respectful, Patrice." I gave her a stern look.

But she continued. "Aw, c'mon, Alice. You know you love that big black dick."

The girls laughed.

"Patrice, please take a time out," I pointed toward the door.

Alice lurched out of her chair and took a clumsy swing at Patrice.

Karen placed a hand on Patrice's shoulder. When Patrice reared back to punch, Karen grabbed her arm. I loved having a jock as a co-therapist.

We separated the two while they slung insults at each other. I hit the intercom button to call for backup.

When Jim arrived with one of his male staff to escort Patrice to the dorm, he shot me his "I told you so" look. Patrice looked over her shoulder and flashed a mischievous smile as he led her away.

Alice took a walk with one of the female staff to cool off.

We wrapped up the meeting, walked the girls to the dorm, and retreated to my office.

Karen slouched on my sofa and looked around at shelves full of sand play miniatures. She picked up the wizard and polished his dusty crystal ball with the tail of her shirt. "This is crazy." She looked up and laughed. Her dark eyes glistened. "But I think it will be fun. If they don't kill us."

I sat down at my desk and kicked off my Doc Martens. We'd survived tougher kids. Karen and I were war buddies from the psych hospital, where we had both taken plenty of blows. One of the patients broke Karen's wrist during a take down, and another brandished a broken beer bottle in my face. And yet another hurled a huge potted plant at my head during a family therapy session. I thought twice before making an interpretation after that one.

You might say we'd been broken in.

Our first group task was to create emotional safety, which seemed impossible.

Patrice could not resist tormenting Alice, and Alice had the world's thinnest skin. Their cycles of retaliation never ended.

Jillian drove wedges between the other girls with gossip and manipulation. She envied Patrice's queen bee status and maneuvered from every angle, hoping to take her down a notch.

Nicole made cruel comments just to watch the girls get riled up. She had that creepy telepathy for sniffing out open wounds and poking them.

The Snotrockets were like popcorn popping. As soon as one kernel settled down, another would go off. Safety seemed elusive, but we would get nowhere without it.

Karen and I decided to appeal to Patrice's leadership potential. She was smart, sassy, funny, and well-liked by adults when she wasn't being evil. And this group would never work without her buy-in.

Alice admired Patrice and longed to be accepted by her. The two girls lived at opposite ends of the social galaxy. Alice was developmentally delayed, heavily medicated, and lonely. Abandoned by her father and neglected by her mother, she believed no one cared about her. A few times, when her hopelessness felt unbearable, she tried to kill herself.

On a Thursday afternoon before group, Karen brought Patrice to my office to meet with Alice.

Alice and Patrice sat side by side on the worn, sagging sofa. I kept the lights low, and Carlos Nakai's Native American flute covered the ambient noise from the hallway. Patrice sank back into the cushions and made herself at home. She picked up a candle and sniffed it.

A framed certificate on the wall above the girls' heads read *Nester Award*. My colleagues had presented it to me one morning in staff meeting after watching my little bare room metamorphose into a cozy art therapy cave.

Alice perched on the edge of the sofa and fidgeted. Her eyes darted from me to Karen. She was one of those kids who never felt safe. I had met her mother and understood why.

Karen and I had coached the two girls privately before this meeting, and they both wanted to please us.

"Alice," Patrice spoke in a sweet, contrite voice. Not very convincing. "I'm sorry for being mean to you in the group."

Alice looked like a frightened mouse about to dart around the corner.

"Okay," Alice said, holding her breath.

"I didn't mean to hurt your feelings." Patrice began to sound more like herself. "I was just playin'." She smiled sweetly at Alice, then at me.

"Why do you treat me that way?" Alice confronted Patrice with tears in her eyes. Her voice quaked. This was a first. She must have felt brave with two therapists at her side.

"I don't know. Maybe because of my mother."

"Oh." Alice grew quiet and sober. She understood.

It was true. Patrice was doing to Alice exactly what her mother had done to her. Sometimes these kids had stunning moments of insight which did not necessarily translate into better behavior.

We talked awhile till the tension dissipated.

Patrice promised to be kinder. Alice agreed to check out her assumptions before going ballistic.

We returned to group that evening and began our first project, a group quilt. Each girl created a square that represented her contribution to the group.

Patrice used fat markers to draw a church with a cross and a heart on the front door. Three stick figures smiled and waved. In one corner of her square, she drew some gang graffiti and the name of her favorite rap group in bubble letters.

Alice drew stick figures to represent her and her mom, and her mom's car. She put the Porsche in the middle, which made sense. It was her mother's true love. Alice tried to copy Patrice's graffiti, but she got it all wrong. Patrice stifled her laughter. Alice looked wounded, but kept her cool.

Nicole drew a portrait of a furby with pink hearts all around it. Her picture looked sweet, but it made me sad. I got the impression that Nicole's furbies were her only family.

The Snotrockets' artwork ranged from preschool crayon drawings to sophisticated graphics, but when we sewed all the squares together, it worked. We marched over to the dorm together and hung the group quilt on the wall in the T.V. room. Then we huddled up and admired it for a few minutes. The girls pointed out details they liked. I'd never seen them so proud.

The following week, Karen and I herded the girls from the conference room to a private room on the dorm. The group formed a circle, sitting cross-legged on the floor while Karen and I darkened the room and lit candles.

We gave each of them a big chunk of clay, and guided them through a visualization we had learned from Lali.

Close your eyes. Take a deep breath.
Fill your lungs as full as you can. Hold it.
Now release the breath as slowly as you can...

They looked so cute sitting Indian style with their cheeks puffed out.

...picture yourself as a small child, innocent, untouched...
before anything bad happened to you...

The room grew still. Candle flames danced.

...now picture another child. The survivor in you,
with all of her self-protection in place...

The girls squirmed and tried to get comfortable on the floor.

... picture your allies, the friends who helped you survive...
They sat still.

...when you feel ready, slowly begin to open your eyes
and come back to the circle.

One by one, they opened their eyes in the candlelit silence. A sense of the sacred flooded the room and fused their circle.

The clay pieces Karen and I had created at Lali's house sat in the center next to a candle and cast shadows on the floor. We picked up some clay and joined their circle.

I explained the assignment. "We're going to use the clay to sculpt the images we imagined: the innocent child, the survivor child, and the allies who have helped us.

Each girl sculpted a set of clay figures, some abstract, some realistic. Ry formed a shield and carved it with Wiccan symbols. Jane created a tiny beret and a painter's palette for her little clay girl.

Most of the girls sculpted weapons and fortresses. Shelly made a small sphere and surrounded it with a circle of spikes. Jillian built a Rapunzel-esque tower for herself.

Alice made a baby and a puppy dog. She didn't really get the assignment.

But I knew about the puppy dog. I'd met him before when Alice played in the sand tray. He was a symbol of how Alice felt with her mother - a needy little puppy trailing after a mommy who couldn't be bothered.

Patrice used every bit of her clay plus some of Alice's to form a church and a family. She arranged the figures in a circle with a girl in the middle.

Nicole sat next to me. She had not bonded with her peers during her twelve months at the group home, and she was in imminent danger of being sent to Juvenile Hall. She assaulted staff and peers every week, and did not express the kind of remorse that victims want to hear.

Funny thing about moral development -- children who receive little empathy in early childhood have little to give to others.

Nicole reminded me of Jesse, but less frightened and more street smart. And she craved stimulation, unlike Jess, who easily became over-stimulated. Nicole seemed like an out-of-control toddler in the body of a lovely young woman.

I tried to apply what Harry taught me about Attachment Theory. Whenever I consulted with him about one of my kids, he would listen to my long, complicated story, then say something like, "Sounds like a disorganized attachment pattern." That was about as pathologizing as Harry ever got.

In Jesse's case, that label fit. She had been abused and abandoned by so many different caregivers that her patterns of relating to others were all over the globe. More like a pinball bouncing around inside a pinball machine than a pattern.

Nicole, on the other hand, seemed to have a cold wind blowing through the void where an attachment pattern should be.

Karen and I sat on the dirty carpet with the girls and worked the clay by candlelight. While they chatted and asked questions, Nicole sat hunched over, absorbed in her work. A softness came over her that I had never before seen.

Her long, auburn hair fell forward and framed her creamy complexion. Nicole was a beautiful girl, and so young. She didn't look like a teenager yet. Her fingernails were chewed down to the nub. She massaged the clay with the tenderness of a new mother while the other girls presented their pieces. When her turn came, she sat back and looked at her sculpture, a thin, wavy container in the shape of a womb. Inside the container lay a tiny, newborn baby, its eyes squinted closed, hands folded on its chest, and legs bound up in a blanket.

The girls remained silent while Nicole gazed lovingly at her sculpture. They all knew the punching, kicking Nicole who spewed profanity and told gratuitous lies, and they had learned to distrust her and keep a safe distance.

Who was this person?

Nicole didn't say a word. She looked at me with sad eyes and tried to smile.

Jane tiptoed across the room and laid a gentle hand on Nicole's shoulder. She was the only girl who wasn't afraid of Nicole. "It's beautiful," Jane whispered.

Nicole looked up at her with hopeful eyes. "Really?"

Nicole *was* the newborn in the container. While the other girls depicted themselves with weapons and fortresses, Nicole's only defense was the womb around her.

Her aggressive behavior came directly from that intense vulnerability.

Marinated in drugs and alcohol in the womb, born with methamphetamine in her system, and abandoned by her mother in infancy, Nicole had searched in vain for secure bonds in foster home after foster home. Her demons and her own physiology tormented her day and night. Like an egg without a shell, the group home became her container.

The girls responded with reverence.

It was dinnertime, so we cleaned up. I scooped up Nicole's sculpture in my palm and carried it to my office for safekeeping.

At the next Case Conference I showed the sculpture to the staff and talked about a developmental model of treatment - a model that would allow us to understand Nicole's outrageous behaviors as messages to be decoded rather than crimes to be punished.

I was surprised by their openness. Even Maggie. They all wanted to help her. They just didn't know how.

Nicole's sculpture changed our perspective. As we came to understand her vulnerable infant self, we were better able to meet her needs and not be fooled by the tough-talking 12-year-old facade.

Nicole was unformed, unattached and unmothered. But when we stuck by her through all of her turbulent testing, she felt safe enough to attach. Once that connection was secured, she caught up on some of the development she had missed out on.

Nicole saved her allowance to buy more furby babies. She kept them in a nest in her room under a blanket, and carried one with her everywhere she went.

I had my own fur ball at home, who bore a striking resemblance to one of Nicole's babies.

Nicole met Shnuckie one day during a brief visit and became obsessed with her. She pestered me to bring her again.

I made a contract with Nicole. If she could go 30 days without assaulting anyone, she could spend one of her sessions playing with Shnuckie.

Once again, Shnuckie the Dog proved to be the secret weapon. Nicole made it a whole month. With a lot of good coaching and parenting from the staff and teachers. And daily contact with a supportive therapist she trusted.

Karen joked about the evolution of attachment in our kids. At first, they only attached to inanimate objects, like furbies. Or like drugs and alcohol.

Then, they graduated to reptiles, like Mario and his lizards.

Later, if we were lucky, they would advance to *creatures with fur*, Karen said.

And, if we got a miracle, eventually they would attach to us.

On the day of Shnuckie's visit, Nicole became a freed puppy. There was no containing her once she knew the doggie was nigh. She bolted out of the double doors of the girls' dorm and sprinted to my office shouting, "Shnuuckiee!!!"

Maggie glowered at me.

Oh well. She made it thirty days.

Shnuckie bounced around, danced, and wagged her tail. Her soft Shih Tzu hair was clipped short in a style that made her look like a little black and white gremlin. Nicole lit up with an exuberant smile. We played with the puppy, took her for a walk around the neighborhood, and then retreated from the desert heat back into my air-conditioned office for a Coke.

I couldn't believe that people actually lived there. It seemed too hot for humans. No wonder the rent was so low. The crime rate was low too. It was too hot to enjoy being bad.

Nicole turned out to be one of those kids who needed extra time to test us before she felt safe enough to settle in and attach. Understandably. Fourteen months after she made her sculpture, she was finally stable enough to graduate from Canyon Ridge and live with a foster family.

We gave her a graduation party and sent her on her way.

Four years later, back in L.A., I would walk through the waiting room of a clinic where I worked and hear a familiar voice.

"Cate?"

I turned and recognized Nicole's foster mother. "Lois?" I was surprised to see her. "How are you?"

A proud smile warmed her face. "Nicole is a senior at Lincoln this year. She's on the honor roll."

Joy whished through me. "Wow! That is wonderful." I stood in the middle of the waiting room and grinned. "Is she here?"

"No, I'm here with my son. But she still talks about you."

We chatted for a few minutes before I walked down the hall to my office. Once inside, I took a deep breath, and exhaled a load of emotion.

Nicole's amethyst ring dangled from a pushpin on my corkboard. She had given it to me on the day we parted. Her sculpture sat on my desk, a daily reminder to see through the fault to the need.

⌘

The art therapy group continued and gained momentum. The staff respected and supported the group's work. After the Snotrockets finished their sculptures, we prepared for the next project.

Karen and I brought in stacks of magazines and other materials for making collages.

During one of her individual sessions with Karen, Patrice decided that she wanted to make a collage of mother figures. Her mother had worked as an escort in L.A. until alcoholism and mental illness disabled her. Patrice was taken from her at age six and placed in a foster home where her behavior became more and more aggressive.

Every few weeks Patrice called her mother on the dorm pay phone where we could all hear their conversations. Patrice felt sorry for her mom and wanted to help her. When she tried, her mother attacked.

Her mother's abuse left Patrice feeling fatally flawed. She believed that she was a bad seed and that it was only a matter of time before she would go crazy as her mother had.

Shame overwhelmed her.

One evening in group Shelly was itching to pick a fight. Instead of grieving her own losses, she beat people up. Sort of like a tomboy version of Will Hunting.

Shelly was hurt and bitter about being abandoned by her mother and abused by her father. She welcomed any opportunity to focus on someone else.

"Patrice, how come your mom never comes to visit?" Shelly asked with faux innocence in the middle of group.

"How come yours don't?" Patrice sassed back. Her hackles rose.

"Is it true that she's a whore?" Shelly asked in her sweet voice.

Patrice dived at Shelly and clamped her powerful hands around Shelly's throat. "Shut up, you fuckin' bitch!"

Karen grabbed Patrice's wrists and tried to pull her off. "Patrice! Let go!"

Patrice's dark eyes blazed with murderous rage. I tried to pry her thumbs loose while Jane called for help.

"Patrice!!" Karen shouted louder, an inch from her ear.

Patrice jerked and turned to look at Karen. She released Shelly's neck.

Shelly scurried across the room, wide-eyed.

Patrice mad dogged her until the staff arrived to escort both of them to separate time out rooms.

Karen spent a lot of time with Patrice, and their attachment grew strong. They cut out pictures from magazines and searched for small objects to glue to Patrice's collage.

One morning, after their individual therapy session, Karen and Patrice knocked on my door. They wanted to show me their work.

I liked Patrice and she knew it. I got a big kick out of her brassy attitude and wicked wit. But the shy girl who stood before me was a whole other being. She looked up at Karen with the adoring eyes of a little girl. Karen laid the round, mandala style collage on my desk.

"This is my grandmother." Patrice pointed to a picture of Maya Angelou. "And this is my social worker." She showed me pictures that represented the people who had mothered her. Some were men. Billy D. Williams represented her pastor. She chose symbols for some of her favorite staff and teachers.

The red rose in the center symbolized her mother.

Patrice looked deep into my eyes. "I want to do the psychodrama," she said.

For several weeks, Karen and I had collected clothing and accessories for our new psychodrama wardrobe. The staff were generous with their donations. We had three chests full of goodies but no Snotrocket brave enough to use them.

I was no actress, but I had been amazed by the power of psychodrama at Lali's house. Watching my friends enact truth from my life took me deeper than any talk therapy ever had.

Patrice was a natural actress. It made sense that she would be the first volunteer.

She and Karen worked together behind closed doors to write a script. Their secrecy created suspense that grew from week to week while we waited. By opening night, we were all dying from curiosity.

Karen reserved a special room across campus for privacy. Patrice instructed me to bring the girls over at 7:00.

It was a warm night, and the girls had been playing volleyball outside after dinner. They were sweaty and relaxed, ready to be entertained.

Jim and Maggie helped me corral the girls and seat them in the back of the room. Maggie was Patrice's special guest. As the mom of the dorm, she was closer to Patrice's daily struggles than any of us.

Karen appeared behind the podium and began reading a Mary Oliver poem. The girls grew quiet and listened.

> *One day you finally knew what you had to do,*
> *and began, though the voices around you kept*
> *shouting their bad advice -- though the whole*
> *house began to tremble and you felt the old tug...*

Halfway through the poem, fabric rustled. A flailing woman burst through the curtain behind Karen. Ice klinked in her highball glass. She flung a fly swatter around her head in wild circles.

It was Patrice in costume. She wore a short, hot pink nightgown and an animal print duster. Bright red lipstick was smeared on her chin and her glass. Her fishnet stockings were faded and torn, and her fuzzy slippers looked like dirty dust mops.

"Who took my handbag?!" she shouted at the group of girls, moving closer and closer to Alice's face. "YOU took my handbag!" she snarled at Alice.

Alice stifled a laugh. Patrice had clued her in about the play ahead of time - a special honor.

The wild woman reared back to slap Alice. Alice ducked. Karen returned from behind the curtain dressed up as the crazy woman's daughter.

"Stop it, Mama!" the daughter yelled. The wild woman/mother lurched backward and went after the daughter.

"You little whore! How dare you raise your voice at me!" The mother swung at the daughter. The daughter blocked the punch and grabbed her mother's wrist.

The girls giggled. Maggie shushed them.

"You worthless piece of trash!" the mother screamed. "I wish you'd never been born! You ruined my life! You make me sick! Get out! Get out! Get out!"

The daughter grabbed a suitcase, stomped out, and slammed the door.

The mother crumpled into a chair and wailed. "Oh, my baby. My poor baby. Come back, baby. I love you, baby."

The door opened. The daughter walked back in with her suitcase.

The mother started raging again and hit her with the fly swatter.

Two more times, the daughter left. Two more times she came back.

The girls squirmed in their seats.

The last time the daughter came back, she brought a doctor in a white coat who carried a medicine bag. It was Jim with a stethoscope around his neck. As the doctor walked toward the mother, the daughter walked out and quietly closed the door.

Doctor Jim looked at the mother with compassion and led her off stage.

The girls sat in silence, holding their breath.

After a long moment, Patrice walked on stage in jeans and a t-shirt, as herself. Her hair was a mess, and she still had traces of red lipstick on her face.

The girls cheered.

Patrice picked up the poem that Karen had started reading at the beginning. It was a story about leaving home.

...there was a new voice
which you slowly recognized as your own,
that kept you company as you strode
deeper and deeper into the world,
determined to do the only thing you could do –

determined to save
the only life that you could save.

Tears poured down Patrice's cheeks.

Alice swiped at her own tears with her shirtsleeve.

Maggie struggled to hold it together in front of the girls.

Patrice's tears transported me back to that hot September day in Lali's living room, lying on the floor with my mountain of soggy tissues, watching our psychodrama.

Neither Patrice nor I had ever mourned like that before. A very old iceberg finally began to melt.

My play had been the story of a young dancer and the angry man who beat her with a club. He pummeled her legs till he broke them. Her friends carried her away and took care of her.

After her friends healed her, the girl danced more beautifully and powerfully than before.

Karen had played the part of the dancer. She wore flowing, pale blue, sheer fabric that made her look like Scheherazade.

I had never taken a ballet class in my life, though I fell in love with dance at an early age. And I had never been beaten with a club, at least not a physical one. But when I watched my friends enact that metaphor, the ice began to thaw.

Our unconscious minds work out their conflicts in the cinema of our dreams and on the canvas of our creativity.

Art lives in a different realm of healing and speaks from a deeper place than words. In that realm, a child can find a refuge, and a voice to tell her story.

Children tell us their stories in mysterious ways.

And they keep telling them till someone hears.

CANYON GIRL

"We do, doodley do, doodley do, doodley do,
what we must, muddily must, muddily must,
muddily must..."
        - BOKONON

I'm walking through a desert canyon with a pair of Wiccans, about to perform a ritual in the middle of my workday. Hot, brittle brush crunches under our sandals. Crows caw from bare tree branches as we pass.

What's a nice Christian girl like me doing in a scene like this?

Rhiannon came to Canyon Ridge for long-term residential treatment after she slit her wrists. She'd been carving on her arms since she was twelve but now, at fifteen, she cut deeper.

Ry's mother would not allow her to return home until she saw radical change in her attitude and behavior. The two together were gasoline and flame. Their violent fights had resulted in two evictions, and their new landlord now threatened a third.

The group home staff at Canyon Ridge called Ry *cold-hearted* and claimed she had no empathy. When one of her peers almost died from a suicide attempt, Ry laughed at her.

I liked Ry. I saw a softness in her. Under her baggy men's XL shirts she wore frilly cotton dresses. She reminded me of those little monster finger puppets with the huge buggy eyes that look more scared than scary.

During Ry's first six months of residential treatment, her mother refused to take her on passes. She wanted to punish her, and she also wanted to keep her safe.

Susan, a tough, practical woman, did not understand her sensitive, artistic daughter. Susan had grown up with a psychotic mother, and dropped out of school at sixteen to work. She wanted to give Ry a better life, and she worked hard to be a good provider.

Ry adored her dad and blamed Susan for driving him away. Dad called Ry on the dorm pay phone every week, badmouthed Susan, and sent frivolous gifts. He never paid a dime of child support.

Susan agreed to participate in family therapy sessions every other Friday after work. She drove her pickup truck over an hour in heavy traffic and arrived early for our first session.

She sat on the couch, arms folded, jaws tight, and watched Ry with suspicion.

Ry pleaded with her mother. "Give me another chance! Pleease!" Tears streamed down her face. "I want to come home."

"Don't give me your crocodile tears," Susan snapped. "We've been through this too many times before. You cry and say you're sorry, and then you go out and do the same things."

"But, Mom..."

"I can't believe anything she says anymore," Susan said to me. "She's a compulsive liar."

"She left me all alone!" Ry wailed, "What was I supposed to do?"

"Well, maybe you could take some responsibility for helping out around the house instead of carving yourself up and running off with hoodlums," Susan said.

"She won't let me do anything," Ry said to me. "She treats me like a prisoner."

"You mean I grounded you for running away and doing crystal?" Susan confronted her. "Why don't you tell Dr. Shepherd about your little tantrum?"

Ry slouched into the sofa and folded her arms across her chest.

"I came home from work late one night, and she screamed at me, called me a cunt, and broke two of the dining room chairs," Susan said. "The next day, she shaved her head and pierced her nose while I was at work."

"You leave me all alone in that fuckin' apartment!" Ry yelled. "You act like you don't even care about me."

Susan rolled her eyes. "Drama," she said, and shook her head.

I examined Ry's nose. "You did that by yourself?"

"Yeah," she said, with defiant pride.

"That must have hurt."

She looked at me, puzzled. "Yeah, I guess."

The accumulated pain and rage between them seemed endless. Neither could empathize with the other's perspective. Both wanted revenge.

Susan could not empathize with Ry because her mother had never empathized with her. And Ry was desperate for a little empathy.

We met twice a month, and I searched for some point of connection between the two. Susan seemed hard. "She's totally shut down," Ry explained to me after a few weeks. She must have learned that language from the staff.

It was difficult to discern how much of Susan's armor was in response to Ry's abuse.

Ry, on the other hand, was a wound that wouldn't stop bleeding.

I talked to Susan by phone between sessions and tried to form an alliance. I reported Ry's progress in the program, and told her about the Snotrockets' art projects. One of Ry's treatment goals was to communicate directly instead of manipulating the staff. Manipulating was a tough habit to break, but she did it.

Ry worked hard to regain her mother's trust. I served as an interpreter, since they lived on different planets and spoke different languages.

Problem was, Susan didn't trust therapists anymore than she trusted Ry. Therapists always blamed the mother.

After a few months of family therapy, I didn't feel much hope of connecting with Susan, and I worried that Ry would not be able to return home.

Meanwhile, my own happy home had broken up when Karen fell in love with a woman at work and went off to make babies. Will moved to Hawaii where he wore shorts to work and went snorkeling every afternoon.

Shnuckie, Puffy, and I moved to a secluded cottage in the middle of a vineyard, and I embarked upon a relationship with Sensitive Ponytail Man, who brought me long-stemmed roses and took me touring through forest-lined mountain roads on his sexy Italian motorcycle.

It felt so weird to be somebody's girlfriend after eight years of marriage/divorce and another five years of *Will I Ever Recover From That Train Wreck?* The first time we went out to dinner, I practically had a panic attack. You might say I was skittish.

My new boyfriend was a therapist, and he said all the right things. He prepared candle-lit dinners, and wrote songs for me, which he played on my guitar when he came to visit.

But, after six months of motorcycle riding, Pony Tail abruptly morphed into Unspeakable Lying Bastard and ran off with an older, blonder woman who had a prison record. She wore a leopard print mini-dress to the Canyon Ridge Christmas party.

Therapists are crazy. Don't ever date one.

One afternoon Ry stomped into my office wearing her dad's brown work boots, plopped down on the couch, and downloaded her weekend on the dorm. She had taken on Maggie in a battle for religious freedom.

No one challenges Mag.

Ry loved witchcraft. While the other girls kept bibles on their night tables, Ry kept her spell book and tarot cards.

An angry Maggie knocked on my door that evening.

"She's scarin' those girls with all that satanic stuff!" Maggie squawked through vocal chords that had been ravaged by years of drinking and smoking. "They have a hard enough time feelin' safe on that dorm without her puttin' spells on 'em!"

I motioned for Mag to sit, and let her vent her spleen.

"I confiscated all that stuff and put it in a box," Mag said. "You can give it to her mother when she comes on Friday."

She ranted awhile longer, then calmed down. "I'll bring that stuff over here at the end of my shift," she said as she walked out.

I adored Maggie. She had the crustiest crust and the biggest heart to go with it. She was harder on the girls than the rest of us, but she would have given her life for any one of them.

Now, the thing about Canyon Ridge: it was staffed primarily by fundamentalist Christians who all attended the same mega church a few miles up the road.

Ry's magical paraphernalia might as well have been concealed weapons.

That evening Mag brought the box to my office and told me more about her ongoing war with Ry.

After she left, I sat on the sofa and opened up the box. I recognized the dream catcher that used to dangle above Ry's pillow, and her collection of crystals that she kept in a bowl on her nightstand.

I picked up Ry's spell book and leafed through it. It looked like a recipe book with elegant sketches and quotations. Bookmarks stuck out in three places.

I read the titles of the three spells she'd marked: *Breaking A Bad Habit, Forgiving a Wrong, and Letting Go Of Resentments.*

Funny...that's the same language Mag uses in her 12 Step Group.

I looked around my office at the dense crowd of sandplay miniatures and symbols that filled the shelves. The wicked witch of the west sat next to Glinda, the good witch of the east. Jewish symbols sat beside the Virgin Mary, St. Francis, Shiva, and Buddha. Crosses and dream catchers shared the same basket with sage and crystals.

In the world of expressive arts therapies, no one is excluded.

The next day, Ry came to me with a proposition.

"Can I keep my spell book and tarot cards in your office?" She put on her sweetest puppy dog face, cocked her head to the side and batted her long lashes.

Then she brought out the big guns: the dimples.

"We can play with them in session!" she bounced on my sofa, eyes sparkling with anticipation.

I swallowed.

I agreed with Ry that she had just as much right to practice her religion as the other girls, but the group home rules were clear: no witchcraft, no Wicca, no magic.

"I'll think about it," I said.

She smiled triumphantly.

Little shit.

What if she tells Mag?

What if I get fired?

Could I lose my license for this?

I'm supposed to return this stuff to her mother.

Who is she putting spells on anyway?

Ry trotted back to the dorm. I sat and pondered.

I conjured my open-minded colleagues: Lali's adventures with the shaman, Ingrid's charismatic priest who cast out bad spirits, and Rose, whose cancer disappeared after she saw a spiritual healer in Bali.

I thought about Karen's women's group, which Will liked to call *The Coven.* They were like family. Yeah, they played with tarot cards and Ouija boards, but they were so supportive of Karen. I remembered the day she came to work with rose petals all over her SUV. The Coven did a ritual to bless her new car. She was so happy.

I hid Ry's spell book and tarot cards in the bottom drawer of my desk, and we made them part of our work together. Ry became much more enthusiastic about therapy.

She told me about her beliefs. She didn't want to do any harm with her magic, but wanted to do some healing.

Ry poured out her pain. She felt abandoned and terrified at home when her mom worked late, and carved on her arms out of desperation.

They said horrible things to each other in anger, threw dishes and broke them. Ry couldn't remember ever having fun with her mom, who seemed humorless and unreachable. She longed to live with her dad in New Mexico. When mom said "no", Ry ran away for several days.

159

As Ry told her story and cried week after week, her rage quieted down. She gained better control over her emotions.

Mischief replaced her dark brooding, and she bonded with her peers. They started getting in trouble for playing pranks instead of abusing the staff.

Ry stopped carving on her arms, and applied cocoa butter to her scars. The large, red pentagram on her left forearm faded to pale pink, and the tic-tac-toe rows of razor cuts on her wrists shrunk till they looked like scratches.

One Friday before family session, Mag called me from the dorm. "Ry wants to talk to you before her mom gets here," she said.

"O.K. Bring her over."

A few minutes later, Mag knocked on my door, Ry standing beside her. "What's up?" I asked Ry. I suddenly felt nervous.

"Can I come in?" Ry asked. She looked nervous too.

"Sure."

I nodded to Mag, and she walked back to the dorm.

Ry closed the door.

"I want to tell my mom about Wicca," she said. "I think she'll like it."

"Really?"

"Yeah. She used to have a spell book a long time ago." Ry looked away, wistful. "I think it will help us." She looked at me. "Can we show her the spell book in session?"

That evening, Susan and Ry sat side by side on the small sofa, as usual. These sessions were always painful, and I dreaded them.

"Cate, can I show my mom my spell book?"

I tensed up. *Can I trust her? How is her mother going to react? Am I about to make a big mistake? Am I going to get fired for this kid?*

Susan's eyes communicated curiosity. My gut said *go for it.* I opened the desk drawer, pulled out the spell book, and handed it to Ry.

Susan cocked her head and looked at me, surprised. A barely perceptible grin tried to peek out from the corner of her mouth, and the stony veil dropped from her eyes for the first time.

Ry scooted over closer to her mom and showed her the book. She spoke with the sweet voice of a young child. Susan looked interested. Huddled side by side on the sofa, they looked like they were reading a bedtime story together.

After that, when the other girls asked to go to the taco shop, Ry wanted to go to the metaphysical bookstore. She worked hard in the treatment program and earned day passes to go out to lunch with her mom.

One Monday morning when I arrived at work, Ry was lurking in the hall, eager to tell me about her lunch with her mom on the weekend.

Susan had taken her to the metaphysical bookstore where they shopped for rocks, crystals, and goodies for magic potions. She showed me a chunk of rose quartz her mom had given her. "Rose quartz opens the heart," she explained.

Mother and daughter were playing together for the first time.

After a few more weeks, Ry earned her first overnight pass. Maggie reminded her of the rules, and of the consequences for rule breaks. We crossed our fingers and sent her off with mom, hoping she would use the new skills we'd taught her.

The following Monday, Ry looked like a new girl. Her black eye liner and dark lipstick were gone. Fresh scrubbed freckles pooched out above her dimpled grin. Instead of black jeans and baggy flannel, she wore a blouse she had borrowed from her mom.

"My mom bought me a new spell book!" she said. "We're going to share it."

"You look happy."

"And we went to the craft store and got some stuff to decorate the apartment." She bounced up and down in her pink sneakers.

That afternoon, Susan called. During the weekend, Ry had told her about the religious discrimination on the dorm.

"This is our family's religion," Susan said. "Ry has just as much right to have her spell book as those girls do their Bibles."

When I told Ry about my conversation with her mom, she swooned like she was in love.

When Susan arrived for family session on Friday, she confronted Maggie and demanded that Ry be allowed to keep her Wiccan goodies in her room. She had no luck obtaining equal rights for her daughter, but she became Ry's hero in front of all the Snotrockets.

I felt a little duplicitous that evening when Mag stopped by my office to vent about "the crazy lady with the witchcraft."
Oh well. What she doesn't know won't hurt her.

The energy that Ry had once invested in fighting now flowed into projects that she shared with her mom. The pair spent their weekends shopping for magical rocks and making crafts together. They became friends.

On a Monday afternoon, after another successful weekend with mom, Ry came to my office with a protruding shirt pocket. She pulled out a wad of cloth, and reverently unwrapped a chunk of deep purple amethyst.

"I found the perfect ritual for me and my mom," she said. "It's a fire ritual."

"Fire is supposed to be heavy magic," I said.

"Yeah!" She smiled, delighted that I remembered.

Ry explained the ritual. She wanted to perform it during a family session with her mom, and she wanted it to be a surprise.

But, neither matches nor mojos are allowed in residential treatment centers.

We were going to have to sneak.

I knew of a wild desert canyon about half a mile up the road, toward the foothills. Nicole had taken me there one evening while we were out walking. The girls were not allowed to go there because of rattlesnakes and stray, beer-guzzling boys. Mag said devil worshippers met over there on the weekends.

I remembered the day when Harry told me, "Maybe you're too open-minded."

Nah.

This kid had found magic to heal her family that none of us could conjure.

We were going to the canyon.

Besides, wasn't Harry the one who always said that in a good therapy the therapist must change? "The patient needs to feel that she can fix the therapist," he said. "So that she can make use of you. It gives her hope. Especially if she can't fix her mother."

Ry knew that my spiritual beliefs were different from hers, and that made my support more precious to her.

I didn't really believe that her spells were supernatural, but if she believed it, it would probably work.

To me, her rituals looked like expressive art therapy. Lali would have approved.

I helped Ry smuggle her ingredients into my office bit by bit, until she had everything she needed for her ritual. I would provide the fire.

On the first Friday after the full moon, Ry prepared her spell.

She spread a cloth on my office floor and crushed up dried sage and lavender. She added a cup of coarse salt and mixed them all together. Then she sprinkled a few drops of sandalwood oil on top and tied it all up in a bundle.

She reached into her shirt pocket and pulled out a crumpled piece of paper. "These are all my resentments," she said. "We're going to burn them in the fire."

"That is very cool."

Ry packed her treasures into her backpack just as Susan knocked on the door. The three of us sneaked out the back and walked down a dusty road toward the canyon.

We hiked through the grey, crispy desert canyon under the summer sun, past fragrant sage bushes, and out of view of Canyon Ridge.

Ry spotted a perfect place to make a fire, and set her backpack down on a flat, hot rock. Susan and I gathered twigs while Ry cleared a space in the dry streambed and built an altar. A lizard poked his head out from the rocks and scurried away.

We shoved dry twigs under Ry's fragrant, magical bundle. She hid the crumpled list of resentments under the twigs.

I handed her a book of matches, and she built a fire.

The aroma of lavender, sage, and sandalwood rose up in the heat. It smelled like my massage therapist's apartment. I watched a pillar of grey smoke trail up into the sky and wondered if anyone could see it from the group home.

While the fire burned, Ry read her spell aloud.

All hatred and bitterness be gone
Leave me when the fire is done
Fire burn to remove all ill
By the power of my will

We watched the list of resentments shrink to ash. Dried leaves hissed and crackled in the flames.

"Now let us make a circle and join hands," Ry said.

We held hands in silence till the fire died.

Then Ry uttered the magic words: *I forgive.*

Ry released our hands, unwrapped the purple stone, and clasped it tightly between her palms.

"Into this stone I put all of my hurts and mistakes from the past," she said. "I cast it away and it is gone forever."

She held her mother with a solemn gaze for a long moment. Tears flooded Ry's soft, brown eyes. The energy between them gave me a chill.

Then Ry clenched her lips tight, squinted into the sun, and wound up for the pitch of a lifetime. She reared back and hurled the stone as far as it would go.

The three of us stared at the thicket of brush where the stone had disappeared.

A red-tailed hawk screeched in the sky. Ry started and looked up. "Wow…"

We stood together, mesmerized by the majestic creature in flight.

Another hawk appeared, and the two flew together in graceful circles above the thicket.

Ry buried her altar in the sand. She hugged her mom. They held each other and swayed, like a mother rocking a baby.

Mother and daughter swiped at their eyes and noses with their shirtsleeves as we hiked out of the canyon and walked down the road. When we reached the group home, Ry hugged me good-bye and went home with her mom.

Magic is nothing more than a shift in consciousness, and some of the best magic seems to happen *way* outside the therapist's comfort zone. We have a duty to follow wounded children wherever they need to go to heal themselves.

You have to be willing to go to the canyon.

VANDALS

*"I'm sending out an SOS to the world.
I hope that someone gets my
message in a bottle."*
- Sting

It's 9:00 a.m. on a Wednesday morning, and I wish I was home in bed like yesterday. Summer colds are the worst.

I unlock my office, drop my brief case in a chair, and turn on the computer. A puddle of partially dried sticky brown goo creeps out from under my *Ponte Vecchio* mouse pad. My big yellow cup is half full of Coke.

That's weird. I never drink Coke out of that cup.

I walk over to the stereo to put on some Dave Brubeck. A little classic jazz will soothe my sickly soul. When I open the CD compartment, brown fluid flows out onto the oak table and soaks my embroidered white dresser scarf.

I look over at my desk. My cell phone is gone, and another brown puddle is drying in the sun behind the computer.

After a few years at Canyon Ridge I'd grown homesick for the city, and accepted a senior therapist position at a psychiatry clinic in downtown L.A.

Outpatient therapy was a bit of a yawn after years of inpatient work with the severely emotionally disturbed, but I decided to enjoy the quiet. Let the young therapists deal with the *E-Tickets* for awhile.

I first met Angel and his father a few weeks after I started work at the clinic. At the time, Angel was thirteen, and his school had sent him to "work on his anger."

He sat in my office, huddled into himself, his chubby face and forlorn eyes framed by a thicket of black ringlets: the picture of vulnerability. A Latino incarnation of Raphael's cherub.

Tears trailed down Angel's brown cheeks while his father reeled off a litany of his sins.

Mr. Martinez held enough tension in his lean, petite physique to make his own head pop off. Veins stuck out of his forehead while he spewed. "He got arrested two times! He beats up other boys! He got no respect! Won't even do his homework!" He sat on the edge of his chair, clutched a school report in his fist and waved it at Angel.

The teacher's report said Angel was "indifferent to consequences" and "incited conflict to avoid work" in the classroom.

Angel cried while his father ranted. After a few minutes, Angel choked out an explanation. "I want to be good," he said to me, through tears. "It's hard because of my anger."

After the first interview, I read the fat intake packet. Angel had been sexually abused by his uncle. CPS removed him from his family at the age of five, placed him in temporary foster care, and sent him to therapy.

When he returned home after a few weeks, he disrupted his kindergarten class with aggressive outbursts, and earned a reputation as a behavior problem.

Angel's parents never believed that his uncle abused him and, after a few years, Angel himself said it hadn't happened.

He tested as gifted and talented but, in the fifth grade, the school district placed him in a special education class for the *severely emotionally disturbed*. Angel's teachers reported that he yelled at the male staff and called them *cocksuckers* and *motherfuckers* whenever they touched him or got too close.

Fueled by a bloodhound's zeal to hunt down Angel's childhood trauma and extricate the poor boy from its clutches, I thought I knew what he needed. After all, I was an expert, right?

During our first few sessions, when I asked Angel about his family and his childhood, he grew angry. "Nothing happened!" he said. He had memorized the story his father constructed, and he was sticking to it: the records were wrong, the social worker had lied, and there was nothing wrong in his family.

One of the great things about living in the city again was being closer to Harry. I signed up for one of his weekly study groups with a couple of my girlfriends.

After a few weeks of banging my head against Angel's resistance, I presented his case to the group.

"This boy was molested by his uncle when he was five, and CPS removed him from the home for a few weeks while they investigated," I explained. "He did play therapy for a couple of years, but his parents denied the abuse."

I looked up at my friend Emma, a sensitive soul, who had survived a ridiculous amount of trauma herself. She gave me that look: *It is so hard to watch these kids suffer their parents' denial.*

I explained how Angel lashed out at the male staff when they crossed his boundaries, and how he got in trouble for loitering and fighting.

What is it about this kid that has me feeling so stymied?

I thought out loud. "Every time I pursue a direction with him, I run into another blockade," I said. "I can't remember the last time I had so much trouble reaching a thirteen-year-old."

"Your agenda's getting in the way," Harry said.

"I want to help him," I said. "He needs to be able to talk about what happened to him."

"Maybe that's not what he needs," Harry said.

"What do you mean?"

"Why don't you try to stay out of the way, and find out how he needs to use you."

I know this. I preach it to my interns all the time. Why am I on such a mission with this kid? It's not just that I want to help him…I need to help him.

"I'm having a hard time staying out of the way," I confessed. "He's been suffering a long time. Alone."

"Duct tape," Emma said.

"Huh?"

She mimed taping her mouth shut, then smiled her compassionate smile.

I laughed.

Harry nodded and grinned. "There you go." He understood. He was a rescuer like me.

"Don't just do something! Sit there!" I said, and smiled at Emma, my sweet Buddhist friend.

Emma grinned and nodded.

I admired my Zen friends, but I was not like them. Not yet. Too much fire in the belly.

Armed with a big roll of duct tape, I scrapped my therapeutic agendas and started over with Angel.

After a couple of weeks he confided in me that he was getting into a lot more mischief at school than anyone knew. Drugs, vandalism, gang fights. But he was good at not getting caught.

He avoided talking about his family.

Angel was a sensitive, soulful boy. I felt his respect and trust.

We complied with the school's treatment plan and worked on Angel's behavior problems.

After three months of impressive progress with his school behavior, Angel was promoted to a less structured classroom. At the same time, I was offered a promotion at the clinic that would require me to reduce my caseload.

I agonized over choosing which five children I was allowed to keep from the 25 I was seeing. There were several who needed me more than Angel, and would not tolerate a transfer to a new therapist.

The clinic administrators said Angel would be better served by a Latino male therapist.

A few days later, I came down with a miserable cold. On a Tuesday, the day of our regular, weekly appointment, I stayed home. The clinic secretaries could not reach Angel's parents, so he showed up with his sister for their appointments.

While Angel's sister was in session, he prowled the halls.

On that Wednesday morning when I returned to work and found sticky soda all over my office, my coworkers told me they suspected Angel. I disagreed. I felt protective of him. I could not juxtapose such destructive behavior with his shy, baby-faced presentation.

A volatile administrator named Gloria had called the police and stirred up several hours of high drama in the clinic while I was out sick. She had already decided Angel was guilty, and had engaged an ambitious detective named Juarez to investigate.

Two weeks passed before Angel's sister ratted him out. She told her therapist, Mr. Lopez, that Angel had clinic keys at home.

Mr. Lopez told Detective Juarez.

I felt like a sucker.

I worried that Angel would key my new car if I disappointed him again.

I felt a new empathy with Tony Soprano's therapist.

Reactions and opinions bubbled up in staff meetings and hallway conversations.

The clinic administrators wanted Angel arrested.

Detective Juarez wanted me to wheedle a confession out of Angel during his therapy sessions.

The clinic staff wanted protection from juvenile delinquents.

I wanted to understand what had happened.

The following Monday morning, my study group listened to the story, fascinated. Harry was all over it.

"He experienced a disruption in his connection with you," Harry explained. "This left him feeling isolated and dysregulated."

I listened.

"The vandalism was a part of his attempt to right himself - to pull himself together after a breakdown," he said.

"Hm." I considered his interpretation. It sounded a wee bit naive.

When I explained Harry's theory to my coworkers, they thought it was dangerously naive.

I decided to keep Angel when I changed jobs. If I succumbed to the pressure to transfer him to another therapist, he would be sent to Juvenile Hall, where he would not have the opportunity to continue his therapy. Once in the juvenile justice system, his fate would change forever.

J.B., the rotund, red-faced chief administrator called me into his office.

"These egregious acts must be punished!" he spouted. He wanted to make an example of Angel.

I had worked at Juvenile Hall for five years and had an idea about the kind of lessons Angel was likely to learn there. Twelve percent of kids in custody are raped or sexually abused by fellow inmates or prison staff. And those figures were always conservative.

With his baby face and cascading curls, Angel would be an easy mark.

At best, he would receive an introductory course in criminal behavior and fall further behind in school. And in either case, handing him over to the juvenile justice system would constitute a betrayal and set him up to be re-traumatized.

When I felt clear about my course, I met with the eager, muscle-bound Detective Juarez, who fidgeted in his chair, about to pop out of his tight white shirt. He looked like he might lick his chops at any moment

"So, Dr. Shepherd, do you have any information for me?" he asked, with the exact same smile as the guy who sold me my car.

"I'm afraid that everything my clients say is confidential," I explained.

"Well, Mr. Lopez has been very helpful." He puffed up. "He was able to obtain some key information from the boy's sister."

I sat still and gave him a blank face.

"Don't you want some justice for yourself?" Juarez asked. He scooted up in his chair and leaned toward me. "He destroyed a lot of property here." He motioned around my office.

"I appreciate your concern, but I won't be able to talk with you any more." I stood and walked toward the door.

He looked flustered. "Uh...okay." He fumbled with his brief case and shoved a beefy hand at me. I shook it.

"Thank you for stopping by." I smiled and closed the door behind him.

I decided to take Harry's advice and focus on staying connected with Angel. We would continue meet once a week and we would be in it together. I hoped that if I remained available to him, he would use our relationship to process the fallout from the Coke incident.

Angel's sister told Mr. Lopez, her therapist, that Angel had clinic keys and cell phones in his room at home. Mr. Lopez told Angel's father, who blew up. When Angel realized that she'd ratted him out, he began to squirm.

As Angel's therapist, it was not my place to reveal information that Lopez had extracted from the sister in her therapy session.

So, we danced around his secret in our sessions together while Angel considered whether or not to come clean.

Like Angel, I was dependent upon abusive authority figures for survival. Gloria, who was one of my bosses, berated me and my interns in Case Conference meetings. She had a *Queen of Hearts* leadership style and a bad case of PMS. Harry had trained her in med school. Or tried to. He called her *Loose Cannon*.

A swirling vortex of chaos and stress followed Loosie everywhere she went, like Pig Pen and his dust cloud. Her skin-tight outfits, bleached hair, and black roots would have looked more appropriate on a fourteen-year-old *chola* than a forty-year-old M.D., and her fire engine red lipstick never seemed to stay inside the lines. Loosie's interns called her Case Conference *The Mad Hatter's Tea Party* when she was out of earshot.

She could not bear the commonness of her job nor the multitude of details that required her administrative attention every day. So she farmed them out. Mostly to me. And she spent a lot of time shopping for shoes.

Loosie was joined at the brain stem with the red-faced J.B., a lascivious older male boss who was easy to manipulate. I remembered him from the psych hospital, where the nurses scattered when he appeared. When I accepted the position at the clinic, my female co-workers warned me: "Beware of the *The Ass-Grabbing Alcoholic!*"

J.B. was known for his thundering knee-jerk reactions to the misinformation Loosie and other ambitious young women fed him. He used his power like a clumsy Godzilla, stomping on the wrong people. We did our best to distract both of the administrators away from clinic business. *Whatever you do, don't tell the people in charge!*

While the overworked clinic staff filled out productivity reports, Loosie and J.B. went out for long, cozy lunches. The clinic could never afford to buy decent toys for play therapy, but by golly we paid for Loosie's meals.

It was nerve-wracking to watch their inexperienced interns treat high-risk families without adequate supervision. One by one, Loosie's interns sneaked into my office for advice.

"Dr. Garcia is your clinical supervisor," I said to each one when they first came in. I was doing my duty, careful to mind my boundaries. "You should discuss your cases with her."

But they looked at me with eyes full of fear and they wouldn't go away. They seemed to understand how high the stakes were with some of our disturbed families. And I didn't have the heart to leave them alone with their cases.

Lucky for me, I had Harry to hold the ropes.

Meanwhile, I had found a new friend at the clinic. His name was Rafael, and he was the senior psychiatrist.

Rafa was the sanest person I could find in the building. He was also the most eligible bachelor. Or, he would be as soon as his divorce settled.

Rafa knew both Loosie and J.B. from med school, and he railed against their incompetence. Their workload often fell on his shoulders.

Loosie was Rafael's supervisor, but she related to him like a flirty teenager. She sat on his desk with her short skirt hiked up while he tried to work. Rafa was politically savvy, and a good actor, so she never noticed his contempt.

If only I had been so smart.

J.B. got his name because every time Rafa saw him at a party, he was clutching a bottle of J & B Scotch. In the holiday photos, he cradled his infant child in one arm and the bottle of Scotch in the other, his chubby red cheeks glowing like Christmas bulbs.

Over time, we all grew weary of Loosie's shaming rants and her attacks upon our clinical work. When we asked J.B., her boss, to contain her outbursts, he said, "You are imagining things."

Just like Angel's family.

One afternoon Angel and I took a walk. He reminded me of a small child in the "why" stage.

"What happened to your office?" he asked sweetly, like a five-year-old in a husky 5'7" frame.

"Somebody poured Coke into my stereo and computer."

"Can you fix it?"

"No, I can't use them anymore."

"Are you mad?"

"A little. Mostly sad," I said. "I can't listen to my music anymore. And it's kind of scary having somebody come into your office and trash your stuff like that."

He turned his head another twenty degrees toward my face and looked at me intently. It felt like he was on my side.

"Do they know who did it?" he asked.

"They have a suspect."

"Well I didn't do nothing! Fuckin' Lopez is blaming me. I hate his ass. He thinks he knows everything. They always blame me."

"Yeah, I know."

We walked on in the sunshine and chatted about school. After our walk, we went back to my office and had a Coke.

The following Tuesday when I walked into the waiting room to pick up Angel, he looked like a guilty puppy. He looked up at me with big brown eyes that reminded me of Shnuckie after she shredded my W-2 forms. She didn't like being left alone either.

We walked down the hall to my office.

Angel sat stiff. "It was me," he said.

"What do you mean?"

"I poured the Coke in your computer."

"Really."

I grinned. Then I tried not to grin. I wasn't grinning about his behavior. I was pleased with his confession.

Also, he was sitting there with his curls spilling over his big eyes. I couldn't picture him vandalizing anything.

And I had grown fond of him. It was that weird thing that happens when I get attached to a kid. That *love covers a multitude of sins* thing. I was more interested in Angel's emotional experience than I was in my computer and stereo.

"So what were you thinking?" I asked.

"I don't know." He shook his head.

"Were you mad because I wasn't here for your appointment?"

"I didn't feel mad." He looked as mystified as I felt.

"Can you remember what happened before you came here that day?"

He thought about it. "I can't think of anything."

"Did you have a fight with your dad?"

"No."

"Did anything happen at school?"

"No. I don't remember feeling mad about anything. I just saw the open door and the keys."

"Temptation," I said.

"That's it. Temptation." He brightened and nodded.

On Monday morning in study group, Harry gave us a mini-lecture on dissociation and enactment. I was still trying to digest his interpretation of vandalism as *organizing activity;* his belief that Angel's behavior was an effort to right himself after some kind of breakdown.

"When a child's experience of being physically and emotionally violated is denied, invalidated, and erased by the family system, he is left with a need to give the unacknowledged wound a tangible form," Harry explained. He could reel off theory better than any textbook.

Oh yeah, he wrote some of my textbooks.

"While the child may not understand his own violent outburst, his truth is expressed, symbolized, and concretized through the destructive act," he said. "The vandalism is not the symptom. The dissociation is the symptom."

"Sounds like play therapy," I said.

"Exactly," Harry said.

"So his feelings become dissociated because no one validates his experience."

"Right. Dissociation shields him from unbearable pain, but it is also a way he accommodates to an environment in which there is no space for his pain to exist."

"I get it. That fits."

Meanwhile, I discussed consequences with Angel and his parents. I did not want to overwhelm the family by requiring them to pay hundreds of dollars. On the other hand, I wanted to give Angel some meaningful consequences that would help him to learn something.

And I wanted a new CD player.

Angel's family did not like social workers, and Angel was bitter about being separated from his family at age five. The family had felt betrayed, and no longer trusted professionals who were part of the system. As a white, English-only social worker, I was suspect.

How could I possibly understand what these events meant to them?

For several weeks, with the help of a bilingual, bicultural interpreter, I talked with Angel's family. I empathized with their experience and validated their anger at social services. As a social worker, I often felt frustrated by the limitations of the system too. With their ridiculously huge caseloads, CPS workers did not have time to do thorough investigations, and mistakes occurred as a result.

If all of this is crazy-making and infuriating for social workers, imagine how the parents must feel.

As the weeks passed, as we struggled together to understand each other, rapport and trust grew between Angel's family and me.

I wanted Angel's consequences to be growth producing but not shaming, and I hoped all of the adults could be united in implementing them.

We all agreed that Angel would work on Saturdays to pay for a portion of the damage. Their pastor offered to provide odd jobs at the church.

Angel earned money, spent it, then earned it again. As the months passed, he needed a bit of prodding and some deadlines. He responded well to these and, after six months, he bought me a new stereo.

J.B. required Angel to write three letters of apology: one to him, one to Loosie, and one to me. When Angel finally wrote them, he asked to slip them under my door after hours.

I said he could.

Angel's note to me was barely legible, printed in the hand and language of a young child.

I was bad. I don't want to be bad.

His words dripped with shame.

Something told me the letters were a mistake.

On Monday, I showed Harry the crumpled strip of paper torn from a spiral notebook, written with a fat, first grade pencil.

"He's a very bright fourteen-year-old," I told Harry. "What do you make of this?"

"If a child gets sick and vomits, he may help clean up, but you don't ask him to apologize," he said.

Harry did not budge off of his interpretation. The vandalism was Angel's attempt to recover from a breakdown -- from being sick.

Harry's theories flew in the face of everything I had been taught in social work school.

The requirement to write letters of apology was not, in fact, for Angel's benefit. And going along with it was an automatic, compliant response on my part to appease angry administrators who wanted evidence of remorse. I was caught in the same dilemma as Angel, compromising my own truth to maintain necessary ties.

A recurring theme in Angel's individual therapy sessions was his strained relationship with his father. Angel experienced his father as cruel and shaming, and he felt crushed and powerless under his father's emotional abuse. He needed a way to fight back.

Angel's antisocial behavior made sense to me in the context of his relationship with his father.

When I was Angel's age, I felt crushed and powerless under my father's abuse too. Dad was a huge, intrusive man who longed to control me. When I tried to protect my boundaries, he trampled them. There was simply no way to preserve any kind of freedom or dignity in that house. Without sneaking.

So I became *The Sneaky One,* which drove my father completely nuts. I sneaked out my window at night and sneaked away from school during the day to hang out with forbidden friends.

My older cousin, Kathy, came to visit in the summer. She loved to lead me and my brother astray. We were terrified of getting caught and beaten, but Kathy was not afraid of anything.

The three of us went for a walk. Kathy rolled a joint and smoked it.

We walked up a country road to an empty farmhouse where Kathy peered in through a window.

"There's paint in there," she said. "Look."

My brother and I looked inside. Two buckets of paint and two paintbrushes lay on the floor.

"Let's go in!" Kathy said, as she shoved a window up and climbed through.

Before I knew it, my brother and I were painting words like *cocksucker* and *motherfucker* on the walls.

I didn't plan to. I didn't even think it was a good idea. But, after a decade or so of being beaten, demeaned, humiliated, and suffocated by a giant bully, my soul apparently had a few comments to make.

And the paint and brushes were just sitting there.

And my father had just bought the house.
Temptation.

My chart notes after Angel's confession reflected change: "positive attachments forming and behavior stabilizing at school...attendance has improved...patient is enjoying soccer...improved impulse control... Positive relationship with new teacher...resisting negative peer pressure."

Over time, our connection and our dialogue transformed the emotional meaning of Angel's behavior. What had begun as a shame-laden scandal became a story of Angel's struggle for dignity. His self-esteem began to heal, like a dehydrated plant that finally got a drink of water.

Angel asked me what would happen to our relationship after he completed his consequences. He said he didn't want to be in therapy when he turned fifteen, so we discussed graduation. He had shaved his head, which made him look very grown up.

When I gave him the option to graduate from therapy, he chose to stay a little longer.

A few weeks later he asked to leave session early. I said he could. He left early twice, then chose to stay for the entire time, and discussed more intimate material. In fact, sometimes it was hard to pry him out of my office at the end of the hour.

I felt a sense of awe at the vulnerability Angel now risked. I became his consultant about girls, sex, gangs, parents and peers.

He acted like a tough gangster in the neighborhood, but in our sessions he revealed his naivete about girls and eagerly sought my advice about his love life.

Meanwhile, my love life had taken an unexpected turn. Pony Tail Man and his brethren had put me off of older men, so I took to wearing flirty skirts and dating my cute, young hairdresser.

UN COM PLI CA TED.

Well, except for the fact that he developed territorial opinions about my hair.

My friends thought I should date Rafa instead, but that was *WAY* too complicated. The clinic staff teased us mercilessly about our close relationship, and Rafa turned Roma tomato red every time. He was shy.

Rafa did a lot of nice things for me, like alphabetizing a zillion psychoanalytic articles that I never had time to file. And babysitting Shnuckie so I could go to Hawaii and visit my old roommate, Will. And smuggling cold beers in his backpack when we went hiking.

He was a smart and loyal friend. With the kind of dry, vicious, delicious wit that kept me sane in an insane environment.

In my new position as Clinical Coordinator I was up to my eyebrows in team building and morale boosting. I had taken on an impossible challenge with a group of people who despised their leaders and did not like peace and harmony. As *Peace and Harmony Girl*, that was hard for me.

One afternoon while I cleaned up the clinic and inventoried our sad, dirty toys, I found an old friend in the closet.

When Elena and I were social work interns together at the clinic twelve years earlier, a four-foot-tall Raggedy Andy type doll had sat atop Elena's toy cupboard. We had named him Pete, in honor of Elena's fiancé.

When I saw Pete, I remembered Elena's warm presence - just what I needed. I pulled Pete out of the closet, made him an official nametag that read, "Party Pete!" and developed his new position as Social Director.

Pete participated in staff meetings and sent out inspiring memos. He hosted birthday parties for the staff, and launched the *Catch a Star* program and the *Warm Fuzzies* campaign.

Party Pete instituted monthly potlucks, which the staff loved. Every month, we recognized several team members for their unique contributions.

One month, during the award presentations, Rafa made a surprise appearance dressed up as *Dr. Fried*. He wore a purple robe and a mad scientist wig, and spoke with a thick German accent. He waved his arms and ranted, misused psychoanalytic terms, and trailed off on disoriented tangents that left the group in hysterics.

Amazing what a costume will do for a closet performer.

One Friday morning, I came in early to catch up on paperwork while the rest of the staff attended Hospital Rounds. The clinic was eerily silent.

I opened my office door and immediately recognized the scene of a crime.

Pete's little yellow chair was toppled over on its side, and his name badge lay broken on the floor.

Pete was gone.

On my chair I found a fat, manila envelope that said, "Open Me." Inside was a videotape labeled, "Play Me."

Shocked and alarmed, I carried the videotape to the conference room and watched it.

There it was. Pete tied up with duct tape over his mouth. Some horrible men with bags over their heads slapped him around and held an electric drill to his head.

I could tell he was terrified.

In the days that followed, I received ransom notes with clumps of Pete's red hair, polaroids of Pete tied up in a dumpster, and the last, most unspeakable note...one of Pete's eyes.

The heartless kidnappers made humiliating demands. They made me wear a Buckwheat wig to the deli to get their next message. Then they made me wear a hideous plaid polyester sport coat over my white silk suit to the psychiatry department meeting.

They were psychopaths.

I met all of their demands, but they were never satisfied. I began to despair that I would ever see Pete again.

On my fortieth birthday, I stood stooped over in the fax room and wrestled with the antique photocopy machine. My pager beeped.

Come to the staff lounge. STAT. Pete's life may depend upon it.

What now? Hadn't poor Pete suffered enough?

I walked down the hall to the lounge, and opened the door with trepidation.

"SURPRISE!" a crowd of staff and interns shouted. At the head of the table sat a small figure with a bag over his head. Rafa ripped the bag off. It was Pete! And he still had both his eyes.

I can't believe they sent me a fake eye. These people are sick.

On the table in front of Pete sat a chocolate birthday cake with a big *40* candle and a photo of Antonio Banderas on top, because the only thing better than chocolate is Antonio Banderas.

My mischievous friends cracked themselves up telling stories about their kidnapping antics. They had had some close calls when nosey neighbors observed their antisocial behavior.

You try explaining why you're taking pictures of a four-foot-tall bound and gagged redhead in a dumpster.

We laughed until we hurt.

The hazing was over. The new Clinical Coordinator was *in*.

Angel and I were in our second year of therapy when he decided he liked older women. "Someone around forty," he said.

The birthday cards on my bookcase said *40*.

With a sheepish expression, Angel told me his sexual fantasies about older women at school. He wanted to ravish his grey-haired teacher atop her desk.

Then he asked me questions.

"Are you married? Do you have a boyfriend? Who lives with you?"

He seemed surprised and puzzled when he encountered my boundaries.

In the weeks that followed, there was something about the way Angel repeatedly tested my boundaries that reminded me of Luke's play in the sand, enacting his story with Batman, over and over.

I was honest with Angel. I answered his questions when I could, and guarded my privacy when I needed to. Angel continued to come in every week, confide, and explore for an hour. I felt reverence for the trust he placed in me.

After a few weeks, he stopped talking about older women and started dating some girls his own age.

Angel never talked about being molested by his uncle. But when he pushed against my boundaries and watched me enforce them, he learned to construct boundaries of his own.

Speaking of boundaries, Angel's father had a long-standing habit of inviting himself into the individual therapy sessions of his children. He would enter Angel's sessions with me without an invitation and spew a litany of his son's shortcomings. He waved school reports at me and demanded that I fix Angel.

I was distressed about this previously established routine, but under pressure to be culturally compliant in a racially charged milieu.

Meanwhile there was trouble on the other front as well. Loosie was obsessed with expanding her fiefdom. She recruited followers with the zeal of a honey badger and held private meetings with them while the rest of us worked. She used her power to grant special favors to loyal subjects. She even tried to give my office to one of them.

The rest of the staff refused to be seduced by Loosie's gifts and free lunches, and they disliked the divisive vibe that poisoned the work environment. The staff and interns started calling her group *The Mexican Mafia* and complained to her boss, J.B.

J.B. became furious and told them they were imagining things.

Loosie was never subtle about her political agendas. My coworkers told me how she poured over my chart notes in search of errors. On one occasion, she directed a therapist to write a chart note stating that I had given a sharp object to a suicidal patient. The therapist refused to falsify the medical record and hurried to my office to report the incident.

When I reported it to Loosie's supervisor, J.B., he listened to Loosie's version of the story over one of their long lunches. And that was the end of that.

Loosie ignored all feedback about how her behavior impacted the clinic. She used her group to make expert proclamations about so-called cultural issues.

Like how I dealt with Angel's father.

As Social Director, Pete was worried about morale, and he decided to do some bridge-building to diffuse the racial tension in the clinic. He was super white with his red hair and freckles, and he needed some color in his life.

Rafa and I decided to help.

On the weekend, we went shopping to purchase party supplies for Pete's *Celebrate Diversity Potluck!* Pete thought we should all bring a dish that reflected our unique cultural heritage.

That was easy for me. I had my *Country Kitchens Cookbook* from the Warren County Home Extension Ladies Group, and all I had to do was decide between a tuna casserole or a green jello salad.

Rafa planned to show off with his *Nana's* secret *Mole* recipe.

We strolled up and down the aisles of Sav-On Drugs looking for streamers and balloons. I spotted a familiar face on the top shelf.

"Oh my God!" I pointed. Rafa looked up.

"Uh oh." He chuckled.

An adorable, dark-skinned girl, about two inches shorter than Pete, sat on the top shelf.

She was obviously his soulmate.

On Monday morning, Pete was thrilled to meet Lupita. We made her a name badge, and introduced her to the staff, who gave her a warm welcome.

Loosie was not amused.

That evening, as I was putting away charts and trying to exit the clinic, Mr. Lopez, the sister's therapist, cornered me in the fax room. He clenched his brow like a Klingon and spat his expert opinions at me.

He demanded to know when I was going to fix Angel and reiterated to me the importance of allowing Angel's father to enter sessions. He reminded me that he and Loosie and their group had a much better understanding of how to deal with these kinds of kids than I did. From his perspective, I had failed in my duty to reform the boy.

A few days later, Angel's father burst through my office door into our individual therapy session without knocking. He berated Angel, waved his arms, and raved like a lunatic. Angel teared up.

His father called him a *fag* for crying.

That was it. Politically correct or not, I was setting a limit.

I interrupted the father's rant. "Excuse me, sir. May I speak to you outside for a moment?"

Angel's father stopped talking and looked at me with beady eyes full of rage. He stalked out into the hallway in a huff. I held

Angel with a reassuring look as I followed his father outside and closed the door.

I explained to Mr. Martinez that Angel and I would focus on individual therapy for awhile and schedule family sessions with the interpreter as needed.

Mr. Martinez's face grew redder and his veins popped out. He stomped off to the waiting room without a word.

When I walked back into my office, Angel looked startled, like someone had just awakened him from a daydream.

I locked the door.

"You will not be abused here," I told him.

He gawked at me, amazed that I was not intimidated by his father. His dark eyes twinkled.

It felt *so good* to stand up to that horrible man.

I wish someone had done the same for me when I was Angel's age.

A few months later, Angel stood up to his father and demanded more respectful treatment. Mr. Martinez, now several inches shorter than Angel, complied.

When Angel graduated from therapy at 15 1/2, he had matured remarkably. He talked about college, and how he wanted to take care of his mother when she retired from cleaning people's houses.

The chief of psychiatry invited me to present Angel's case at an upcoming conference. He was fascinated by what he had heard from Loosie. Through her efforts to get me in trouble, she had inadvertently piqued his interest and secured a large audience.

I went to Harry for a pep talk before facing the conservative crowd.

"Bad behavior is an expression of the child's spirit," Harry said. "When we respond to the child's broken heart, when the child's spirit is understood and responded to, the bad behavior goes away."

That had certainly been true for me and Mr. O. As soon as I felt understood and validated by him, I transformed from a depressed rebel into a volleyball-playing homecoming court honor student.

That Friday morning, I put on my most grownup suit and drove to the meeting hall with sweaty palms. I walked up to the podium and adjusted the mike. My mouth was dry. A roomful of more than 100 experts and authorities stared back at me. I remembered how Harry used to tease me about my performance anxiety. He seemed to think it was mostly ego. I never told him it was PTSD.

"Like children who work out traumatic themes in the sand tray, teens also struggle to tell a story and to be understood," I began. "But it can be more challenging to explore the emotional meanings in a child's behavior when my office becomes the sand tray, and the toys are my computer and sound equipment."

I looked around the room and spotted Rafa. He was sitting with two of my interns. They smiled and waved. I took a deep breath and read the facts of the case aloud from my notes.

Then, with Harry on my shoulder, I launched into theoretical heresy.

"When a child feels continually misunderstood, he may react to this malattunement in ways that appear *delinquent* or *crazy*. These reactions are not inherent properties of the child's personality, but products of a relational context that is operating in an unrecognized, painful disjunction. Labeling such a child "delinquent" (i.e. bad) and punishing him for his emotional reactions, in most cases, will serve to deepen the disjunction and exacerbate the problematic behavior."

I heard rustling and murmuring from the back of the room. I tried to breathe deeper.

"When a child's SOS is misunderstood, the system repeats the original trauma, failing to hear the child's cry and responding with pathologizing labels." My chest tightened. I realized I was talking to the kings and queens of pathologizing labels.

I paused to swallow and wished for a drink of water. "This process often has an iatrogenic effect, inducing more disruption and desperation, and resulting in more outrageous behavior."

There. I used one of their big words.

"But when a child feels understood and accompanied in his struggle, the need to send behavioral messages fades."

I knew the cognitive-behavioral contingent would have some questions for me. Most of the research with delinquent kids focuses on behavior modification. And most of our psychologists had been trained in behaviorism, not psychodynamics. Therefore I acknowledged the value of cognitive-behavioral techniques before I pushed my agenda: *CBT is not enough.*

"Many of our troubled teens live with an unbearable sense of emptiness and isolation. These overwhelming states often lead to extreme coping behaviors. A boy who has developed a coping strategy of molesting younger children when he feels isolated, or a girl who turns to cocaine when she feels empty, will not readily swap their attachments to these experiences for newly acquired CBT techniques."

I scanned the room. No one looked angry. Except for Loosie and Mr. Lopez, scowling in the back.

"We must accompany them in their emptiness and isolation. When these children internalize new relational experiences, their sense of isolation and emptiness shifts. When they feel connected to a therapist who does not abandon or retaliate, but remains available and responsive in all circumstances, their reality is dramatically altered. Hope emerges and, with hope, so does motivation toward health."

Rafa pointed to his watch. Time was up, so I cut to the juice.

"The defiant boy who poured soda into my stereo was healthier than the stifled, depressed boy who peered out from behind his curls at intake."

Silence.

"Children as young as seven years of age are being held in juvenile detention centers in this country. Many of these children have no charges against them of any kind. Our country's prison population has quadrupled since 1980. What has been reduced, to the point of near-extinction, are programs designed to reach troubled teens."

"A small shift at age fifteen can produce a dramatic shift in life trajectory. One reparative relationship in adolescence often makes the difference between a career criminal and a career helping others."

I could never talk about this stuff without remembering those girls in Unit 400, fifteen years ago, dancing *The Hammer* in their baggy blue uniforms.

That could have been me.

"Sadly, many teens fall through the cracks. Many go on to commit more serious crimes and to raise juvenile delinquents of their own."

I looked up. Rafa and the interns smiled at me. Kind eyeballs.

"As the political pendulum continues to swing away from treatment and toward incarceration, our children are increasingly deprived of the most essential piece of their treatment. And as resources for prevention and treatment continue to dwindle, programs close, caseloads rise, and delinquent behavior increases."

"More than 93,000 juveniles are being detained in prison in the U.S. today. Two-thirds of them have at least one mental illness. More than three dozen of them have seriously injured themselves or attempted suicide while in custody. And at least 12% of them have been sexually assaulted by other inmates or by prison guards."

I couldn't believe it -- the experts and authorities listened with rapt attention.

It resonates. They know it's true. No matter how they were trained. Anyone who works with kids knows.

And those of us who were that kid know.

I concluded, "A child's behavior can only be understood in context. When we decode their messages and respond to their needs children no longer resort to desperate forms of communication." I paused to breathe. "Thank you."

The crowd applauded. Rafa and the interns wolf whistled. The rowdy clinic staff made monkey sounds. Loosie scurried out.

Every question from the floor was respectful. Some even expressed admiration for my work with Angel. The experts were intrigued.

I had gotten through.

I have met many Angels since 1986, when I first went to work at Juvenile Hall. Some were given a chance, some were not. For Angel, having a chance made all the difference.

LIFELINE

"No man is an island."
- John Donne

I'm walking through a festive crowd with my funny friend, Jim, who feels more like family than family. It's a hot July day at the annual LGBT Pride Festival where friends and lovers lounge in the dry, crunchy grass under the shade of sprawling trees.

This community has been my tribe ever since high school when my lesbian friend saved my sanity by singing Bob Dylan duets with me in the incomparable acoustics of the girls' restroom when I was grounded for six months. And my gay friend took me to prom when I wasn't allowed to go with my boyfriend. And pretty much every time my family kicked me to the curb, from adolescence through middle age, my queer friends took me in and healed me. They were far more Christian than my religious relatives who condemned them.

As we near the festival gate, I hear the hubbub from the beer garden, and smell carne asada sizzling on the grill. My mouth waters in anticipation of the tart, cold lemonade that awaits us.

Inside the gate, the first person I recognize is Billi. We've both put on a few pounds since we last spoke seven years ago, and we both look a lot more peaceful. She's passing out free condoms from a large cardboard box and chatting with people. I hear her admonishing a young man to keep himself safe. She's engrossed in conversation and doesn't see me. *Whew.*

I wonder how her son, Michael, is doing. He would be in his early 20's now. I imagine him on a college campus somewhere in Northern California, wearing one of his scary Goth outfits, arguing philosophy with a total stranger, and waving his arms around like an Italian.

I want to talk to Billi, but the thought of looking into her eyes makes my heart hurt. I want to run away from the pain. And I want to protect her from pain. My breathing constricts, my feet weigh fifty pounds each, and sorrow drags me down as I turn and trudge away.

Michael was 16 when he first came to the clinic. He painted his face Kabuki white every day, lined his eyes and lips with thick, black eyeliner, and everything he wore was black. He wrapped his arms in silver duct tape from wrist to elbow. The tape covered red lines and pink welts that marked where he'd carved on himself with razor blades. His intelligent green eyes flashed with anger, and also with mischief.

Michael wrote poems, drew cartoons, and made art of his body and his clothes. The more his creations shocked and offended the adults, the better he felt. The clinic staff were afraid of him.

I got a big kick out of Michael. To me, he was a performance artist, a wise jester, daring everyone to see past the barbed wire barricade to his tender soul. Like so many of my punk and Goth kids, he brandished piercings, tattoos, and other armor in proportion to the softness of his heart underneath. And like other desperate teens, he would practically set himself on fire to get the attention he needed.

In our sessions Michael entertained me with irreverent, dark humor, and bizarre objects he designed, like his Marvin Martian lunch bucket covered with plastic jiggly eyeballs. When he saw that I got his humor and appreciated his creations, we connected. I was honored to be his confidante.

Michael's favorite music group was Nine Inch Nails, so I made a special trip to Lou's Records on the weekend to buy their CD and listen to it. The guitars shrieked and whined a chaotic storm. The bass and percussion hammered a crushing dirge.

Geez...no wonder he's depressed...more like Nine Inch Nails on a chalkboard!

When I saw Michael the following Tuesday, I tried to think of something positive to say about his music. He sat across from me dressed in black cutoff shorts, knee high Doc Marten lace ups, and a skintight black and white striped t-shirt. If he'd painted his face that day, he would have looked like a punk mime. It was the first time I'd seen him wear any white.

"I listened to that NIN CD you recommended," I said.

He lit up with a smile and pushed himself up in his chair. "So, what do you think?"

"It's intense."

"Do you like it?"

"It's kind of dark."

"Yeah..." he sighed. "Feels like home." He sank back into the chair with a satisfied expression.

"What do you mean?"

"It matches how I feel inside," he said. "It soothes me."

"Ahh...I see." I nodded. "That's how I felt about Rush when I was your age."

"You listen to Rush?" He perked up.

"Oh, yeah...best drummer on the planet."

"Neil Peart."

"That's right!"

"He's a badass dude."

"Yes, he is."

Michael whipped out his air guitar, played a riff, and sang off key, "We are the Priests of the Temples of Syrinx..."

I sang along.

He kicked back with a relaxed smile, draped a booted leg over the arm of his chair, and told me about his weekend. He showed off his bruises from the mosh pit like badges of honor. He even peeled back some of the duct tape.

Michael talked about his best friend, Joe, who was a year older. They called themselves brothers even though they weren't related, and sometimes, when the alcoholism and isolation at Joe's house became unbearable, he spent the night at Michael's.

Billi, Michael's mother, urged Joe to see me. She took him to the Medi-Cal office to get an insurance card, and encouraged him to call for an appointment.

"He is horribly depressed and lonely at home," she said. "He doesn't really have anybody. He really needs to see you."

Joe didn't think much of therapy, but he respected Billi. After a few weeks of her persistent nudges, he called me to make an appointment.

He arrived early for his first session wearing navy blue mechanic's coveralls with his name embroidered on the chest, and steel-toed work boots. His shaved head was smooth and perfectly formed, and he wore big, black plugs in his ears, long before plugs were popular. He was only seventeen, but he seemed very grown up. Too grown up for a children's clinic.

Joe had the premature wisdom that is forced on children who are abandoned. His mother was a meth addict, and his father was in prison for drugs and burglary. They left Joe with a grandmother he called BeerMa who drank a twelve pack every night. By her fourth beer she'd effectively disappeared. There was nobody at home.

Billi called me every week to tell me her worries about Joe: how alone he was, how drunk his grandmother was, how he spent most of his time in bed, too depressed to go out.

Except for punk shows, where he loved the sensation of being pounded in the mosh pit. This pleasure he shared with Michael.

Joe liked to work on cars, and he wanted to become a mechanic. He had dropped out of school at 16 - figured it was a waste of time. His boss at the garage was a compassionate man who kept him on in spite of spotty attendance.

Joe and I connected right away. He reminded me of the boys I went to high school with, the emotionally orphaned ones I took under my wing.

He was a gentle soul, a poet and musician. He composed songs on his electric guitar. His vulnerable eyes and pale skin reminded me of my brother's baby pictures. He spoke in a soft, low voice, like he was trying not to wake someone.

I could feel Joe's loneliness in my throat, like the thirst after a long desert hike.

In the weeks that followed, Joe told me about his solitary life at home in his room, where he listened to death metal and punk, and numbed himself with whiskey and heroin. He wrote out song lyrics that revealed his emotional experience. They reminded me of the poems I wrote in high school about my life in *The Cage*.

Thanks to Mr. O, I kept hope alive long enough to get away to college.

But Joe had lost hope.

Like most children who are neglected and abandoned in childhood, he lived with a deep, tenacious belief that no one cared about him.

It can take years of consistent evidence to the contrary to loosen that belief or turn down its volume.

But this boy was such a sweetheart. Surely someone cared about him.

"Where are your parents?" I asked.

"Oh, you mean the Crack Whore and the Invisible Felon?"

I looked at him. His language sounded angry, but his expression revealed nothing but resignation.

"I haven't seen her since I was a baby," he said. "He's been locked up for years."

"Did you ever know your dad?"

"Yeah, he used to come around once in while to borrow money from BeerMa."

"Do you have contact with him?"

"No."

"Wow. That must hurt."

"Not really. It happened a long time ago."

"Do you ever miss them?"

"Not any more."

"Does it make you sad?"

"Nah. They did the best they could. They were just a couple of wild kids." He looked away. "Billi's my mom now. She's nutty, but she's a good person."

I laughed. Billi was like an eccentric angel to Joe. The kind of angel who always shows up when you need her, but there's no telling what she might do to embarrass you to death.

Billi's mood swings ranged from dark despair to giddy mania. She flew into noisy rants at the neighborhood kids one day and invited them over for treats the next.

She lived in a trailer park, drove an old, rusty pickup truck, and wore heavy metal t-shirts with her faded jeans. Her long, stringy hair hung in uncombed clumps, and her holey sneakers revealed her bare toes.

When Joe spent the night at Billi's house, she made pancakes for breakfast and packed a lunch for him to take to work at the garage. She always tucked a funny note in between his sandwich and chips, and sometimes a prize, just like Cracker Jacks. I could see where Michael got his creativity.

Billi was old enough to be Joe's mom, but Joe was the more grown up of the two. With thoughtful detail, he explained to me how Billi had suffered mistreatment from her family and her ex-husband.

Joe's empathy moved me. He made no judgments, but spoke with compassion, like a good son.

After a few sessions, Joe settled into a routine of pouring out his heart. It was like he'd never had anyone to talk to before.

One afternoon he came in looking nervous, his neck and shoulders stiff, and studied my expression with the vigilant eyes of a hawk. He perched on the edge of his chair. "I have to tell you something," he said.

His eyes were wide. He swallowed with his big Adam's apple. So manly.

"I'm in love with Michael," he said. "I've loved him for a long time." He watched me, eager to read my reaction.

"I can see why. He's adorable."

Joe coughed out a laugh of relief and slouched into his chair. "You don't think it's weird?"

"Weird?"

"Yeah, you know, perverted." He fiddled with his skull ring.

"Perverted?"

"Yeah, like there's something wrong with me."

"No, there is nothing wrong with you."

He stared at me.

"*L'amore e cieco.*" I spoke with a dramatic Italian accent and waved my hands.

"Huh?"

"*Love is blind. Love rules without rules.*"

He grinned.

I grinned back at him. "And it will spark in the most unexpected places."

We looked at each other for a moment.

"Does he know?" I asked.

"No way!" He looked scared. "I can't afford to lose him as a friend."

Joe was certain that Michael love him too but just didn't know it yet, and he refused to be discouraged by Michael's steady stream of girlfriends. Joe hoped that if he was patient, Michael would eventually come around. He clung to this fantasy like a lifeline.

The following Tuesday, Michael came in for his regular session.

"You know Joe is gay, right?" he asked me.

Are ALL of these kids psychic?

"Michael, you know everything you guys say in session is private."

"Yeah, I know. Well, he's gay. And he has a crush on me."

"How do you know?"

"I can tell. He's afraid to tell me. He's afraid of being rejected. I'm his only real friend."

"Hmm." *This is why therapists refuse to see more than one family member. Too many secrets.*

Michael explained that he did not welcome the sexual interest, but he was deeply attached to Joe. He didn't mind that Joe was gay, but he didn't want to be wanted.

Despite this tension, their friendship flourished. They were like twins who could neither part nor get along.

"You know he wants to die," Michael said. "He talks about it all the time."

I listened.

"He doesn't really have anything to live for," Michael explained. "His family doesn't care about him, and he doesn't want to deal with the past."

He spoke matter-of-factly, like he was talking about the weather.

Rafa saw Joe twice a month for medication management. I had never seen him so worried about a patient. Joe was taking a man-sized dose of Prozac with no effect. We decided to try Effexor instead.

I sat in the middle of the family triangle week after week and listened to Michael's story, then Joe's, then Billy's. Their lives were entangled in good and complicated ways.

Michael struggled with depression, but he had a repertoire of survival skills that worked pretty well most of the time. He was smart, charming, and had an uncanny ability to land on his feet. Each time he came home from the hospital, following a period of despair and suicide threats, he bounced back and caught up in school. He always met a new girlfriend in the hospital, which helped.

Joe was not so resilient. When he was in pain, he hid in his room. When the pain became unbearable, he numbed it with whiskey and heroin. Joe's ability to resist heroin when he wanted to was one of many ways he demonstrated an indomitable will.

Being Joe's therapist was like towing a barge with a rowboat. His spirit was very heavy. He felt little hope, and the little hope he could muster was easily dashed by circumstances. The hurtful messages that had been carved into his soul by years of abuse, neglect, and abandonment were hard to compete with. His belief that he was alone in the world operated like a powerful magnet that sucked away all the shavings of self-worth I offered him.

Being 17 and gay in a neighborhood where skinhead gangs roamed the streets and mugged swishy boys did not help. When I read an article about the suicide rates among gay teens, I thought of Joe, hiding out in his room, listening to death metal on the headphones and anesthetizing himself.

But despite all the darkness, Joe was a lovable boy. Intelligent and sensitive, with precocious insight and a razor wit. He was a loyal, devoted friend to Michael and Billi.

After a few months of therapy, Joe seemed to feel more hopeful. He found an emotional home in our relationship.

He spoke like a concerned older brother about Michael's mood swings and erratic behavior. Joe saw Michael's talent and potential, and encouraged him to stay out of trouble and go to school. They were family in the best sense.

Meanwhile, Loosie monitored my caseload to make sure it was always overfull. She called me into her office one day to tell me I had to discharge Joe on his eighteenth birthday and refer him to an adult clinic. "We have families on the waiting list who can actually pay for their therapy," she griped, in her snotty middle school tone. Loosie liked to bump the wealthy VIP's to the front of the line.

"Joe is severely depressed," I told her. "He takes the maximum dose of Effexor, and he still can't get out of bed some days."

"Well, this is not a long-term therapy place." She scowled. "He'll have to go to the adult clinic like everyone else."

"I don't think he'll go. He won't to start over with a new therapist."

Loosie rolled her eyes and dismissed me with a wave. She was very busy and important, and I was just a bleeding heart social worker.

So I went over her head.

I called the clinic contract monitor and requested a waiver to continue seeing Joe after he turned 18. I explained that Joe was not stable enough for discharge, and that I was pretty sure he would not follow through on a referral to an adult clinic.

The contract monitor listened with interest. He had helped me before. But this time Loosie had gotten to him before I could.

"I'm sorry," he said, "but this is really Dr. Garcia's jurisdiction."

I called my old friend, Terri, from Casa. She would be great with Joe. She agreed to see him in her private practice.

The next time I saw Joe, I explained the situation. We still had a few weeks before he turned eighteen.

I told him about the adult clinic where I was supposed to send him.

"There is another option," I said.

"What's that?"

"My friend, Terri. She has a private practice. I think you would like her."

Joe slumped in his chair with a flat expression.

"She does art therapy. She's got hundreds of toys, and some really cool drums."

"Oh."

"You can think about it."

Joe remained quiet.

The day before Joe's eighteenth birthday, we met for our last session. He brought his Matthew Sweet CD and played me a song.

> *...there's something in your eyes*
> *that is keeping my hope alive.*
> *But I'm sick of myself when I look at you*
> *Something is beautiful and true*
> *In a world that's ugly and a lie*
> *It's hard to even want to try...*

I teared up. We stared at each other.

"I'm so sorry about this," I said.

"It's not your fault. It's just the stupid system again."

"Even so..."

"I'll be alright. I've made it this far."

"I hope you like Terri."

He didn't say anything, but looked away.

"You know you can call me anytime, right?"

"Thanks."

Joe had no patience left for clueless adults who jerked his life around. He was polite, but he was pissed. Yet another senseless disruption in his life that left him frustrated and powerless.

He gave me a warm, gentle bear hug. His cologne smelled expensive. It must have been a gift from Billi. He sure didn't smell like the auto mechanics I grew up with.

Joe shuffled out and closed the door behind him.

I watched him walk away through my sealed, bulletproof window. The walk home was several miles, but he refused to ride the bus that day.

Impotent rage seared my stomach. I wanted to strangle Loosie. She was a giant toddler playing with hand grenades.

As I watched Joe slump down the road, I called Billi and gave her Terri's address and phone number.

"Be sure he calls, okay?" I could count on Billi to nag him till he followed through.

"I will. Thank you for everything."

"Billi, you and Joe can call me here any time. Okay? The on-call therapist knows how to reach me."

"Thanks. I'll see you Tuesday when I bring Michael in."

Two months later, around the holidays, Billi called me in a panic.

"Joe needs to see you," she said.

"What's happening?"

"He is really depressed. He never called that new therapist."

"Uh oh. Is he still taking his medication?"

"He stopped taking it."

"Do you know when?"

"Two weeks ago."

"Billi, you know I would love to see him, but they won't let him come to the clinic."

"I know."

"Can you get him to come to the phone?"

"I'll try." She set the receiver down. I could hear her knocking on a door and calling his name.

I waited. And waited.

After an eternity of silence, Billi picked up the receiver again. "He won't come to the phone. He's going home to sleep."

"Will he see Terri?" I asked.

"I'll try."

"Will you let me know what happens?"

"I'll call you."

"Thanks, Billi. I'm so sorry about this."

"Me too."

I fumed. I was tempted to sneak Joe into the clinic, but I would never get away with it. Not under Loosie's intrusive scrutiny. She was itching to get me fired.

Every few months, Loosie launched a new smear campaign against a new scapegoat, usually an attractive female therapist who was becoming too popular at the clinic. With J.B.'s support, Loosie harassed each one until she resigned under duress.

It was the most disgusting thing I had ever seen. Doctors who were well paid to take care of sick children, behaving like cutthroat tycoons in an episode of *Dallas*.

I should have quit. The combined stress of Loosie's harassment and the dysfunctional politics was making me sick.

I made an appointment with a psychologist in our EAP program and hoped she could help me manage the stress.

"They eat their young at that clinic," she said with concern and empathy in her eyes. "Why don't you go into private practice?"

"I'd love to, but the timing is not right."

"I think you would do well." She nodded and smiled.

"Thank you."

I planned to go into private practice someday, but the training program at the clinic was my baby. I had invested three years of hard work, sacrificed way too much, and recruited a team of good people. I couldn't leave them alone with Loose Cannon.

Rafa gave me some Zoloft samples and I soldiered on.

"What does it mean that you have to take anti-depressants to stay in your job?" he asked with a smirk. Rafa took Zoloft too.

"I know, I know."

On a gloomy Sunday morning in July, I sat in my reading chair and sipped a latte. The phone rang. It was the on-call therapist at the clinic.

"Billi is trying to reach you," my friend said. "She wants you to call her."

My stomach seized up in a knot. "What is it?" I asked.

"Just call her." She gave me the number.

My heart pounded in my head as I bent over the phone and dialed Billi's number. Shnuckie stood in front of me, ears back, and watched me with anxious eyes.

Billi answered on the first ring. "Hello?" Her voice shook.

"Hi, Billi. It's Cate."

She exploded into hysterical weeping. "Cate!" Billi wailed through the phone. "Joe is dead!"

A wrecking ball slammed into my chest.

"He killed himself last night." She stammered through sobs. "He was at home alone, in his bedroom. He shot himself in the head."

Billi poured out her story between bursts of tears. "I loved him so much!"

I submerged a mass of overwhelming emotions and spoke to her in the most soothing voice I could muster. "I know, Billi. He loved you too."

Billi wept.

"I wish I could have helped him." She spoke through heaving and tears.

"You did help him, Billi. Joe knew how much you cared about him. He thought of you as his mom."

I comforted her and absolved her as well as I could.

"Ohh..." she moaned. "Cate?"

"Yes?"

"I'm worried about Michael. Can he come see you?"

"Absolutely. I can see him tomorrow after school. Can he come to the phone?"

Michael had graduated from therapy a few months earlier, but losing Joe would knock the earth out from under his feet.

"He's not here right now." Billi sniffled. "He's out with his girlfriend."

"Okay. Tell him he can have the clinic page me when he gets home if he wants to. I'll see him tomorrow at 4:00."

"Thank you, Cate. I'll see you tomorrow."

"Billi?"

"Yeah?"

"Take good care of yourself."

"I will. I promise." I heard her hang up.

I sat down, stunned, like the time I ran into an electric fence with my head.

Is he really gone?

Can I please have another chance?

Did I abandon him like his parents did?

Sorrow filled my throat and flooded my eyes.

Then fear clenched the sorrow.

Oh no. Loosie will exploit this.

I called Rafa on speed dial. He had a remarkable ability to provide a calm, competent presence in the fire swamp of clinic politics.

We were like siblings trying to survive in a crazy, alcoholic family.

He answered his phone.

Thank God.

"Rafa?"

"Que pasa?"

"Do you have a few minutes?"

"Sure." I pictured his face. Rafa's kind, dark eyes, giving me 150% of his attention. "Are you okay?"

"No." I swallowed my tears. "Do you remember our boy, Joe?"

"The one in the coveralls?"

"Yeah, that's him. Rafie, he killed himself last night."

"*Dios mio, no!*"

I told him everything. I paced as far as the phone cord would let me. He listened.

When I was done talking, Rafa said all the things I needed to hear. He absolved me.

"Thank you," I said. "I have to get to the clinic before any more time passes."

"Right."

"You know what Loosie will do with this." It disgusted me that I could not even mourn in safety.

"Not if she doesn't know about it." He spoke with an authoritative tone that made me feel protected.

I drove to the clinic in a daze. I had to make sure Joe's chart was in good shape just in case.

When I arrived, Rafa was waiting by the door. His son and daughter rode their bikes around the clinic's wide, empty parking lot in eerie silence.

He examined my face, concerned about my emotional state.

I played the part of the stoic warrior, but my eyes gave me away.

Rafa didn't say much, but he hung around while I finished my business. Like that red-shouldered hawk who always perches outside my window when I'm in trouble.

Later that night, Rafa made a house call. We sat out on the deck and talked awhile. I made a fire in the chimenea. Shnuckie curled up on my lap.

We didn't say much about Joe. There wasn't much to say. And Rafa was not a big talker anyway.

And I was still in shock.

Michael came to see me a few times after Joe's death. We both needed it.

"He always wanted to die," Michael said. "It was just a matter of when."

Suicide had been a long-cherished dream of Joe's. Like an inmate making his hash marks on the wall, he had counted the days till his spirit could fly free.

Our reaction to Joe's death seemed strange. We mourned him and the massive injustices of his life. But, there was no rageful protest, no screaming at the sky asking why.

We let him fly away in peace.

My acceptance puzzled me.

Harry had taught me to trust my patients and respect their agendas. Joe's suicide felt like the ultimate test of those tenets.

Michael and I both felt a strange respect for Joe's choice. He had thought about it for a long time, and he had suffered. It was his life.

In retrospect, I wonder if Michael and I really felt acceptance, or just the insulating numbness of denial. The psyche can be merciful in that way.

Or maybe we could bear it because we were in it together.

As Jim and I mosey around the Pride festival, I realize how far my perspective has shifted in seven years. I wonder...if Joe had met me later in my training, would he would be here at the festival today, handing out condoms with Billi?

In a few years' time, with Harry's help, I've traversed a paradigm shift from following orders to forging life-saving bonds with desperate people in whatever way is needed.

In social work school we learned the importance of maintaining clear boundaries. No crossover between a professional relationship and a personal one.

It's not personal - it's business.

We make the rules, and patients are expected to follow them. If they don't, they're *acting out* or *non-compliant*. If one therapist is no longer available, the patient is transferred to another. And another. And another.

Therapists are not interchangeable for the same reasons that mothers are not.

My patients have taught me the power of connection. Our attachments and the nourishment they provide are the most powerful medicine. A healing relationship can fill some of the emptiness. The result is new resilience.

And we are only as resilient as our relationships.

If I could have a do-over, I would find a way to stay connected with Joe. I would make house calls when he was too depressed to come to the clinic.

I would give him my pager number, even if Loosie fired me for it. And if he couldn't keep himself alive over the weekend, I would put him in the hospital, even if he hated me for it.

I would not allow clinic rules to dictate our relationship.

It's not that I want to take away Joe's right to die; I just want to buy him some time. Time to find hope again. Time to find new reasons to live.

He was only 18.

My best do-over might not save Joe, but he would know that I was right beside him in the darkness. He would feel me fighting for his life. He would know, for once, that someone really cared about him.

It's true what they say: if a person is intent on suicide, we don't have the power to stop them.

But it is also true that one person holding a lifeline can make the despair bearable. Humans can bear an incredible amount of pain if we don't feel alone with it.

With Joe, I am the student who learned about the cure for the disease after the patient was already gone.

The year after Joe's death, I spent Christmas Eve in the E.R. with a suicidal 19-year-old. She intended to snort gram after gram of cocaine until her fragile heart gave out.

I intended to keep her alive until she had a better idea.

So there we sat, for three hours, admitting her to a psychiatric hospital against her will, her worst nightmare.

I swear Joe's spirit sat right next to me the whole time and kept me company.

AFTERNOONS WITH HARRY

"Had just one person understood what was happening
and come to my defense,
it might have changed my entire life."
- Alice Miller, Ph.D.

Two months after Joe's suicide, one of Rafael's patients, a sweet ten-year-old girl, was shot and killed by her father. Rafa had worked intensively with the family for two years and forged an unprecedented bond with the unstable father.

He brought his case notes to my house, and we sat on the deck, reviewed every treatment decision Rafa made, and tried to understand how the tragedy had happened. The police were eager to talk to Rafa. So were the press.

Rafa sat rigid on the edge of his chair, wide-eyed. Shnuckie jumped into his lap to offer support.

I listened to his clinical rationales. The father had suffered from chronic PTSD as a result of his own traumatic childhood and, while he had made good strides along some developmental lines, he remained vulnerable to fragmentation and psychotic states when under stress.

A stable pattern of instability, as Harry would call it.

When Rafa was done talking I said, "You did everything right, my friend. Good work in an impossible situation."

He studied my face like he wasn't sure I was telling the truth. We hadn't realized how disturbed the little girl's father was. He had been famous for his histrionics, but he had not seemed dangerous.

Trauma and psychosis can be unpredictable that way, like a twister that hops over one town and demolishes the next.

Sometimes it's easy to forget how dangerous this work is. If we remembered all the time, we probably wouldn't do it.

Rafa locked up his notes, and we walked uptown to decompress at our favorite Italian restaurant.

The press hounded Rafa. The story was all over the news.

Rafa and I met with the clinic staff who were traumatized by the murder. I would have preferred to hide out and conserve my emotional resources, but our coworkers needed to process their experience before they could move on. And they couldn't do it alone.

The Chief of Children's Mental Health commended Rafa and me for our work on the case. He had referred the family to us two years earlier, calling them *high risk*.

Sometimes the patients we pour ourselves into the most don't get to enjoy the results.

After a few weeks, the clinic settled down, and we all moved on. Except for Loosie.

She'd been eerily quiet for weeks. I thought it was just her usual mood swings. Or perhaps her lust for drama had been momentarily sated by the tragedy.

But she was just getting started.

On a Monday morning, I arrived at work to find a memo in every mailbox.

Mandatory Morbidity & Mortality Conference
Wednesday, 9:00 a.m.

I felt an urge to vomit.

No one at our clinic even knew what a *Morbidity & Mortality Conference* was. We counseled children and families.

I hurried to my office and shot an email to Harry.

Loosie and J.B. have called an M & M

Harry understood. He knew these characters. He responded in an instant.

Stay calm. Don't get defensive.

Harry was my lifeline.

A few minutes later, I heard Rafa's coded knock on the door. He padded in, closed the door with care, and perched on the edge of a chair. He'd been waiting.

My breathing was shallow. Rafa nodded toward the memo on my desk. "Well, I guess it was too good to be true," he said.

"What's that?" I asked. I tried to breathe deeper and lower my shoulders.

"You know she's been quiet lately."

"I know. It's been lovely."

"I thought maybe she was trying to act like a decent human being for once. But *NOOO*."

Loosie had harassed and slandered me throughout my three and a half years at the clinic, and accused me of all the crazy things that she did. The stress of the hostile work environment had become toxic. Some days it felt just like the stomach flu.

But I couldn't even have the flu in peace. One morning as I sat in a bathroom stall, bent over with stress-induced stomach cramps, Loosie scampered in with one of my colleagues, stood at the sink, and trashed me for five minutes while my colleague put on makeup. As usual, she accused me of the kind of abusive behavior that she routinely perpetrated.

If she wasn't my boss, I would have thrown a roll of toilet paper at her head.

Every week, my friends and colleagues urged, "You need to get out of there." But I had invested a huge amount of work and heart in the training program, and it was coming together beautifully.

The more I succeeded, the more Loosie seethed and sniped.

Rafa stood by me through all of it, made me laugh, and invented nicknames for our nemesis. He was disgusted with J.B for hiring her. He said anyone who talked to her for five minutes could tell she was insane.

Rafa pointed at the memo. "She's been talking to the department heads about *inadequate supervision at the clinic*. Never mind that it's her job – she's trying to blame you."

"I figured." I frowned.

"What are you gonna do?" Rafa raised his eyebrows and scrunched up his forehead.

"I've got two days to talk to the department heads and tell them what's been going on here. This is ridiculous. We just got the staff through this nightmare. They've finally calmed down, and now she wants to rip open the wound."

Rafa's face went blank. He tried to hide his emotions, but the color drained from his face. "Be careful," he said.

"I'm tired of trying to run a training program with a giant five-year-old stomping around. We pay her to supervise, not to terrorize."

I felt a familiar surge of energy. *Righteous Indignation.* My long fuse had reached an abrupt end.

The following day, I met with the vice president of the psychiatry department and asked him to help me deal with Loosie. He had always supported me, though his hands were often tied by hospital politics. It seemed bizarre that I had to go three levels up the org chart to find a sane, competent administrator.

My V.P. friend empathized and promised to help, but he was outnumbered.

Meanwhile, J.B. sent me a letter that said I was imagining things. To his mind, Loosie was wonderful and I was just paranoid.

Every time one of the staff therapists reported Loosie's destructive behavior, it was the same routine: the *You Are Imagining Things* letter, followed by a smear campaign, followed by Loosie and J.B. meeting privately with their Special Friend in Human Resources, followed by the whistle-blower suddenly resigning under mysterious circumstances.

It was the most abusive system I had ever worked in, and that is saying something.

I showed Rafa the *You Are Imagining Things* letter. He looked amazed.

I requested a meeting with the department heads, Human Resources, Loosie, and J.B. to confront the craziness. I had met with all of them the previous year, and succeeded in getting Loosie contained enough that we could get some work done for a few months.

The meeting was set for Tuesday afternoon, before the M & M. Maybe I could talk some sense into them.

When I arrived at the meeting, Loosie was not there.

J.B. was. With his Special Friend from H.R. And a list of unethical and unprofessional behavior that described Loosie pretty well.

Problem was, Loosie's name was not on the document.

Mine was.

No evidence, just Loosie's word against mine. And Loosie was the boss.

I sat stunned with disbelief. How could these people take Loosie seriously?

I looked at the H.R. lady. "Can you please give me some examples of these behaviors I'm accused of?"

"No. The staff are afraid of retaliation."

"What? My staff? Afraid of me?"

This is nuts. My staff are always teasing me about spoiling them...

I looked at the head of my department. He should know better. "Bill, I thought you guys understood what I was dealing with here."

Bill gave me a blank stare, his eyes fixed like he had a gun in his back. He said nothing.

It felt like a scene from *The Godfather*. Loosie had woven her web long before the meeting, and sent her emissary to do her dirty work.

I was meant to sleep with the fishes.

I returned to my office and called Rafa.

"I'll meet you at your house in an hour," he said.

We sat on the deck where we had reviewed Rafa's case notes a few weeks earlier.

Grief convulsed out of me. Me who rarely cries. "I feel like I just spent three years in hard labor, and as soon as I gave birth, she stole the baby."

"That's exactly what happened," he said. He looked at me with such tenderness.

I held on to his gaze.

"Just remember: It's not you." He spoke with authority. "No matter what they say, *it's not you.*"

I understood the wisdom of his words. He was trying to insulate me from further trauma with his validation. But it was too late. Three years of abuse had already triggered all of my worst nightmares and activated every chunk of trauma shrapnel in my bones.

Loosie didn't realize at the time that stealing my baby would kill it. Worse, she didn't care.

Exile is a dreadful thing for one who knows her rightful place.

In a moment of weakness, I called my mother. Maybe she would be there for me this time.

She scolded me in her angry church lady voice:

> *You should be more thankful!*
> *You should have more faith!*

I had forgotten that feeling anxious was a sin.

A few days later I received a packet of Bible verses in the mail.

The hospital gave me a fat severance package in exchange for signing a paper that said I would not sue them.

In my absence Rafa attended the M & M Conference and fought for my honor. My friends said he shut Loosie up in the first two minutes.

Then he loaded up all of my art therapy and play therapy supplies in his truck and drove it to his storage garage.

Loose Cannon inherited a sinking ship full of frightened staff and students, and no one to do the work for her.

My old friend, Sarah, co-owned a retreat center on the Caribbean side of Costa Rica. She attached a V.I.P. tag to my battered carcass and shipped me to a paradise called *Samasati* for some long overdue R & R.

After umpteen hours in coach, and another two hours in the back of a minivan, I collapsed into a colorful hammock that overlooked the lush mountainside rainforest and turquoise sea. Sarah had arranged for me to stay in a secluded cottage close to the hot tub.

At 4 a.m. a loud roar jarred me out of a nightmare.

Is that a lion?

Disoriented, I tried to make sense of my surroundings. I couldn't find even a speck of light in the black night.

Howler monkeys!

I had read about them in my Costa Rica travel guide. Tiny little monkeys that sound like great big lions. Their roars jolted me into a familiar state. *Unsafe.*

Once awake, troubled thoughts intruded. *What am I going to do when I go home? Where am I going to work? How much damage has Loosie done?*

Before I left L.A., Rafa had told me that Loosie forbade my colleagues to write letters of recommendation for me. When Rafa ignored her and wrote me a glowing recommendation, she confiscated it from the outgoing mail.

When I rose on my first day in paradise, I felt like I'd been wrestling all night. But I was in a safe place. Finally. At least for a week. God bless Sarah.

I opened the cottage door to hike down to the dining hall.

When I stepped out onto the porch, a six-inch-tall hummingbird with an engine like a Cessna zoomed up to my face and hovered a few inches from the end of my nose.

VRROOOMM!!!

I could feel the wind from his wings on my cheek. He stayed there, in my face, humming like crazy, his vibrant, metallic colors shimmering in the sun. He wasn't going to leave until I listened to him.

Aggressive little bugger.

I remembered what Lali, our art therapy and shamanism teacher, had said about hummingbirds: *a symbol for accomplishing the impossible; a reminder to find joy and savor the sweetness of life.*

I detoured around my intense little friend and walked through wet jungle to the kitchen. Beside the path sat a tiny, neon orange frog.

The bright colored ones are poison.

I gave him a wide berth.

A little further down the path, in the middle of a stepping-stone, sat a massive toad, the size of a small ham.

Now I grew up on a farm, and I've seen some big frogs, but I never saw anything that size.

Did I just step into Wonderland?

I ventured into the dining hall in search of coffee. A dirty white cat climbed around on the pristine, polished wood of the open deck. He hopped up on the snack bar and sniffed the coffee pot.

Ahh...there it is.

I looked out at a calm sea framed by dense jungle. Toucans flew to and fro, like crows with bananas sticking out of their beaks. Several of them posed on bare tree branches, arranged like quarter notes on sheet music.

"Buenos dias." A tall man with curly hair and a radiant smile walked up to me. "Welcome to Samasati. I'm Luc, and this is Chico." He stroked the head of the Australian sheep dog, whose tail wagged his whole body. Chico raised his paw and smiled. "May I join you?" Luc motioned toward a chair.

"Please." I smiled.

He poured himself a cup of aromatic Costa Rican coffee and sat across from me.

"Your accent..."

"Paris," he said.

"Ahh. What brings you to Costa Rica?"

"I've been traveling a long time. I got tired of the Paris attitude."

"What attitude is that?

"Arrogance."

Luc told me stories about his adventures. He had worked on boats and organic farms, tended vineyards in Tuscany, and managed a resort in Provence.

He looked about forty years old, with a few silver hairs accenting his long, dark curls, but he spoke with the wisdom and conviction of an old man.

I talked about my work with kids and my travels. We philosophized, shared experiences, and reflected on lessons we'd learned.

"It's all about growing up," he said.

"What do you mean *growing up?*"

"If I didn't want to grow up, I would be laying in a hammock in Jamaica, smoking a spliff."

I laughed.

"You have to do the work," he said. "Whatever it is that you're afraid of, you have to face it. And whatever you are clinging to, you must let go."

I nodded. Seemed reasonable enough.

That week, Luc and I hiked to the waterfall in the rain, rode a zip line through the treetops up high where the monkeys play, watched a sloth climb down a tree. Well, part way down. It would have taken him two days to climb down at that rate.

We saw bright yellow snakes and gigantic brown ones. We took a boat out and snorkeled in the warm, clear sea. Transparent jellyfish floated around us like streamers hanging from the ceiling of a high school gym. It was so early in the day, I didn't think to put sunscreen on my back. That night, a bright red sunburn kept me awake.

I explored the nearby beach town, chatted with locals, and bought gifts for my friends at the clinic. I found a four-foot long, hand painted rain stick for Sarah's little girl. I couldn't wait to see her face when she played it. It really did sound like the rainforest.

Every day I sat in the hammock, wrote pages in my handmade Costa Rican journal, and sketched the critters I met in the rainforest.

I wrote questions. Questions about my life and my future. Lists of options. Maps of options.

And I prayed. Not the fancy prayers of the religious, but the down and dirty prayers of the desperate.

I tried to forget the nightmare that awaited me at home, and immersed myself in the beauty of the rainforest. But I was haunted.

Every morning I hiked through the jungle to the yoga hut for the 6 a.m. class. My body remained clenched, full of impacted emotion.

Every night we enjoyed a delicious gourmet meal prepared by our visiting chef. I made friends with the owner and with one of the residents, an expat social worker who had left the U.S. after her divorce and built a house on the Samasati grounds. When I saw her beautiful cabin style house in the rainforest, I fantasized about running away from home.

On my last night at Samasati, I soaked in the hot tub while Luc played Brazilian folk songs on his tiny guitar. He sang to *Imanja,* goddess of the sea.

We sat up late telling stories, like the time he got malaria in India and nearly died. But there was one story that grabbed me.

Luc had worked in Calcutta with Mother Teresa for two years. "They were the most joyful people I ever met," he said. "These children who lived in extreme poverty, understood what matters."

I had always admired Mother T, but I couldn't imagine living there for two years. I don't think Shnuckie would have fit in very well in the slums of Calcutta.

"I didn't see her often," Luc said. "She stayed very busy from dawn until bedtime. But one day she talked to me. I asked her, 'What should I do to develop humility?'"

"What did she say?"

I was a big fan of humility, though not a regular practitioner.

"No shoes." He smiled.

I looked at his leathery feet. I had noticed that Luc went barefoot a lot, but I figured it was a hippie thing.

"It's been interesting to travel with no shoes," he said. "To get into a restaurant, to walk in the snow..."

"How long have you been without shoes?

"Six years."

The last morning at Samasati, I choked back tears during yoga practice. Luc came over and placed his palms between my shoulder blades. The accumulated stress and trauma of the past three years erupted in my chest. It was coming up. He seemed to know somehow.

He scooted up beside me, laid a hand on my shoulder and looked at my face. "Let it go," he said.

I looked into his kind eyes, too proud to cry in class. I knew it would be loud and snotty. And embarrass me.

After class, I walked out of the yoga hut into the freshly washed morning. A deep turquoise butterfly with an eight-inch wingspan floated past, leisurely flapping huge, metallic wings that gleamed in the sunlight. I half expected the March Hare to come sprinting up behind him.

At breakfast, we listened to my Cat Stevens CD. The young man in the song poured out his heart to a father who never understood him.

How can I try to explain?
When I do he turns away again.
It's always been the same, same old story.
From the moment I could talk
I was ordered to listen...

...it's them they know, not me...
Now there's a way and I know
that I have to go away...
I know I have to go.

As I listened to the lyrics, a sledgehammer cracked dead center into the breastplate of my old armor. Grief pierced my heart. A torrent of tears washed my face while the eggs got cold.

Epiphany.

I had done it again: chained my life to another abusive family. Re-created my family to postpone the pain of losing them.

I couldn't wait to talk to Harry. What he taught me was true: *Talking about the darkness transforms the darkness.*

For the past three years I had sat across from Harry once a week and poured out my clinic stories with wide eyes and high anxiety. One Thursday afternoon I was so terrorized when I arrived at his office, I slammed the door on my fingers.

Harry fetched an ice pack, and my fingers throbbed while we talked.

A few weeks later, I smashed them again.

Psychoanalyze that.

The clinic had been famous for its incompetent administrators and psychotic politics. I was a fool to think I could make a difference there. I built beautiful sand castles on shifting sand.

Just like trying to fix my family.

But no matter what harrowing tale I brought to Harry, he listened with unflinching calm. He held the ropes for me while I climbed ill-advised trails.

The following Thursday, back in Los Angeles, I drove to Harry's office for our weekly consultation. I told him all about *The Gang Rape,* as Rafa liked to call it.

"It's a smear campaign," Harry said. "They turned on you, attacked you, and replicated your trauma history."

My innards relaxed in response to his validation.

Harry had always admired my dedication to the programs I directed, but he thought my idealism was dangerous.

I'd heard it a hundred times: *Cate, if you wear your heart on your sleeve, you're going to get hurt.*

"Why don't you go into private practice?" He asked.

I looked at him, and tried to veil my cynicism with politeness.

"You are well suited for it," he said.

"I wish." *And who will pay the bills while I chase that pipe dream?*

I had enjoyed a small practice for the past ten years, but I couldn't imagine supporting myself with it. I felt unworthy.

But Harry believed in me. And sent me lots of new clients. So did my friends at the clinic.

Every week I received distress calls from the clinic staff and interns. I found jobs for some of the therapists and secretaries. A few of the interns hired me for private supervision.

A group of Loosie's victims invited me to join their class action suit. I was tempted for a moment, but I had fallen in love with my new, peaceful life.

Oh, sure, I fantasized about how I would: key her car, slash her tires, vandalize her house, dump dog poop on her porch...

But sadly, I was not the type who could enjoy revenge. I would suffer more than she did.

Then fate intervened.

Early one morning I stepped outside to take Shnuckie for a walk, and saw the sky darkened by ash. A round, red sun glowed through smoky haze.

Huh? Armageddon? I didn't hear anything...

We walked a little, then retreated from the ash-filled air back into the house. I checked my voice mail.

One of the clinic secretaries had left a message at 7 a.m. *Old Loosie was evacuated from her house last night. The wildfire came up to her back yard. It's karma!*

It did seem like the kind of karma Loose Cannon had created for herself. But then I pictured her seven-year-old daughter, Sofia. The fire would terrify her. So would the sight of her brittle mother melting down under stress.

I remembered the night my own house burned down. I was nine. We lived in the woods of rural Ohio, fifteen miles from the nearest small town. I sat in the station wagon with my blanket while Dad helped the firefighters.

My mother, who was easily overwhelmed, had shut down. She stared at the fire, absorbed in herself. I couldn't reach her. I felt alone, and my little body erupted with that stomach flu thing from too much stress.

"Mom, I have to go to the bathroom." *If I can make it that far.*

"No, stay in the car." She frowned and scolded with her mouth, but her eyes stared off into a black hole. My mother could go a million miles away without moving an inch.

I knew that look, so I ignored her, jumped out of the car, and bolted for the ditch.

I was on my own.

While I was still working at the clinic, Sofia liked to hang out in my office and draw pictures. She seemed more relaxed with me than she was with her mother.

A few weeks after I left, when Rafa and I unpacked my stuff from storage and moved it to my private practice, I found a note from Sofia in a box of toys. She had drawn orange and yellow flowers, a big pink heart, and printed,

To Cate,
You are amazing.
Love, Sofia

Talk about validation.

I remembered the day when Loosie walked up to me in the lunchroom and asked, "Why am I so mean to you?" She stared at me weirdly, like she was in a trance. "You're so on top of things," she said, "you give me the creeps." In that moment, she seemed guileless, like she'd seen a fleeting glimpse of her own reflection.

Loosie had grown up with a psychotic mother. She still behaved like a traumatized little girl in many ways. When she berated me in meetings, Rafa said, "She's mothering you."

Little Gloria became a loose cannon because she never had a stable mommy to attach to. Her psyche grew up distorted around her mother's disorganized personality. She terrorized us the same way her mother had terrorized her.

That's what happens when wounded therapists don't get their own therapy.

I was beyond grateful to be free from the noxious environment at the clinic. I felt like I'd been rescued by the Hazmat Team and sent to Costa Rica for decontamination. But I mourned the destruction of the training program. And the staff and interns kept calling. It became harder to listen to their stories about Loosie's ongoing abuse. Validating, but painful. I longed to put it all behind me.

Harry provided a true compass as I found my way in private practice and launched a new training program. He took up residence in my head, and accompanied me while I worked. I could hear him.

Staying calm is half the battle.
The other half is staying connected.
Trust the process.
Trust your patient.

Harry was right. Private practice was my element. I felt like a happy pig in her favorite mud hole.

But the clinic ordeal left scars. For the next two years, I suffered from nightmares and moments of post-traumatic stress. It didn't help that the clinic dynamics were so similar to my own family's. That craziness had awakened every old ghost that lurked in my soul.

My practice filled up fast, without much effort from me. My brilliant marketing strategies ended up in a desk drawer. I was too busy seeing patients to network much.

Two years later, ready for a break, I took my dream vacation in Italy and visited Luc on an organic farm in Tuscany. We stayed in an 800-year-old villa, secluded in a womb-shaped forest on *La Montagna Magica.*

Magic Mountain.

From my second floor window, I watched the sun rise over the pristine Tuscan countryside. Rows of tall, cigar shaped Italian cypress trees, fields of red poppies, and the ancient stone of a medieval walled city all glowed under the pink sunrise. Abundant star jasmine crawled up the villa walls and filled the moist morning air with a luscious aroma. Five white doves flew circular laps above the vineyard then landed in a noisy flurry on the barn roof. They cooed and flapped around in the golden light. The largest dove struck a regal pose against the blue sky and sienna tile.

I crept downstairs before the other guests rose and found the espresso machine. Then I snooped around the private kitchen in search of a coffee mug. As I exited the kitchen with my illegal mug, Luc walked through the front door of the villa with a radiant smile and wet hair. His damp shirt hung loose, unbuttoned, revealing his dark, toned torso.

"*Bella!*"

"Hey!" I gave him a big hug. He kissed my face. I sniffed. "What's that smell?"

"Sulfer," he grinned. "The hot springs at sunrise. *Molto bella...*"

"Mmm...that sounds good."

"We'll go," he said, "but now... breakfast!" He disappeared into the kitchen. I heard him singing a Brazilian song while he cooked for a houseful of guests. Two sleepy-eyed farm workers shuffled past and joined him.

That evening, several fellow travelers and I sat at a picnic table in the cool shade of a massive cherry tree. A soft breeze animated its sunlit leaves. I surveyed miles of rolling Tuscan hills, farms, villas, and vineyards. We reached up and picked ripe cherries, and moaned with pleasure as we savored the meal prepared by our hostess: homemade pasta, fresh pesto, vegetables from the garden, warm homemade bread. Nirdosh, owner of the farm, decorated her pasta dishes and salads with orchids and other colorful blossoms, and served them in large, ceramic bowls created by local artists.

We talked and laughed and sipped Chianti while the rich Tuscan sun set over an idyllic landscape. The valley at dusk looked like a plush quilt of varied textures and vibrant colors.

After they served us, the farm staff relaxed at a separate table, accompanied by a furry mountain dog named Fanicula, who smiled and wagged her tail constantly. A roving herd of ten cats, ruled by an old, yellow tomcat named Mustafa, enjoyed table scraps atop a vine-covered stone wall about four feet tall, and several hundred years old.

I picked up my plate and joined the staff. Luc introduced me to his friends.

A middle-aged couple from Poland spoke no English, but listened attentively and smiled, eager to connect. A nineteen-year-old know-it-all from Germany pontificated and flung her skinny arms around. She railed against the *fat, stupid Americans* who had ruined the world.

For some reason, they all assumed I was Canadian.

A fair-skinned beauty from Boston told us her plans to become a pastry chef and open a bakery back home. She'd been studying in Paris, and she intended to practice on us. Her lemon tart awaited us in the kitchen.

Nirdosh, a 70-year-old Italian matriarch who looked like a 40-year-old California blonde, walked up to the table. Luc rose to introduce us. I stood.

"Cate, this is my friend, Nirdosh. She is queen of all this." He made a grand gesture toward the forest, the vineyard, the gardens.

"*Buonasera*," she said. Her hazel eyes twinkled, and a huge smile bloomed across her face. She moved closer and put her face in my face. She studied my eyes. "You're a witch," she said. She nodded and laughed. "A very powerful one."

I smiled, unsure what to say. She clearly intended this as a compliment.

She took my hands in her hands. "You must come visit me." She motioned toward a cottage up the road. In front of the cottage, a great horned owl peered at us from her perch inside a spacious cage that had been built around several small trees and bushes.

"*Si.*" I nodded.

Nirdosh squeezed my hands, then sat down and poured herself a glass of Chianti from the carafe on the table, and greeted her friends. Luc winked at me.

Luc was true to his word. He took a group of us to the mineral hot springs after we spent a day swimming in the warm Mediterranean, and picnicked on the best brie, Pinot Grigio, and other delights that he could find in Siena.

After we lounged in the hot springs awhile, and let the massage jets of the mineral waterfall pound our shoulders, Luc appeared with a giant steel bowl full of cold watermelon. He scampered around on the rocks with his leathery feet like a mountain goat and delivered chunks of cold watermelon to the guests sprinkled throughout the steaming pool. When the bowl was empty, he turned it over and played it like a *djembe*. Luc's music echoed across the hot springs and down the river. We baked in the sun.

Ahh...Paradiso.

On other days, Luc and his friends drove us to the hill towns of Tuscany for leisurely lunches, gelato, and cappuccino, and to a nearby winery for a lazy afternoon of wine tasting.

When I tired of togetherness, I spent hours hiking Magic Mountain. Several circular trails climbed high enough to view the valley and the walled city through the trees.

It was good to have time to think. So much had happened in the past few years, and I never really had time to sort through it. My psyche worked hard at night to sort and integrate the past. My dreams were often dark, and sometimes I woke up spooked.

But then new dreams emerged. Dreams that felt more hopeful. At last.

One night I awoke from a joyous dream about a huge graduation party. All of my friends and loved ones, past and present, celebrated with me. Harry stood by my side.

The next morning I took off on a trail dotted with white tee pees. Luc explained that a group of Native Americans had visited the previous week and performed their annual ritual on the sacred ground of Magic Mountain. It seemed like a long way from home, but I could see why they chose it.

I immersed myself in the overwhelming beauty of the mountain, and photographed surreal views of the valley, the walled city, and close-up portraits of Italian flowers. I walked and walked through the cool, shaded forest, and assumed the trail would circle back to the villa like all the others.

About four hours later, I bumped into some German hikers who spoke English. "Do you know where this trail goes?" I asked them.

"France."

Uh oh.

I began a long hike home, with no idea where I was.

During those hours, my mind wandered. The forest reminded me of the woods back home, and memories of childhood arose. My thoughts wove in and out, from the past to the present.

I thought about Harry. I'd come to depend on him like family, and I couldn't wait to surprise him with the perfect bottle of wine from Tuscany.

My country girl radar got me to the main road. On the way down the mountain, I discovered a winery in the forest, built inside an old castle. From there, I found my way back up the other side of the mountain to the villa.

I've never been so happy to see home. After hours of wondering what had happened to me, Nirdosh greeted me with a big smile, a glass of water, and a dish of pasta. I kicked off my sandals and collapsed in the shade of the cherry tree. Fanicula came over and leaned into me. She liked to lean. And I clearly needed to be herded. She propped her chin on my thigh and looked up at me with love eyes.

Several geese waddled past and honked their way across the yard. Julio, the rowdy peacock, screeched from behind the villa. Luc yelled back at him, "Julio!" Julio screeched some more.

I told Luc about getting lost on the mountain. He had shown me the circular trails. "Ah, yes, that trail is not a circle," he said.

I gave him my cute, incredulous face. He laughed.

Lucky for me, an Italian masseur named Adriano was passing through that evening. I had just enough time for a hot bath before I received what I will always remember as the *No Stone Unturned Italian Massage*. Mmm.

Luc and his friends prepared a celebration for our last night at the villa. Several guests planned to leave the following morning, and Luc was going to play in a Didgeridoo Festival in Volterra.

Our hosts roasted pizzas in the gigantic stone oven behind the villa. Fresh mozarella, homemade pesto, organic herbs and vegetables from the garden, fragrant basil, and Nirdosh's magic marinara sauce. Luc played the didge while we dined, and two local girls belly danced in sheer pale blue gowns and veils with dramatic makeup on their eyes. Bells jiggled and jingled on their ankles and wrists.

After dinner, Nirdosh laid a warm, gentle hand on my shoulder. "You must come see me tonight."

"*Si*." I nodded.

A dozen travelers and a few neighbors laughed and danced for hours. Our Paris pastry chef surprised us with the flakiest chocolate puff pastries in the history of baking. No one wanted the celebration to end.

After awhile, I left the merry party and hiked up to Nirdosh's vine-covered cottage. Her pet owl, Athena, monitored my movements.

Nirdosh greeted me at the door with a warm smile, and scooped up a tiny, grey kitten who was too young to go outside.

"Can I hold her?"

She handed me the kitten, who purred and looked up at me with huge, intelligent eyes.

"Sit down," Nirdosh said, and handed me a small square of paper. "Write your name, date of birth, and place of residence." Nirdosh knew I was an American, but she didn't hold it against me.

I set the kitten in my lap and followed her instructions.

Her messy, cozy kitchen reminded me of my great-grandmother's house where I used to hang out as a child. Grandma Rosie had been an artist and a spiritual healer. AKA: *Weirdo* in that part of the world.

"Let me see your hand," Nirdosh said. She took my hand and turned it over with authority. Her skin felt cool and smooth. She studied my palm, then picked up a small crystal on a string and swung it back and forth.

I didn't understand what she was doing, but I had grown fond of Nirdosh during our week together, and this was her gift to me. She picked up the square of paper, turned it over, and drew several symbols on the back. "Put this under your pillow when you sleep," she said. I recognized one of the symbols as the eternal *Om*. Then she swung the pendulum some more.

After a moment, she laid the crystal on the table, and handed me a pad of paper and a pen. "Write this down," she said.

"You are carrying anger at yourself," she said. "It destroys your life and your beauty. You must express this anger and *let go*. Now. Top priority. Don't postpone."

I listened with respect and took notes. *Does this woman know I'm a therapist? Does she realize I've had more therapy than God?*

"One false belief recurs," she said, "a false problem. Your mind playing a trick..." She held my hands between her soft palms, closed her eyes for a moment, then opened them. "It's not you," she said. "Every day, twice a day, a.m. and p.m., you must look into the mirror and say *It's not me*."

I nodded.

She continued. "60% of your being is tied up with pain."
That is the last thing I want to hear right now.

"You must pay more attention to your spiritual life. Develop your spiritual gifts. Your healing power will give you extra energy," she said. "What kind of work you do?"

"Terapista."

"Terapista? What kind of *terapista?"*

"*Analista.*"

"Ahh..." she smiled and sat back in her chair. "I knew you were a witch."

We laughed together and talked awhile. She told me about her years in the ashram in India, and her travels with her wild teacher. She invited me to come back and visit in the spring.

After awhile, we grew tired. I hugged her and walked back to the villa.

In the morning, we all gathered for a bittersweet breakfast together. Tears welled as I looked out over the Tuscan countryside. It's heartbreaking to leave heaven and return to earth.

On my way out, I stroked Fanicula's head, and she dropped and rolled for a belly rub. When I squatted and rubbed her belly, she reached up with her front legs and hugged my neck.

I'll bet Nirdosh taught her to do that.

When I returned home, I threw a party for my friends. So much to be thankful for.

The next time I called my mother, I reported the good news about my thriving practice and the new training program. Surely she could be happy for me after all I'd been through with the murder, Joe's suicide...

"We can't see you as a professional," my mother said. She spat the words at me with that righteous condemnation of hers that leaves no room for discussion. *The Church Lady has spoken!*

A familiar old poison seared my stomach.

Of course they can't see me as a professional. They can't see me at all.

All they can see is the gelatinous muck of the projections they've dumped on me.

Why did I call her?
What was I thinking?
Why do I continue to smash my face against that wall?
Why can't I just give up on them?
Keep hope dead!
Keep hope dead!

I remembered a poem about a girl who tried to please her mother. The girl played the clarinet brilliantly in the Philharmonic. Her mother didn't like music. The girl made a delicious souffle. Her mother didn't like food. The girl performed all kinds of amazing feats, eager to earn her mother's approval. Each time, the girl's mother crushed her spirit with annihilating invalidation.

So, the girl cut off her own hands

Then, the mother bought her a pair of gloves.

Nirdosh was right. My family still had their hooks in me.

SCAPEGOAT

I'm fucking up, does anyone care?
I didn't prepare, does anyone care?
I'm over here making a mess of myself...
Is anyone there?
Does anyone care?

Look at me!
I'll slash my wrists
Look at me!!
I'll slit my throat
Look at me!!!
a bloody mess,
a worthless, faceless scapegoat

Look at me.
I'll dance around
Make a spectacle,
macabre clown.
Paint my face and run amok
because no one could give a fuck.

Why not be a crazy fool?
Eat and drink, laugh and die,
if no one cares, I cannot care.
If I can't win, I cannot try.

Can you see the sin you've done?
Can you see the pain I've had?
Never seen by anyone,
I'll shoot myself with your gun, Dad.

Audrey sits huddled on my cotton couch, her fingers tucked under her legs, and stares at the sculpture she created over the weekend. Her long, dark curls cascade over tanned, slender shoulders. She could have stepped out of Vogue magazine in her flowing, flowered dress, silk scarf, and platform shoes that lace up the calves.

Audrey is one of the sweetest people I know, and also one of the most self-destructive. And at 29, after several years of intensive psychotherapy, she still believes what her family says about her.

Bad. Crazy. Hopeless. Evil.

In fact, she's just received a letter from her father that reiterates these labels. He says she can't visit home until she *takes responsibility*.

Audrey is the family scapegoat, a required role she has filled since early childhood.

The irony is that she's done nothing *but* take responsibility for her parents' sins throughout her life, and it has nearly killed her. She drank the family Kool-Aid again and again to stay connected with them. As long as she agreed with her parents' judgments, and pretended to be bad, crazy, etc., she could pretend to have a family.

But betraying herself in this way led to despair. And despair led to desperate coping strategies like substance abuse, self-mutilation, and starvation. Sometimes Audrey believes that the only way to hold on to her true self is to die.

Audrey is haunted by memories. From age three to six, her parents left her alone with a sadistic male babysitter who molested and terrorized her. At five, when she finally asked for help, no one believed her.

Little Audrey served as an emotional caretaker for her mother, whose mood swings and debilitating depression made her a volatile and often absent parent.

At thirteen, ghosts from the past emerged full force, and Audrey suffered from nightmares, panic attacks, and suicidal thoughts. Her parents admitted her to a psychiatric hospital against her will, then sent her away to a long-term residential treatment facility in another state.

When Audrey finally came home at 15, she anesthetized her pain with alcohol. Again, her parents sent her away. This time to drug rehab.

And when she came home six months later and continued to numb her pain with alcohol, they kicked her out of the house.

Audrey survived on the streets for a few months, developed a drug habit, panhandled for change, and suffered additional sexual trauma at the hands of drug dealers.

At 17, her parents finally allowed her to come home and finish high school.

Audrey has some abandonment issues.

She leans forward and turns the sculpture so that I can see inside. A black box, three feet tall sits on the coffee table. I look in through a five-inch square window that Audrey has carved.

"It's dark," she says, "very dark," and sinks back into the couch.

I peer in through the window. The inside of the box is painted black, and a red rubber heart hangs from a string, exactly in the middle. Arrows of fire in silver, orange, and yellow aim at the heart. Three double-edged razor blades pierce the heart, and red paint drips from their shiny steel.

Audrey scoots up to the edge of the couch and points inside the box. "This is how I feel when they attack me."

Sorrow swells in my throat. Then anger. I've grown attached to Audrey during the past few years, and I feel fiercely protective of her.

Tears wash over Audrey's smooth, olive cheeks. She drops her face into her palms and sobs. "It hurts so much," she wails. "I just want to die."

"I know." I swallow my own tears. If Audrey sees them, she'll dry her eyes and take care of me instead.

"Why do they hate me so much?" She wails louder.

"It's not you that they hate, Audrey. They can't see you."

"I know." She wipes her nose with her forearm. "But why do they always have to say those horrible things about me?"

I study Audrey's lovely, youthful face, her soft brown eyes full of pain, and I marvel. *How could anyone be so cruel to their own child? They don't deserve her.*

"Look at their projections, Audrey. Your father is an alcoholic...he calls you alcoholic. Your mother is mentally ill...she calls you crazy. They abuse you, then call you abusive. The labels don't fit you."

"But I still believe them. They still have power over me." Audrey swallows and grows quiet. "I have to leave them, don't I?"

I nod.

"They're never going to change." Her big eyes look so sad.

"I don't know. Maybe not. But sacrificing yourself will not make them change."

Anger flashes in her eyes. "And it's making me sick."

"Yes. It's toxic."

We sit together in silence for a moment. Birds chirp near the open window, and I can see a clear, blue sky though the tree branches. A warm, spring day awaits outside.

"Audrey, you deserve to be loved. And to be seen. And to be appreciated for who you really are."

"Will I ever have that?"

"I believe you will. And as you give the abusers less access to your heart, you will create more space for people who care about you. The more you surround yourself with safe people who respect you, the more you will heal."

"I'm so sick of being blamed! I wish I could live in a bubble where they can't touch me."

"Maybe it's time to take back some of your power."

"How do I do that?"

"Refuse to tolerate any more abuse. Refuse to be their victim."

"But whenever I try to stick up for myself, they say I am hurting them."

"I know. It's crazy-making."

"And when I try to live my own life, they just attack harder."

"When you step out of that black sheep role and take care of yourself, it leaves them without a scapegoat."

"Well, they're busy grooming my little sister to be the next one. It's so sick. I wish I could get her out of there."

"That's sad."

"Can I leave this here?" She points to the box.

"Of course."

"And this?" She hands me her father's letter.

I watch Audrey rise from the couch and take a graceful turn toward the door. The fresh scent of shampoo lingers behind her.

At the door, she spins around and stares at the box.

Audrey attacks the box like a kitten pouncing on a toy. She tears open the lid, rips the razor blades out of the heart, and throws them into the box. Then she cradles the heart between her palms and holds it tight against her chest. "I'm guarding it from now on," she says. "It's mine."

During the past twenty years, patients and students have asked me, "How does a family choose a scapegoat?"

I answered different ways in different contexts. Some families choose a child who is vulnerable in some way, or one who is different, *The Outsider*. Others select *The Strong One*, who is sturdy enough to bear the projections of the family. A *Sin Eater*.

After practicing psychotherapy for a few years, I noticed that the scapegoat was often the healthiest person in the family, *The Truth Teller*. One who could see through disturbed dynamics and refuse to participate.

Sometimes it's *The Sensitive One*, the one with a heart, who cares about the feelings of others and tries to stay connected at any cost. Or *The Compassionate One* who refuses to hurt the abuser with retaliation.

And sometimes it's the child who most resembles the abuser, who mirrors unacceptable and despised qualities that must be disavowed and projected.

Some of these dynamics have become archetypes: *Cinderella*, who sweeps the chimney and serves her siblings while she longs to be part of her family. *Jane Eyre*, whose aunt was eaten up with envy and hatred: "Jane is mad! She's a fiend!" the aunt said of the orphan in her care when she shipped her off to a hellish institution.

But Jane knew who she was, and that truth kept her sane.

Anger can also keep a child sane – that pure outrage that rises up in response to injustice.

Laura Esquivel captures this kind of power in *Like Water for Chocolate*. Young Tita's mother berates her and treats her like a slave, then haunts her from the grave. Mother's venomous ghost appears outside Tita's window, calls her a slut and tells her she's going to hell for her sins.

Of course, the mother actually *did* all the things she accuses her daughter of.

Tita lives in terror until the night she confronts her mother's ghost. *You did all those things, not me. I hate you. I've always hated you.*

With those magic words, the ghost evaporates, never to return. After a lifetime of persecution, Tita is no longer vulnerable to her mother's curses.

It's like Harry says, "The burial of truth is the source of suffering. The unburying of truth is our salvation."

Harry and I have an ongoing argument about one thing. He says *Trauma Recovery* is an oxymoron; that trauma never really goes away.

I don't want to believe that, so I found a theory to support my preferred belief. According to Non-Linear Dynamic Systems Theory, a dynamic system, such as a human being, can be perturbed in various ways until a state shift occurs. I apply this theory to traumatic states and other states of mind. New relational experiences can facilitate state shifts, and new attractor states can, in time, overtake old patterns. Emotional memories may not go away, but their chattering can sometimes be drowned out by new memories.

Harry says Invariant Organizing Principles govern the psyche and determine our perceptions of reality.

I say, "Nothing is invariant." And I intend to prove it. By reorganizing myself.

So there.

But here I was, ensconced in my new, peaceful life, still harassed by ghosts from the past.

What I really needed was *Yoda* to complete my training.

So, I asked Harry to analyze me.

"It would be an honor," he said.

Being in psychoanalysis is like being remodeled. I sat across from Harry four afternoons a week and felt my psyche rearrange itself, bearing walls and all.

At first, kid fears haunted me: *What if he morphs into a monster like the others? What if he betrays me like my family? What if he looks inside me and doesn't like what he sees?*

Then I had a dream:

Harry and I were camping in the desert with our study group. We stood together, nude, in the campground shower. Me, completely naked, completely safe, with a father figure.

In our Monday afternoon session, I told Harry my dream.

"Cool!" he said.

No interpreting, no analyzing. Just *cool*.

God, I love that man.

Harry provided new relational experiences in analysis that I had missed out on in childhood. He believed in me. And he respected me.

With Harry, I found an emotional home.

I told him about the men I dated and asked his advice. He validated my perceptions and laughed at my jokes. And when I arrived sleep-deprived after a decadent weekend, he made me a cappuccino.

A few months into analysis, I had another dream:

I sat next to Harry in a recliner, the way my little sister always sat with my Dad. It was awkward because I was bigger than Harry, but you know how dreams are. Somehow it worked.

For the first time in my life, I had a father.

I used to think therapeutic transformation was all about insight. But, after twenty years of training, I had insight out the wazoo and still needed a father. Lucky for me, it's never too late to have a happy childhood. At least not when it comes to finding an emotional home.

Things with my own family were never good. Harry helped me understand what had happened to me.

I was four years old when I first asked, "Why does Daddy hate me?" That question whipped my heart around like a nasty Midwestern tornado for forty years.

When I started psychoanalysis, my father had not spoken to me in ten years. My mother blamed me and insisted that I make peace at any price. I refused and held the line: "I will not tolerate any more abuse."

My family made me crazy, but I decided it was time for a visit. I don't remember why. Perhaps because of my mother's poor health. Maybe to measure my progress. Or to say good-bye.

Probably for all kinds of reasons that I was not conscious of. In any case, I booked a flight and planned to visit the crime scene.

As soon as I purchased the ticket, a vault of bad spirits busted open and spewed into my soul.

For three months leading up to the trip, hecklers in my head harassed me. The old nightmares returned. I woke up in the middle of the night screaming, being beaten and strangled in my dreams.

Poor little Shnuckie didn't know what think. She sat at the foot of my bed at 2:00 a.m. and stared, her dark eyes intense with concern.

I found myself in strange states of mind, sometimes in the midst of a peaceful weekend. One afternoon, while walking in the park, I suddenly felt caged, isolated, and hopeless.

I took it all to Harry.

"I thought I worked through this garbage ten years ago. Now I find myself in traumatic states in the middle of a sunny day. What is happening to me? I feel like I'm dying."

"You are what is called *dying in the truth*, which means feeling all that has hurt you, in its total intensity, and it is motherfucking deadly."

I nodded. Then I grinned. "And what theoretical framework is that?"

"I call it *Agony Therapy*," he said. "People come to me feeling a little blue, a little blah, and then we go deeper into the truth of what happened to them: agony."

I laughed.

We looked at each other in silence for a moment. The energy of our connection reverberated through my bones.

"I feel haunted," I said.

"The ghosts and the darkness are emotional memories taking physical form," he said. "A gut level remembering of all you were made to feel."

"It's true. It's like I'm snapped back in time. I remember exactly how it felt to be that scared little girl, all alone."

"It feels awful when these things are stirred up, but it's an opportunity to heal it."

I nodded. "What about this horrible shame?" I asked. "I keep thinking about how they call me a *piece of shit*, and then I start feeling like I really am a piece of shit. It feels like a curse."

"You are allowing yourself to be defined by their projections. Don't take it on. Whatever you do, don't turn against yourself."

"It's hard."

"I know." He gave me that familiar look: *we are siblings in the same darkness*. Harry had been an abused kid too. He understood.

"I feel stuck. Stuck, stuck, stuck. I want to move on."

"The most profound way to move on is to not move on at all, but to be very present. Embrace it all. Hold it in your heart. But, do not be its victim. Be friendly to your own feelings, and you'll move on far more profoundly."

I nodded. I knew it to be true. I preached it to my patients. Why was it so hard to practice?

"Once you get to the purity of those feelings, that truth will make you immune," he said. "The projections won't penetrate you anymore."

I listened and tried to absorb his wisdom.

"*Moving on* is a recipe for dissociation." He crinkled up his forehead. "A time bomb."

"I know." I had seen it many times. The ones who say *the past doesn't affect me...just leave the past in the past*. They were the ones who went on to repeat their parents' mistakes and become their own worst nightmare.

"The pathway to forgiveness and compassion is through all of the anger and rage," he said. "Even murderous hatred."

I thought about it. I remembered when I first learned this truth, fifteen years earlier, the poems I wrote. Why do I always have to be reminded of these things?

"What can I do to get unstuck?" I asked.

"You've got more grieving to do."

"Ugh. Not that again. I'm tired of grieving. Why is this stuff coming up again after all these years?"

"This is how we heal: in layers. When we enter a new phase of development, we revisit the same themes again, on a deeper level."

I scrunched up my face and stuck out my tongue.

Harry smiled. "You're *Grief Girl*," he said.

"I don't want to be *Grief Girl*. I want to be *Happiness Girl*."

"You will." He looked at me with loving eyes. "You will."

I had healed myself through many different means over the years, but nothing loosed the truth quite like the combination of walking and writing. Long walks that allowed time to free-associate, compose, and listen to the ever-louder voice of truth in my soul.

It's hard to cry when no one is there to catch your tears. And Dad beat them out of me at an early age with his *I'll give you something to cry about* program. But, twenty years later and 2000 miles away, after I walked and wrote enough, eventually I could cry, usually at a really inconvenient time.

I used to think crying was essential for healing trauma, but my patients have taught me otherwise. They each find their own unique way to release pain. Some rarely cry. Others can't stop crying. Some rage. Some paint. Some write music. Some talk. Some just walk and walk.

Forrest Gump ran. Neil Peart rode his motorcycle.

Mourning has a life, rhythm, and timetable of its own, and it is not linear. Loss and grief ebb and flow, up and down, all around. More like a roller coaster ride than like the Five Stages of Grief I learned in grad school.

The thing about loss and trauma: the only way out of it is through it. We have to acknowledge the pain and feel it if we want to heal it.

Going deeper into the truth can frighten and overwhelm, but the truth will set you free.

After three months of demons and dread, accompanied by Harry's empathy and validation, I bucked up and got on a plane.

238

Whenever I visit my family I feel like a black woman at a Klan rally. It's always the same routine. My brother rails against *Those Damn Librals* while Fox News blares from three T.V.'s: two upstairs, one downstairs. I sneak through the house and turn off the T.V.'s. Ten minutes later, they're back on.

On my first day in Ohio, I sat in my brother's back yard while he held court. He followed his usual script. First, he ridiculed my life's work, and counseled me to abandon those *losers* to work with *positive people* like he does in his sales job. Then he bragged about his big income and brilliant investments. Then he washed down his *happy pill* with a beer. His happy pill gets bigger every year.

Finally, he discussed politics:

"That Hillary Clinton's tryin' tuh start uh *Adopt a Nigger Program,*" he said. "One uh these days we're all gonna git one in a crate with a note on it sayin', *this one's yers - take care of it.*"

My nine-year-old nephew shot at birds with his new BB gun while my brother's wife pecked at me like an enraged turkey and demanded to know why I didn't vote for George Dubyah Bush.

But there is one bit of logic the clan has grasped -- it is their own version of Aristotle's syllogism.

Major Premise: All Liberals are evil.
Minor Premise: All Californians are Liberals.
Conclusion: Cate is evil.

Oh, well.
If they liked me, I'd have to talk to them.

When I arrived at my parents' home, my father walked past me as though I did not exist. He gave my nephew a big hug, glared at me with fiery hatred, stomped into the next room, and slammed the door behind him.

Dad did not speak to me at all. So I left.

When I got home to Santa Monica, I kissed the ground. *There's no place like home. There's no place like home.*

Then I kissed Rafa, who met me at the airport and took me to the pub for Shepherd Clan Cult Debriefing.

A couple of hours later, we emerged into the sun, giggling like a pair of teenagers playing hooky from school.

Harry and I continued to meet four times a week. I brought him my dreams and insights, and told him some of the horrors and humiliations of my childhood: the beatings, the trash wagon, the sexual harassment, the murdered kitten, the disappeared horse.

He listened and resonated.

"It felt like they *wanted* to traumatize me," I said, "like they took pleasure in it."

Harry frowned.

"Why do they need to be so cruel?" I asked.

"They enact their own trauma on you," he said. "They treat you the way they were treated."

"I could write a dissertation on the unconscious enactment and intergenerational transmission of trauma, but I still can't get past how it feels: it feels personal. My father looks at me with such hatred, like he wants to kill me."

Harry listened.

"Dad was horribly abused, and my mother had a neglectful, narcissistic mother, though she'll never admit it."

"Those things they can't admit, they pass on to you."

"It's so frustrating. I feel like the boy in *The Emperor's New Clothes*. I've watched this craziness my whole life while the rest of the clan looks on in denial."

"Dissociation."

"You really think they can't see it?"

"They can't bear to see it. That's why they project it onto you."

"Well, it's toxic."

"It certainly is."

"Sometimes when Dad whipped me, he looked like he was in a trance. I screamed louder and louder to snap him out of it. I felt like Luke Skywalker, yearning to reach the traumatized young man encased in the scary Vader suit."

"Do you think he was in a dissociative state?"

"Probably. Flashed back to his own father's violent outbursts. But how can my dad be so loving and accepting of my sister, my cousins, some random girl at my wedding..." I stopped to breathe. "Why does he have to devalue *me?*"

"He must feel very vulnerable."

"*Vulnerable?*" My face heated up.

"Yes, vulnerable."

"Vulnerable to what?"

"I don't know...what do you think, Doc?"

I thought about it. I didn't want to think about it, but I wanted to give him a smart answer. "I don't know...shame? His sister always said he was afraid of me. I could never figure out why. Maybe he's afraid of being exposed. A preemptive strike?"

Harry nodded. "Maybe."

"Maybe closeness feels dangerous to him. When he was a little boy, his mother chased him around with a butcher knife. When he was a teenager, his father threw him through a window."

"No wonder he feels so vulnerable."

If that old man says that word one more time, I am going to scream.

But he kept saying it. Week after week. And deconstructed my belief that my parents' abusive behavior had something to do with me.

It had very little to do with me.

It wasn't personal.

They treated me the same way their parents had treated them. Automatically. Unconsciously.

That's what happens when parents don't heal their own wounds.

My family was more fragile than I had realized. Their aggression was self-protective. Kill or be killed.

Just like my kids.

If my theories were true for the emotionally orphaned kids I loved, were they also true for my emotionally orphaned parents?

SNAKE MEDICINE

*"When I have been traumatized, my only hope
for being deeply understood is to form a connection
with someone who knows the same darkness."*
- Robert D. Stolorow, Ph.D.

"To have suffered much is like knowing many languages."
- George Eliot

"Some of the best medicines are derived from poisons."
- my buddy, Ben, age 14

"Is there anybody out there? Is there anybody out there?"

George leans forward in his chair, terror in his eyes. His long arms reach out to grab the invisible. The muscles in his face and neck pull taut.

He is remembering.

George is 54, a talented M.D. and devoted father who sees me four times a week for psychoanalysis. He finds himself snapped back in time into states of terrifying aloneness. His belief, based in his childhood experience, that there is *no one out there* who cares about him creates hopelessness and depression that shackle his life in the present.

I watch him wave his hands, and I feel echoes of his fear in my chest. He looks like he is about to cry. I hope he can.

I want George to feel understood and accompanied in this moment.

I search my emotional memories for an experience akin to his:

I'm thirteen years old, curled up on the hardwood floor in my bedroom, struggling to protect my body from the punches and kicks of a bullying brother. I scream, "Mom! Help! Mom!"

I can hear her in the kitchen. I panic when she doesn't respond. The panic turns into hopelessness.

I use this memory to help George put words to his emotional state.

Terrified. Abandoned. Invisible...

I empathize with George's experience of feeling alone throughout his life.

He looks at me with vulnerable eyes, filled with tears. "That's exactly how I feel," he says.

He takes a deep breath and exhales. His body relaxes. He falls back into his chair.

"When did you first feel there was someone out there?" I ask.

He closes his eyes and searches his memory. After a few moments of silence, we both realize the answer is, "Now."

Lali, my Art Therapy mentor, once told me a story she heard from a Native American shaman. A young warrior who wants to become Medicine Man must be bitten by poisonous snakes in a ceremony. His survival is the sign of an authentic healer.

A true shaman possesses the power to transmute deadly venom into life-saving medicine.

Living through different kinds of trauma is like learning many emotional languages. Or, as Harry says, "The best training for this work is going through a lot of bad shit."

Traumatized patients need to sense that the therapist has *been there* in some way, and confronted the ghosts that terrify them. They need someone to go into the darkness with them and help bear the pain while showing the way through it.

Some therapists maintain an emotional distance from the suffering of their patients and call this *objectivity*.

But if I distance myself for my own comfort, my patient may feel I've left him alone in his nightmare. Like his family did.

Some trauma survivors cannot bear to confront the truth of what happened to them and choose instead, consciously or unconsciously, to identify with their abusers. They pass on their unprocessed trauma to others.

Many survivors get stuck in a loop of enactments and unconsciously play out their traumatic tale with new characters in the hope that the story will end differently. They try to master it by living it again.

Some turn against themselves and take on the deadly projections of their families as a way of staying connected to them. One precocious young woman told me, "Treating myself like shit is the only way to feel connected to the people who call me a *piece of shit*."

Others live a life of numbness, walling off the pain, but also walling off joy, aliveness, and intimacy.

And some just give up and end the pain for good. Like Joe.

I asked Harry one day, "Why do abused children hate themselves?"

"It's because they've been treated like they are worthless," he said. "It is so hard to set that aside; to deny its all-defining truth."

Abused and neglected children believe that no one cares about them.

As a child, I found teachers who cared about me, and I sponged up their emotional nourishment. I fared pretty well for a few years, in spite of everything.

Then, when I was nine, my baby sister was born.

Rebecca was a blue baby, and she lived in an incubator for six weeks at a Children's Hospital 100 miles from home. She was tiny and fragile, and when she finally came home, everyone was nervous. Rebecca had suffered severe brain damage, but no one knew why, and her terrible seizures required frequent trips to the E.R.

Every time Rebecca learned a new trick, like crawling a little or holding her spoon, she had another bout of seizures that made her forget everything she had learned.

Dad's rage ramped up under the burgeoning stress.

Farming didn't provide enough income, so Dad drove long hauls for a trucking company. Sometimes he stayed away for several days.

Mom was anxious and overwhelmed, so I took care of her as well as I could. The shadow of her depression fell on me, and my nine-year-old needs got lost in a crowd of more important things.

Our family pediatrician expressed concern about my developmental needs and asked how I was coping with the sick baby. I told him what my mother required me to say: *she's a blessing*.

I found refuge at church and at school, and created a colorful world of art and music in my bedroom. But, I never knew when my father or brother would burst through the door in a violent rage.

"It was like living with a terrorist," Harry said.

It sure was.

I loved my baby sister. I called her Pooh Bear, and bought her a stuffed Tigger. She chewed on him when she was teething.

My father loved her too, and showed her tenderness that I had never known.

I took care of Pooh Bear when my mom went to town. It was nerve-wracking to be alone with a fragile baby in such a remote place. I grew into a sensitive, anxious caregiver, grateful for my bond with my sister, an oasis of tenderness in a dangerous family.

By the time I got away to college at seventeen, my self-esteem had been demolished by years of abuse. I barely spoke. I sat in the dorm cafeteria frozen in self-conscious silence and waited to be ridiculed. My new friends were puzzled.

One thing I felt good about was my skill as a caretaker. So I went to work as a nurse's aid. My family did not help pay for college, so I had a lot of work to do.

I worked at Styrest Nursing Home, where I earned $3.75 an hour in 1981. At the end of each eight-hour shift, my feet and legs felt like they'd been beaten with a bat. It was the hardest work I'd ever done, and that includes heavy farm labor.

As low girl on the totem pole, I inherited The Ghetto, a wing of patients with persistent bedsores, who did not speak, and had no family. I learned to change adult diapers and clean out bedpans without gagging.

I tried to connect with my patients. Most of the time, they just lay there all day in silence. Few made eye contact.

I talked to them, sang to them, combed their hair, and rubbed lotion into their dry skin.

I looked out for them. When other staff were too rough, or took my patients' belongings, I confronted them. Maybe these people didn't have any family, but they had me.

One day, while I chatted and sang to Mary, a mute stroke survivor, she looked into my eyes and burst into a radiant smile. She held my gaze a long time and teared up. So did I.

Over time, some of my people appeared to come back to life. I can still see the light in their eyes. They responded to the power of connection.

I thought of Mary years later when I met my first catatonic adolescent patient at the psych hospital. I talked to her every day. Then, one day she looked deep into my eyes and spoke. And cried. The incest secrets she told me were enough to explain her breakdown.

Once I settled into the safety of the university environment, I began to heal and thrive.

When I visited my parents during semester break, they crushed me down to size and threw me back into the trash wagon where I belonged. How dare I try to climb out.

I realized that I would need more distance to heal.

About 2000 miles.

After I moved to California, I visited my parents every year. I thought I had to. My mother didn't have any other friends. She needed someone to talk to about her problems.

Going home was like smashing my face against the same concrete wall again and again.

I don't know what I was thinking. The same thing as every other abused kid, I guess: *maybe they'll change.* Clinging to the hope that keeps us stuck.

But they didn't change. And every time I went home, my family ripped open my wounds. The nightmares started up again. Depression dragged me down again.

Back in California, I took long walks on the beach and wrote dozens of poems.

emotional orphan

I wish I was an orphan for real.
Then I could make a family out of what I choose,
make my own dynamics, my own rules.

I wish I had a slate wiped clean.
Then I could paint reality, paint it as it should be,
something that is fitting for the likes of me.

I wish I had the power to heal.
Then I could fill these caverns with light,
never return to the dark night.

Then I'd find a home for all I feel.
I wish I was an orphan for real.

I had spent my life serving as little mother to my sister, psychic nurse to my mother, punching bag for my brother, and garbage receptacle for my father's overflow.

I always had a roof over my head, but I never had a home.

Harry helped me make sense of all of it. He understood my family, and he wasn't afraid to talk about my sainted sister. "It's a strange message," he said, "that you have to be a vegetable to be loved."

I hadn't thought of it that way before, but it did seem odd that my brain dead sister was so loved while I was so hated.

I realized all the weird ways I had unconsciously tried to cripple myself throughout my life. Now it made sense.

Worse, I thought Pooh Bear's suffering was my fault. I just didn't know that yet. Harry sniffed that one out early on, but it eluded me for years. He watched me doing penance in other relationships. He analyzed my dreams.

For years, I had nightmares about babies. I left a baby on top of the car and drove off, sat on a baby and squashed it, gave birth to a deformed baby, left a baby in the bathtub and let it drown.

"What's with all the babies?" I asked. I knew the answer, but I loved to listen to Harry wax psychoanalytical. And I really loved the validation.

"You must have been terrified," he said, "left alone to care for such a fragile infant when you were only a child yourself."

I nodded.

"You were so neglected," he said.

"They say I was spoiled."

He shook his head. "Amazing."

On the morning of my last analytic session with Harry, I sat in my reading chair with a cup of coffee and pondered the closing of my case. A poem popped out. It was about my baby sister.

aquittal

I didn't kill her.
She was already dead.
A lifetime undoing crimes not committed.
She's still dead, and I have a life to live.
Another case closed:
accused -
aquitted.

Funny how children make sense of things. Usually by blaming themselves.

When I had mourned enough, I wrote a letter to my father.

Dear Dad,
You will always be that tall, handsome young man
I fell in love with when I was four…

I told him how hard it had been to live with his abuse, and what it had been like to heal from it.

I told him about my life in California the past twenty years. Not that I expected him to be interested. I told him anyway. For myself.

I told him how much I still loved him, how I had always longed for a father, and how I hoped we could be friends someday while we were both still on the planet.

And I meant it. Finally, miraculously, I was done.

It's funny how the poison drains away quite suddenly. An overnight cure after twenty years of hard work.

I proofread the letter, sealed it, and walked out into a sunny summer day. As I watched my engraved business stationary slide down into the mailbox, I felt whole.

It no longer matters how he responds.
It's not me. It never was.

My family did not change. I went on with my life feeling more free. I gave up on trying to reach my father, and accepted the fact that I would never have a father.

"Some problems in our lives, Cate, are best dealt with by walking the fuck away from them," Harry said.

He had such a way with words.

not broken

little girl toddling through
smoldering stench, aftermath
bodies strewn, eerie silence, hissing fire

shell-shocked, paralyzed,
staring at the truth of
an all-pervasive, personal funeral pyre

she can't fix them.
they lay lifeless.
bewildered little child, so alone;

time to leave
this tragic mess
and find herself a new home.

ME TOO

*"Then you will know the truth,
and the truth will set you free."
- Jesus of Nazareth*

On a January morning, five months later, my mother left a
message on my answering machine. Pooh Bear had died.

I looked out at the trees from my canyon cottage on a cold,
grey day, and pulled the shawl tighter around my shoulders. A
red-shouldered hawk stared back at me from his perch, a few feet
from the deck.

Shnuckie hopped onto the sofa and molded her warm body into
my thigh. I stroked her velvety fur. My throat hurt from crying as I
took a deep breath and forced myself to dial my mother's number.

"Hello?"

"Hi, Mom. How are you doing?"

Her sisters and nieces chatted and laughed in the background. I
could picture them. Aunt Susie, giggling and flirting with the men
while her ditzy daughter mimicked her. My brother's wife,
glowering in her Catholic corner, judging everyone.

Dad quietly dying from grief in a crowd of relatives.

It's so strange how he can be the designated asshole of the clan
and also the only one with a heart.

"I'm doing great!" Mom chirps. "We're having a good time."

I hate that phony voice she dons to ward off any honest emotion,
and to warn me that I had better fake it too.

I know it's dangerous to be vulnerable with my mother, but the
little girl in me thinks *maybe she'll be different this time*. And I am
finished with faking it.

My colleagues had sent me home from the hospital where I was
working an on-call shift that morning. My old pal, Karen, saw the
pain in my eyes and asked what was wrong. Her kindness loosed
my tears, and then I couldn't turn them off.

I told her Pooh Bear had died.

"I'm so sorry," she said, and hugged me. Karen had lost her own sister to breast cancer a few years earlier.

My coworkers hugged me and said, "You should go home and take care of yourself."

My friends said the things that I had always longed to hear from my mother.

So, the naïve child in me tells my mother, "They sent me home from work because I couldn't stop crying."

A long moment of silence. I can hear her breathing, her sisters giggling, then her signature sigh of annoyance. "You should be rejoicing! You should be happy for her!"

Smack!

Snapped back in time, I become that little girl again. I reach out to my mother for comfort and slam into a religious iceberg.

From age nine to seventeen I cared for Pooh Bear, changed her diapers, held her bottle, sang her lullabies. Our favorite was "Rock and Roll Lullaby" by B.J. Thomas.

She laughed when I shook out the clean sheets in the laundry, and chuckled uncontrollably whenever I danced or did jumping jacks. She would have loved to watch me bounce around with the girls on Unit 400.

Pooh Bear had a great laugh. A deep, wicked cackle from her tiny, broken body. She never learned to talk, but her gorgeous, dark eyes shone with love when she smiled.

She wasn't meant to live past eighteen, with her bad heart and seizures. She made it to thirty-six in Depends diapers, drinking liquified baby food from a bottle.

When Pooh Bear died, she pulled my heart out of my chest and took it with her.

My brother picks up the phone and blusters, "Yuh know, I was closer to her than anybody."

Right. That's why you haven't touched her in thirty years.

I do not respond. I can hear the ice klinking in his highball glass.

He continues. "Yuh know, she shoulda died years ago."

Ahh...now I see how close you were.

"Let me talk to Dad," I say.

My father comes to the phone. He hasn't spoken to me in ten years.

Dad drops feelings like hot coals. Whenever I had tried to hug him, he pulled away. When I said, "I love you," he clenched his jaw and stared his steely stare.

Why is he always so angry at me?

But now Dad's heart is busted open. He's choking on tears and can hardly talk.

"I don't know how you and Mom have survived all these years," I say.

They almost lost Pooh Bear many times. Midnight trips to the E.R., round the clock vigils in the ICU.

"This is how it's felt for thirty-six years," he says. His voice is soft and tired.

There it is. A glimpse at my dad. One I've waited for like Haley's Comet.

I always knew he was in there. Like an earthquake survivor trapped under the rubble.

Dad's vulnerability reminds me of that day in my office when Mario finally dropped his Satanist act and sobbed.

"Do you have room for a couple of old farts out there?" he asks me.

Oh my God. He's desperate. They haven't been here in twenty years. He hates California.

This is the man I've longed to know for forty years. All those years I watched him cuddle Pooh Bear and talk baby talk to her. All those years he called me *That Piece of Shit Sister of Yours*. Or so my brother says.

For forty years I longed to reach him, flung my heart at him, mauled it on his barbed wire, picked it up, flung it again.

I never understood what was wrong with me. Why he didn't like me.

I lived out the drama in endless reruns. Then I wrote it out and cried it out and talked it out until finally the pain loosened its grip on me.

"You're always welcome here," I say.

My body floods with warmth and hope that both excite and scare me. My father is not a safe person to be close to.

But I don't care any more. What's he going to do to me that he hasn't already done?

"I'm here if you need anything," I say. "I love you, Dad."

"Me too," my father says.

They never made it to California, but that didn't matter.

I had found an opening in his armor.

Two weeks later I visited my parents in Ohio. As I carried my suitcases into Pooh Bear's room, memories engulfed me. Pooh Bear's little stuffed Tigger sat on the shelf, thirty-six years old now. And the quilt Grandma Cate made for her covered the foot of the bed. Tears flooded my eyes and poured down my cheeks.

Mom came in. I hugged her.

She held me for moment, then looked at my face. She smiled. "We've been looking at her pictures," she said, and motioned to a scrapbook of Pooh Bear's life.

In that moment, I caught a glimpse of the mother I had always longed for. A woman who could respond to me instead of whacking me with a Bible.

Bless her heart. She has her moments.

That night I slept in Pooh Bear's room. I had a dream:

I'm walking out of a warm, cozy coffee shop on a cold, windy night in Chicago. As I pull my scarf tighter around my neck, I run into my old friend, Carol. We walk together for a few blocks through a festive uptown district, joyfully chatting and catching up. She is excited about matchmaking me with a friend of her husband. Out of nowhere, a man appears and starts harassing me. I try to get away from him, but he is aggressive and persistent. He is angry.

I don't recognize him. He's wearing white jeans and a white sweater. He looks a few years younger than me. What is his problem? Carol disappears into the dark and, before I realize what has happened, I am on the sidewalk, on my back. The man is sitting on top of me, punching my face. He tries to strangle me. I scream, "HELP!" as loudly as I can, over and over, in different tones, desperate to attract attention. A group of elegant party guests, all dressed in black, watch from the balcony above. When they turn to walk back inside, I scream louder, frantic. I try to summon them. They watch in silence. The man strangles me. I try to scream...

I wake up and find my 70-year-old father standing in the doorway of the bedroom in the dark.

"Are you havin' a *bad* dream?" he asks. He puts the accent on *bad* like Bob Dylan does. It's a Kentucky thing.

"Was I shouting?"

Dad says nothing, but turns and walks to the bathroom.

I pad to the kitchen for a drink of water. On the way back, I pass Dad. He squeezes my bicep. "You're havin' bad dreams, girl."

My mind is confused, working to reconcile colliding narratives at 3:00 a.m.

For years I had nightmares about my scary father lurking in the dark. *How did the monster of my childhood become my protector?*

I can smell my brain circuits smoking.

I go back to bed. My mind reels.

The terror was that no one cared.
No one responded, no matter
how loudly I screamed.
Terror is being left alone with the attacker.
When my brother was hurt, it was a tragedy.
When I was hurt, it was insignificant.
When you're a piece of shit,
it does not matter what happens to you.

I can take a beating. The real trauma arose out of the lack of response from the onlooking environment. From feeling dehumanized and invisible. From looking to a mother who was not there.

I lie awake while my mind tries to sort itself. I remember Heinz Kohut's last speech, the one he made a few days before he died. He talked about the emotional suffering caused by emotionally absent mothers. And he talked about the Nazi war camps. He believed the lion's share of psychological damage to survivors resulted not from the overt abuse, but from being treated as less than human.

Like a *piece of shit*.

I returned to Los Angeles feeling discombobulated and skeptical. I told my friends about the change in Dad.
Do you think it will last?
I don't know...

Two months later, I booked another flight to Ohio to support Mom and Dad in their grief.

I purchased the ticket and braced myself for the usual haunting. But the ghosts never came.

I no longer found myself in traumatic states. Nor did I feel defined by my family's projections.

Instead, I felt angry.

And happy. Sometimes downright joyful.

Hmm.

I couldn't wait to tell Harry.

I had graduated from analysis two years earlier, but I still discussed cases with him every few weeks. Including the case of my family.

"Our first case is always our mother," he said. "And it is always a failed case."

Harry had brought a bottle of *Veuve Clicquot* to our last analytic session, and we drank champagne while we chatted.

I thanked him for his priceless investment in my life, and told him the most important thing: "For the first time in my life, I feel like I have a father."

He gave me a bear hug with sound effects and kissed me on the cheek. "I'm very proud of you," he said.

Coming back to Harry's office for consultation made me feel all grown up. I brought him the gossip from our psychoanalytic institute and gave him pages to read from my writing projects.

His 1970's velvet psychoanalytic couch still looked new, with a tissue paper cover on the pillow. I had never used it. I preferred to sit up and look at him.

I grinned as I remembered a joke Harry once told me:

> *A patient says to her analyst, "Kiss me."*
> *The analyst says, "You know I can't do that.*
> *I shouldn't even be lying here next to you."*

"I'm going to Ohio again," I said.

"Uh oh." He crinkled his forehead.

"I don't feel haunted anymore."

He looked curious.

"I feel like a big wound that has finally closed up."

He nodded.

"I feel happy and strong."

He listened, as though waiting for a shoe to drop.

"And *PISSED*."

He grinned.

"I've been brewing with fury that I haven't felt for twenty years. I went back and dug out some of the poems I wrote when I first went to therapy. It's all there."

"Did you bring them?"

"Of course." I pulled the old pages out of my briefcase.

"The thing that still drives me nuts is how my mother plays the victim and refuses to take any responsibility for her behavior."

Harry nodded toward my pages. "Let's hear it."

I read aloud:

where were you?

"where was I?" you always say,
"when all these things were going on?"
feigning childish innocence.

Stymied mute, I play along...

...where were you when Daddy came
and smashed my brother's precious head
into the jagged, dirty rocks
until the boy was nearly dead?

...the red and blue of welt and bruise
we learned young to accessorize
while mother hid her bloody hands
beneath a shroud of holy lies.

"Wow." Harry raised his eyebrows.
I studied his expression.
"You skipped some verses."
"Yeah. It was a long litany."
"I'll bet."
"I asked her one time why she let them beat me up."
"And?"
"She said she would rather be hit than criticized."
"Huh?"
I nodded.
"Has she ever been hit?"
"No."
He just stared in disbelief.
"Her response is always the same: *I have it worse than you so stop complaining.*"
"You were never allowed to have any needs or feelings of your own."

"When I express a need, it triggers her. And she responds with rage. The rage she was never able to express toward her own narcissistic mother."

Harry looked at me with the compassion of a concerned father. "That is so profoundly true that it just gave me a chill."

"One of the times when my brother burst into my room and attacked me, I curled up in a ball on the hardwood floor, covered my head with my arms to block his punches and kicks, and screamed for help. She was in the kitchen, at the bottom of the stairs. I could hear her."

Harry looked riveted.

"She ignored my cries. I screamed louder and louder. He kept punching and kicking."

"What a nightmare."

"But the most awful part was, after he left, while I cried in my room, I could hear them in the kitchen. She badmouthed me while she cooked him a cheeseburger. He was her little agent."

"Whoa."

"Well, not little. He was a six-foot-tall football player."

"How old were you?"

"Thirteen."

Harry teared up. "She fed you to the wolves."

I felt more angry than sad. "When I am honest about who she is, I don't get triggered."

"You're becoming immune."

I smiled. "Anger is the antidote to feeling terrorized, isn't it?"

He nodded. "The truth will set you free."

"It's a painful truth. I can see now why I denied it for so long."

"It's becoming clearer to you that none of this was your fault. No more sacrificing your truth to maintain the tie."

I shook my head. "No more."

Two weeks later, I met my parents in Ohio and we took a road trip to Kentucky to visit Dad's sister who was dying from cancer. She had always been a good friend to me.

It felt weird to travel together as a family after twenty years of estrangement.

Dad reminisced about his childhood in rural Kentucky.

"I once started the same school three times in one year," he said with a bitter laugh.

"How did you manage that?"

"The old man had to move every few months."

He talked about the hardships and humiliations of growing up in poverty with a violent, philandering father and a volatile, neglectful mother. I had heard these stories before, always steeped in rage. But now he laughed from a distance. He was a good storyteller.

While in Kentucky, we visited Pooh Bear's grave. She was buried beside Grandma Cate, my other childhood buddy. It felt good to be near both of them again.

We moseyed around the quiet cemetery on a windy autumn afternoon. I inhaled deep, full breaths of freshly washed country air as my boot heels sank into the moist Kentucky soil. Piles of wet, brown leaves gathered in wreathes around the headstones. Dad looked for familiar names, and talked about the ones he knew.

Then we took a drive through the countryside to see where the old one room schoolhouse used to stand. Dad had dropped out of school after the sixth grade and worked to support his family.

As I listened to Dad's stories, I noticed parallels between our lives. The losses. Lessons learned the hard way. Our resilience. Our temperaments: both too loyal, and both with a ridiculously long fuse that ends abruptly.

We traveled together for three days. My father did not utter one hurtful word. I enjoyed his company.

But if passive-aggressive behavior ever becomes an Olympic event, my mother will do her country proud.

At the end of a mostly pleasant, albeit surreal visit, I packed my bags for L.A.

It's before dawn the next day, a chilly November morning in Ohio, and we're headed for the airport in Dad's truck. I dread going to the airport with him. He always dumps me off at the curb way too early like he can't wait to get rid of me. If I try to hug him good-bye, he turns into a 6'5" pillar of stone.

As we slow down at the curb, my stomach knots up in anticipation of pain, and I brace myself for the ritual rejection. This never stops breaking my heart.

I climb out of the truck, point to the *5 Minute Parking* sign and say, in a gruff voice like Dad would, "Gimme a 5 minute hug."

My father wraps his arms around me and pulls me close. I lay my cheek against his chest and inhale the scent of fabric softener from his soft knit shirt. I exhale and relax into his big, warm body.

My Dad holds me and scratches my back softly, the way he used to scratch Pooh Bear's back.

This is where I always wanted to be.
Home.

That hurt we embrace becomes joy.
Call it to your arms where it can change.
A silkworm eating leaves makes a cocoon.
Each of us weaves a chamber
of leaves and sticks.
Like silkworms, we begin to exist
as we disappear
inside that room.

- Rumi

.

Made in the USA
San Bernardino, CA
30 June 2013